MELVILLE
and the THEME
of BOREDOM

DATE DUE

NOV 1 7 2014	

MELVILLE
and the THEME
of BOREDOM

Daniel Paliwoda

McFarland & Company, Inc., Publishers

Jefferson, North Carolina, and London

LIBRARY OF CONGRESS CATALOGUING-IN-PUBLICATION DATA

Paliwoda, Daniel, 1973–
    Melville and the theme of boredom / Daniel Paliwoda.
      p.   cm.
    Includes bibliographical references and index.

    ISBN 978-0-7864-4154-9
    softcover : 50# alkaline paper ∞

    1. Melville, Herman, 1819–1891— Criticism and
interpretation.   2. Boredom in literature.   I. Title.
PS2387.P35   2010
813'.3 — dc22   2009036801

British Library cataloguing data are available

On the cover: Portrait of Herman Melville from the frontispiece
to *Journal Up the Straits*, 1860 (Library of Congress); background ©2010 Shutterstock

Manufactured in the United States of America

McFarland & Company, Inc., Publishers
  Box 611, Jefferson, North Carolina 28640
    www.mcfarlandpub.com

For Jacob and Ariel Paliwoda

"He took the children in his arms, placed his hands on each of them, and blessed them." — Mark 10:16

Acknowledgments

To my students, especially from the Holocaust course at Stony Brook: Marisa, Terri, Dina, Sarah, Brianne, and Jason, from the Intro to English Studies, Melville and Conrad, and American Literature courses at U. Albany: you all were great, and from West Point: Mary Ann, Emily, Chuck, Carson, Stephen, Peter, Logan, Haley, Grant, and Caroline. Each of you has motivated me to become a better teacher.

To Dr. Kathleen Kier, who served as an initial midwife to this project at its earlier, more rudimentary Master's level infancy.

To Dr. Ira Livingston, who read the manuscript of a stranger and whose generosity was heartening.

To Dr. Nicholas Rzhevsky, my Slavic brother, whose Dostoevsky course healed and inspired, and who was there at the right times.

To Dr. Stephen Spector, whose timely and essential arrival to the committee provided the invigorating energy and resolve to complete the project.

To Dr. Susan Scheckel, who encouraged and heightened the fever pitch intensity necessary to write an ambitious and colossal project on Melville.

To Dr. Steve Ressler, my secret sharer, who has become like family, and who provoked and spurred me to ask and dare to answer the big questions.

To my parents, Matthew and Maryann, and my sister Yvonne, who tolerated and survived the turbulent storm named Daniel.

To my son Ethan, whose love for life roused me at key moments. The *Moby-Dick* chapter is dedicated to him.

To my son Nicholas, whose arrival inspired me to see the dawn. The "Bartleby" chapter is dedicated to him.

To my wife Ania, who wrestled with and persevered during the writing process and more as much as the writer. The *Billy Budd* chapter is dedicated to her.

This project indeed was baptized with sweat, tears, and blood. This work is dedicated to my children Jacob and Ariel, who passed away; even though I did not get a chance to know you, Daddy loves you very much and thinks about you every day.

Looking into Fayaway's eyes, chasing after the whale, staring at the wall, wandering over spiritual deserts, and singing about a handsome ideal both humbled and terrified me. Melville's artistic madness and genius excited me, seducing me completely. His tragic strains deepened my perspective, and his jovial and affirming undertones lightened my own skepticism. Reading Dante, Shakespeare, Dostoevsky, Chekhov, and Milosz, all have expanded my understanding and respect for Melville, and added to my love for literature. Thank you to all the artists who have enriched and shaped my life.

Table of Contents

Preface

This book traces how boredom becomes a major preoccupation in Melville's art. Although very few commentators have noted the appearance of boredom in Melville's art, they have not recognized its significance. Mentioning boredom only in passing, these observers fail to examine in detail its role shaping Melville's larger imaginative and intellectual concerns. Unlike most critics who have plainly ignored boredom's importance in Melville's art, I focus on the centrality of boredom in Melville's oeuvre. I examine the effect this malady has on the interior landscapes of his literary figures, and sound the abyss into which boredom drives these characters. I show how boredom increasingly becomes a significant force shaping not only Melville's characters but also his approaches to literature. As his characters become more complicated, especially in their experiences of boredom, Melville varies narrative voice, genre, tone, and other artistic devices to express the meaning and force of boredom in his art.

Theorists believe that distinctions between boredom and ennui align with distinctions of class, race, and gender; however, Melville finds no differences in meaning. He finds boredom on a whaler or naval ship, at home or on a tropical island, and in a Wall Street office or in the Holy Land, which indicates that neither social nor economic constructs protect against this debilitating condition. Most serious attention to boredom involves examining British and European literature, while American articulations of this problem virtually have gone unnoticed. The general absence of any in-depth attention to the centrality of boredom in the American imagination can be understood because it was never considered an American problem. As Emerson points out, "This discontent — this Ennui for which we Saxons had no name, this word of France — has become a word of terrible significance, a disease which shortens life & bereaves the day of its light." Focusing on Melville's lifelong literary preoccupation with boredom, I have identified his work as offering the most pronounced insights into the role of boredom in the American nineteenth century.

Even when it seems Melville has reached an endpoint in his artistic rendering of boredom with Bartleby's death, he still perceives boredom's dark, life-robbing shadow which still appears in his later art. As Melville begins to question his confidence in man and faith, and as he learns to tolerate and then to recognize as undeniable, real, and inescapable, the realization that evil undermines his literary-philosophical musings, boredom then becomes an index for selfhood. Boredom functions more and more as an agent of both affirmation and destruction in Melville's art; boredom attacks core values, thus revealing their inadequacies, or, through that extreme assailment of beliefs, virtues gain greater meaning. Melville gains affirmation, no matter how fragile, of his core values through the action of boredom. The patterns of development which had led to the scrivener's suicide branch off into more complicated, frightening, and elusive representations, as they now enter the realm of the spiritual-religious, psychological, and moral.

Boredom confounds because there is no clear cause; there may be many underlying causes, but they are vague and can overlap. Despite the efforts of cultural critics, there can be no exact or meticulous definition for boredom. This project disputes and amends the theoretical tradition of viewing boredom as somehow less dignified, hazardous, and significant than ennui. Given the rather complex nature of boredom, to splinter it into disparate notions and bewildering lexicon and to insist on rigid constructs and abstruse diagnoses is to deny, constrict, and blunt its restless and existential complexion. Boredom is a force in its tidal-like action against the self: it ebbs and flows over the Melvillean protagonist's well-being, either pummeling the self's integrity or rising it toward consciousness and strength. Boredom may vary in its strength and duration, but is an unified, although complicated, existential state. Melville's literary vision of boredom reveals the awesome power of this beguiling and oftentimes confounding crisis. In its most basic sense, boredom is the decisive point in Melvillean consciousness when meaning is eroded; the absence or destruction of meaning, whether it be short-lived or sustained, is the threat that sinks or swims Melville's major heroes. Boredom is a kind of psychological and moral crucible in which Melville tests his literary protagonists, measuring authenticity, maturity, and values. Not all of his work can tolerate this stress, and therefore functions as a kind of index of artistic integrity, thus measuring the strength of his art. There is no major resolution of the theme of boredom toward the end of his career; one cannot say that *Billy Budd* is the culmination of his lifelong artistic struggle with boredom. There is no "final" statement. Melville achieves muted victory, partial faith in the backdrop of a devastating skepticism.

Only when Melville abandons his pretensions and crude conceptions of evil, renounces his irresolution concerning the darker implications of his material, and forsakes his own reliance on ill-defined and illusory expressions for boredom, does he then arrive at maturity as artist, becoming more philosophic and artistic in his creative representations of boredom's devastating effects. With *Moby-Dick,* he begins to accept that boredom is not something to be ignored; thereafter, it becomes clear that boredom kills not only time but souls. The uncertainties in his early art — execution, coherence, and impact — suggest hesitation, skepticism, and unconsciousness concerning how the theme of boredom should function in his art; in his better art, to explore boredom means to confront his worst fears, which is to stare into the abyss, and to articulate a tragic vision — to go against his own romantic impulses. This staggering not only marks his juvenilia but even his more advanced work. At times his optimistic straining and his heartbreaking drive to prevent his beloved heroes from succumbing to tragic insight due to boredom and even death itself will become the artistic (and emotional) tension determining his art. Coming between Melville and his artistic aim for boredom in his earlier career is himself. Melville's "shock of recognition" finally will allow him to contain his self-antagonisms, and give him the confidence no longer to wander about for his theme of boredom, but now to pilot over the difficult course of boredom and to record that harrowing trip in his art. Melville achieves muted victory, partial faith in the backdrop of a devastating skepticism. To believe, and not to believe: yes.

Introduction

Herman Melville's Noontide Demons

[L]ulled into such an opium-like listlessness of vacant, unconscious reverie is this absent-minded youth by the blending cadence of waves with thoughts, that at last he loses his identity; takes the mystic ocean at his feet for the visible image of the deep, blue, bottomless soul, pervading mankind and nature; and every strange, half-see, gliding, beautiful thing that eludes him; every dimly-discovered, uprising fin of some indiscernible form, seems to him the embodiment of those elusive thoughts that only people the soul by continually flitting through it. In this enchanted mood, thy spirit ebbs away to whence it came; becomes diffused through time and space; like Wickliff's sprinkled Pantheistic ashes, forming at last a part of every shore the round globe over.

There is no life in thee, now, except that rocking life imparted by a gently rolling ship; by her, borrowed from the sea; by the sea, from the inscrutable tides of God. But while this sleep, this dream is on ye, move your foot or hand an inch, slip your hold at all; and your identity comes back in horror. Over Descartian vortices you hover. And perhaps, at mid-day in the fairest weather, with one half-throttled shriek you drop through that transparent air into the summer sea, no more to rise for ever. Heed it well, ye Pantheists! [*Moby-Dick*, 159].

The rolling sea of life undulates. It rises, cresting on energy, potential, and exhilaration; however, with each swell, there also is a lull. The ocean most definitely surges, deluges, and overcomes both sea creature and seafarer. The wave can pummel and then caress, and the wind can howl and then whisper. Poseidon's dominion simultaneously nauseates and vitalizes with its same saltiness and vastness. Tempestuous waters that splinter the mainmast, crack the leviathan's back, and break a tar's will also can, in seconds, give way to calm, sunny ripples which spontaneously can turn into deadening stillness, unblinking sameness, and total silence. "There is no life in thee, now." Nothing stirs; work is nearly, if not, impossible. An unwillingness to exert oneself at first is gratifying; a wistful pensiveness glazes one's eyes, until, that, too, becomes boring. In boredom's shadow hovers death.

Like the sea, boredom is fluid. It ebbs and flows in the soul, exposing life to the harshness of the elements and suffocating the sources of life. It dampens, clogs, and washes away the joie de vivre. Stepping on shore does not soothe a queasy soul, and chasing after Fayaway ("Far Away") or the Great White Whale as well does not refresh the dulled out, dissatisfied, and disconnected adventurer. Plunging into the depths or skimming on the shallows equally can kill: one can plunge deeper and deeper into the abyss, or one can run ashore, stranding oneself on an island in the middle of the Pacific Ocean. Boredom begins innocently and deceptively, like the tides commencing or as gentle disturbances on the water's surface. At first, it may appear as if nothing is wrong, or as if nothing is happening; in fact, it may not even seem as if one is bored. Lying underneath the spell of languor or reverie, dullness and inattention wear away consciousness; the warm caress of tropical breezes and sun rays stroke one into deadly calm. What seems to be an enjoyable moment — and in the beginning it truly is gratifying — really only seems to be, until boredom does finally emerge from nowhere, somewhere, and everywhere.

Boredom often is characterized as tiresomeness, weariness, and disinterestedness, but these elements fail to capture its essence. Boredom is a complicated psychological state. The condition involves metaphysical and moral factors concerning consciousness, growth, and meaning. Among other cultural and ethical critics, Lars Svendsen believes:

> boredom involves a loss of meaning, and a loss of meaning is serious for the afflicted person. I do not believe that we can say that the world appears to be meaningless because one is bored, or that one is bored because the world appears to be meaningless. There is hardly a simple relationship here between a cause and an effect. But boredom and a loss of meaning are connected [17].

Boredom is a vaporous, opaque, and equivocal condition that has troubled many critics, artists, and philosophers trying to define it. Reinhard Kuhn interprets boredom as a "vague disquiet" (9). The problem in assigning a comprehensive and invariable definition of boredom is that it is such a uniquely personal experience; it is indeed an existential crisis. Elizabeth S. Goodstein notes, "My desire, or its failure, is revealed: Boredom isolates, individuates, even as it blurs the world gray" (1). One may be totally fascinated, absorbed in something, while the other may be indifferent, incurious. There can be no reliable or categorical tenets of boredom. Subject matter may be too easy and therefore tedious, or may be too abstruse and consequently irksome. To each his own. Something or someone can trigger boredom: aversion to certain activity or people, inertia induced by the environment, fatigue brought on by dullness or exhaustion in one's patience and/or fancy. These variables do not even capture the possibilities for boredom. Subjects and objects lose their vigor and freshness; they no longer provoke or satiate. Boredom may last intermittently or what may feel like an eternity. Although clinically distinguishable, boredom, it may be said, is a kind of unacknowledged depression.

Boredom's effects on the self are various, ranging from mild irritation, to chilling numbness, to existential nihilism. Rather than affixing a consistent and facile definition of boredom, I understand boredom as a continuum. Among those cultural critics who view boredom (and ennui) as a rigid and unbending construct rather than a coherent whole characterized as a sequence or progression of moods and actions varying by minor and deceptively inconsequential steps, Sean Desmond Healy distinguishes between boredom and *boredom*, defining the former as a normal response to an uninteresting life situation, and explaining the latter as a state of mysterious and incomprehensible existence. Moreover, Healy characterizes these two moods into "boredom" and "hyperboredom." Such a forced, rhetorical, and fragile binary serves to confuse, segregate, and glorify one hypothetical state over another. Boredom is not easily dissected and contained. What may seem to be a shallow, inconstant, and provisional experience of boredom to the observer may in fact be terrifying, hidden, and erosive. This critical approach to boredom is not vague or broad. Often times the bored do not and cannot admit or describe their own boredom. Boredom even touches upon many other emotional and moral states, and therefore, its boundaries and very definition always will be in flux. I too would like to pose to critics Lars Svendsen's question: "What is the difference between profound boredom and depression? My guess is that there is a considerable overlap" (15). The protracted terminology and classification of boredom that some postulate also illustrates the typical theoretical lines separating boredom from ennui, a critical problem I will discuss below.

Minute and subtle changes in attention span or interest, boredom can be understood as a kind of slippage: one gradually loses one's hold on life. At first, boredom may seem pleasurable. Many of Melville's earlier characters use their boredom to avoid tedious work, and imagine a paradise filled with excitement, plentitude, and women. Boredom is a means to distract the mind. Some Melville protagonists, sickened by their soul weariness, take flight, but soon realize that their boredom follows in their wake. The pleasurable feeling that their boredom-influenced stupor brings is short-lived, and these men's life problems, existential in nature, exacerbate their other dilemmas. Instead of confronting these issues, some continue on their flight, sailing away from their boredom, until boredom finally engulfs them. Bartleby's "I

prefer not to" is Melville's most extreme case of boredom's blackness and finality.

Although commentators have noted the appearance of boredom in
Melville's art, they have not recognized its significance. Mentioning boredom
only in passing, these observers fail to examine in detail its role shaping
Melville's larger imaginative and intellectual concerns. There is a small but
important minority of critics who have gone beyond just calling a Melville
hero bored. Paul Brodtkorb, Jr., for example, has made keen insights into the
problem of boredom in *Moby-Dick*, and has suggested that Ishmael's recurrent boredom is a possible reason why he goes to sea. Brodtkorb asks, "But
why is he recurrently bored?" (106). Brodtkorb does not answer his own question sufficiently, an unanswered inquiry that obscures the graveness of boredom. Brodtkorb's study is limiting because his discussion of boredom in
Melville's work plays an extremely minor role in his argument, and is one
of many factors Brodtkorb studies in his phenomenological reading of
Moby-Dick. Likewise, Christopher Sten lists boredom as a common problem
facing many Melville heroes, but severely downplays its importance in
Melville's art. Sten seems to minimize the intimate relationship between boredom and despair; moreover, Sten understands boredom only to be a temporary, less harmful condition than despair. Boredom is as dangerous as despair,
and boredom is not only typical in the early stages of Melville's art; it is a
recurrent, ever-powerful force robbing Melville's figures of joy, sanity, and
life.

Unlike previous critics who have plainly ignored boredom's importance
in Melville's art, I focus on the centrality of boredom in Melville's oeuvre. I
examine the effect this malady has on the interior landscapes of his literary
figures, and sound the abyss into which boredom drives these characters. I
trace how boredom increasingly becomes a significant force shaping not only
Melville's characters but also his approaches to literature. As his characters
become more complicated, especially in their experience of boredom, Melville
varies narrative voice, genre, tone, and other artistic devices to express the
meaning and force of boredom in his art. From *Typee* to *Billy Budd*, Melville's
preoccupation with boredom becomes increasingly linked to his other crucial literary themes, particularly his religious concerns.

Focusing on Melville's lifelong literary preoccupation with boredom, I
have identified his work as offering the most pronounced insights into the
role of boredom in the American nineteenth century. No other major nineteenth-century American artist has established the permanence, insidiousness, and destructiveness of boredom as thoroughly as Melville. Even when
it seems Melville has reached an endpoint in his artistic rendering of bore-

dom with Bartleby's death, he still perceives boredom's dark, life-robbing shadow which then appears in his later art. The patterns of development which had led to the scrivener's suicide branch off into more complicated, frightening, and elusive representations, as they now enter the realm of the spiritual-religious.

Melville's attitudes toward religion have become critically less important in current years, a problem which still confounds a serious and full understanding of Melville's work (Sherrill 1986), particularly when examining his treatment of boredom. Many critics have accepted or questioned slightly the classic study, *Melville's Quarrel with God* (1952), as the definitive critical statement on Melville's personal and artistic faith, or rather lack of it; however, a closer examination of key Melville texts suggests that Melville is ambivalent toward God, a characteristic that goes straight to the heart of boredom. One cannot easily proclaim Melville either as doubter/believer, or atheist/agnostic; Melville continually has varied, ironic, and complicated positions and treatments of religion in his art; to trace Melville's ever-changing and elaborate expressions of faith or disbelief is a monumental task. There exists no "final statement or testament" by Melville, or by literary critic that is satisfactory. I share Rowland A. Sherrill's (1986) frustration and confusion over some of the labels placed on Melville's relationship(s) toward religion. The question of Melville's stances toward religion, indeed, has remained unanswered or rather has not been dealt with for a long time. I agree with Judy Logan who also believes that Hawthorne's private insight into Melville should be taken into account when considering Melville's religious literary expressions. In *The English Notebooks*, Hawthorne enters his last meeting with Melville — the famous assessment: "He can neither believe, nor be comfortable in his unbelief; and he is too honest and courageous not to try to do one or the other. If he were a religious man, he would be one of the most truly religious and reverential" (651). Hawthorne also adds, "[he] will never rest until he gets hold of a definite belief" (651). Whether Melville ever achieved a "definite belief" is not clear. Hawthorne's understanding of Melville's crisis of faith allows for doubt and faith to coexist. Melville's relationship with God is restless; it is a troublesome faith but faith nonetheless. Along this line, Christopher Sten believes, "Melville was not a traditional Christian believer" (85). Melville does not deny, but questions God; he does not curse, but cries out for recognition. God's aloofness most frustrates Melville's art. To believe or not to believe is Melville's question. Why he wants to believe is as baffling as why he cannot assert disbelief, and boredom's role in complicating this task for the artist to untangle the religious knot is even more frustrating.

Siegfried Wenzel, Michael L. Raposa, and Lars Svendsen all see how loss of meaning, religion, and boredom are interrelated, and I see these problems shaping Melville's art. As Melville begins to question his confidence in man and faith, and as he learns to tolerate and then to recognize as undeniable, real, and inescapable the realization that evil undermines his literary-philosophical musings, boredom then becomes an index for meaning. Boredom functions more and more as an agent of both affirmation and destruction in Melville's art; boredom attacks core values, thus revealing their inadequacies, or, through that extreme assailment of beliefs, virtues gain greater meaning. Religion is one of these key principles that are subject to boredom's attack. Melville gains affirmation, no matter how fragile, of his core values through the action of boredom.

Melville's Christianity was an uneasy and wavering creed, one that molded his art, especially when it touches upon his theme of boredom. Boredom indeed has religious origins, going back to the medieval concept of *acedia*. *Acedia* was a gloomy and despairing condition that haunted medieval monks, causing them to grow bored with religious matters. Blaise Pascal observes, "We do not grow bored with eating and sleeping every day, for we soon feel hungry or sleepy again, otherwise we should grow bored with it. Likewise if we do not hunger for spiritual things we find them boring" (299). True hunger is spiritual, one that is satisfied only if one hears, sees God; unfortunately, Pascal himself was skeptical as evidenced by his famous wager. Melville did bet that God exists, but his gamble also involves the probability of God's nonexistence; it is not firm or abiding belief. Jonah and Job from the Hebrew Bible were examples of varying ambivalence toward God, and both figures influence the dynamics of *Moby-Dick*. These prophets test the limits of faith and disbelief, a contest which Melville tested himself for a lifetime.

The religious stakes of boredom could then be understood as a kind of ambivalence, a position developed by Michael L. Raposa. A religious scholar, Raposa examines the contradictory feelings toward God known as acedia or spiritual boredom. During medieval times, it was understood that boredom may be a gift from God, a necessary means to ignore worldly things so as to focus on God. On the other hand, boredom can be a curse, an indifference to the love that God has for His creation. For Raposa, it is "important to distinguish between good and bad species of indifference" (19). Acedia could be either a gift from heaven or an invitation from hell because one led to concentration on God and the other led away from God; in essence, hell is the distance from God. In Melville's art, the equivocal nature of boredom deepens his characters' life dilemmas, exacerbating their integrity and consciousness. Whether confronting or dodging this spiritual ambivalence, the Melville protagonist is making a statement on the self, the world, and God; even in inaction, he is facing the void.

Encounters with Boredom

Although Melville uses the terms *boredom* and *ennui* sparingly in his earlier art and never mentions *acedia*, this moral and spiritual disease becomes a somber and looming life and death crisis that shapes his work. He finds boredom on a whaler or naval ship, at home or on a tropical island, and in a Wall Street office or in the Holy Land, which indicates that social or economic constructs do not protect against this debilitating condition. Boredom is a progressive and precarious soul sickness that corrupts many Melvillean characters. There is no figure afflicted by boredom who is not altered by this disease of the spirit. The changes manifest themselves both in the inner and outer life. Boredom attacks the very foundations of the self, and functions as an index of consciousness, measuring recklessness, immaturity, and other failings as forerunners of existentially calamitous outcomes. Boredom torments many of Melville's protagonists, and how each responds to the problem reveals his character and values. Recognizing, braving, and confronting boredom is an infrequent victory, one that truly characterizes the Melville hero.

Most critical analyses of boredom insist that it is a temporary, superficial, and harmless condition, and postulate that ennui, in contrast, is a persistent, intense, and lethal variation. Commenting on the individual who suffers ennui, Patricia Meyer Spacks posits, "the defining element of his situation is its irremediability; nothing can cleanse the poisoned element" (12). For most theorists acknowledging differences between ennui and boredom, boredom is not poison for the soul. Key theorists believe that differences between boredom and ennui align with distinctions of class, race, gender, and history; Melville however finds no clash between these two terms. A representative proponent of this view that boredom and ennui are contrasting, opposing experiences is Reinhard Kuhn. Kuhn's selected and selective examples of undistinguished, prosaic, and humble manifestations of mere "boredom" prejudice the reader's understanding of boredom. Kuhn's examples are so superficial that, quite logically, one would tend to agree with Kuhn that "boredom" is not worthy of study. However, what is going on in the person's mind and spirit while bored in this fashion? Could such a "superficial" boredom give rise to a version that is deeper? Is boredom then a given for a commuter, student, or shopper staring blankly? Is the lecturer himself boring or the topic itself boring, or is the student boring, finding everything boring? Kuhn's

reliance on French expressions of the higher, more dignified state of boredom, ennui, demonstrates that there is a cultural bias when discussing/think-
ing about boredom. Although she concedes that there is also a need to explore
"working-class" boredom, Patricia Meyer Spacks contends, "Middle-class
boredom, often associated with idleness, and middle-class attributes of boredom to members of other groups reveal with peculiar distinctness certain
forms of boredom's social utility, forms that have changed over the course of
two centuries" (6). Spacks quickly realizes, "I do not, of course, mean by my
narrow focus to suggest that the working classes fail to suffer psychic malaise
comparable to that of those higher on the social scale" (6). However, Spacks
then insists, "Boredom was not (*is* not) the same as ennui, more closely related
to acedia. Ennui implies a judgment of the universe; boredom, a response to
the immediate. Ennui belongs to those with a sense of sublime potential,
those who feel themselves superior to their environment" (12). Patricia Meyer
Spacks insists that "boredom" did not occur before 1750, but what makes
1750 a turning point in the history or lack of history of boredom? Elizabeth
S. Goodstein also is firm, declaring, "Boredom is an experience of modernity,
of modern temporality" (6–7).

Melville equally employs each term to signify in varying degrees the
numbing and deadening consequences of confronting or evading boredom.
In *Omoo* (1847), he specifically uses variations of *boredom*, and in *White-Jacket*
(1850), he mentions *ennui* at least twice; in his later work, Melville does not
employ either *boredom* or *ennui*. Melville did not struggle to resolve which
term to use to signify this life-robbing condition. The fact that, at least only
in his earlier artistic career, he did not rely on these terms suggests that his
project was more concerned about dramatizing the psychological state of being
rather than theorizing or semantically determining its historicism. Also, there
was no consensus during the nineteenth century in America on which term
to use. In fact, many periodicals of the day used both *boredom* and *ennui* inter-
changeably, even within the same paragraph, to connote the state of feeling
weariness, dissatisfaction, and restlessness.

Melville does not privilege ennui to bear the weight of the condition's
profundity, nor does he relegate boredom to its shoals. The vital question or
artistic concern for Melville is to dramatize the emotional or metaphysical
aftermath of the encounter with boredom. He identifies the problem immediately in the opening sequence of *Typee* (1846). The art leading to *Moby-
Dick* (1851) clarified and reinforced the fact that boredom was deadly, and was
a threatening specter. Thereafter, Melville's art grows darker, troubled by
boredom's destructive force. As Melville matured as an artist, he found more
direct ways to pronounce boredom's appearance, severity, and damage in the

soul. Rather than limiting himself to phrases or words, Melville actually illus-trates the devastating effects; increasingly, he becomes more philosophic and artistic in his creative representations of boredom. Melville's concerns are empirical: he emphasizes the uniqueness and isolation of the individual in a hostile and indifferent universe. Boredom intensifies this crisis.

Boredom confounds because there is no clear cause; there may be many underlying causes, but they are vague and can overlap. Despite the efforts of cultural critics, there can be no exact or meticulous definition for boredom. Boredom is not like clinical depression, which can be treated with medicine and psychotherapy. There is no medicine for boredom. Melville was not a scientist/psychiatrist, essayist, historian, or theologian; he did not want to be perceived as participating in any of these professions. He did not scrutinize competing terminologies for boredom, question their application, or trace their historical and cultural relevance. Melville was an artist, illustrating what boredom does to the soul; dramatization, not definition, was Melville's larger, more meaningful goal as artist.

Melville's juvenilia, however, demonstrates a wavering in that higher ambition to represent boredom in his art. A significant obstacle in his art is his initial reliance on euphemisms for boredom. These substitutes for bore-dom indeed screen the problem's direness; they instead tame and neutralize the deadly associations of boredom, minimize the implications and deeper causes, and trivialize the condition. "Whiling the time away" is one such example. Despite their violent-sounding and suggestive tones, "killing time" and "bored to death" have domesticated boredom. The state of mind these two phrases attempt to capture has been taken for granted. Even when Melville utilizes the phrases in *Omoo*, there is a nonchalant, complacent, and over-stated inflection in describing the humdrum lifestyle in the islands; the men who are "bored to death" are not on the verge of dying. Melville's own inex-plicit, ill-defined reliance on these illusory and inoffensive expressions sug-gests his own hesitant and unsure understanding of boredom in his early artistic career. Only when seizing upon the evil nature of boredom and when comprehending the harm to the soul does Melville articulate a mature vision. Overcoming his fear and irresolution concerning the darker implications of boredom, Melville begins with *Moby-Dick* to accept that boredom is not sim-ply to be ignored or downplayed. Boredom kills not only time but souls, and the death of Bartleby certainly testifies to that menace.

Only Ishmael attains self-knowledge, articulates the perils of boredom, and lives its consequences. While acknowledging the real danger of boredom to their well-being, the earlier characters evade any serious moral confronta-tion with boredom; rather than any personal action or responsibility, circumstances largely save them from doom. These figures prior to *Moby-Dick* are not mature, expressive, and engaged as is Ishmael. Thereby, Ishmael affirms himself and achieves the highest consciousness. Another protagonist who comes close, perhaps even surpassing him, is Rolfe of *Clarel*. An older ex-mariner-roamer, Rolfe is a balanced and confident "deep-diver" who has moral strength to face the worst and accept it; however, the narrator of *Clarel* does not say whether boredom is a problem for Rolfe. Nonetheless, Martha C. Nussbaum praises such a literary character as engaging a morally challenging task, yet being admirable for doing so. Nussbaum observes:

> "The effort really to see and really to represent is no idle business in the face of the constant force that makes for muddlement." So Henry James on the task of the moral imagination. We live amid bewildering complexities. Obtuseness and refusal of vision are our besetting vices. Responsible lucidity can be wrested from that darkness only by painful, vigilant effort, the intense scrutiny of particulars. Our highest and hardest task is to make ourselves people "on whom nothing is lost" [148].

Ishmael and Rolfe are characters on whom nothing is lost. Bartleby is a special case who also confronts the full forces of boredom, but silently and tragically dies with that knowledge. Ahab's boredom is a judgment of the world, of life itself, and he expresses a kind of joylessness that has profound spiritual and religious implications.

It seems a logical conclusion in Melville's art that the theme of boredom dies with Bartleby; because of his evolving treatment of religion, however, Melville continues his exploration of boredom through *Billy Budd*. Tracing the appearance and importance of Biblical allusions in Melville's art, Nathalia Wright explains, "By actual count they increase from a dozen in *Typee* to 100 in *Mardi* to 250 in *Moby-Dick* and then decrease, to rise again in *Clarel* to 600 and in *Billy Budd* to 100.... There thus appears to be a correspondence between the most ambitious expressions of Melville's genius and his use of the Bible.... It was in his most profound thought and his most distinguished style that he relied most heavily on Scripture" (9). To fetter one's boredom and discover spiritual fulfillment can be a victory of religion; it was for the desert monks who fought the noontide demon. To come to terms with the profundity of boredom is to validate life. Achieving a higher level of being is the goal of religion. Melville initially criticized institutional Christianity in *Typee*, but gradually focuses on the more personal expressions of faith. *Omoo* focuses on the perils of meddling with spiritual lives of the Tahitians, who ultimately experience boredom as a result of their religious crisis. *White-Jacket* can be seen as the first determined exploration of religious faith as a response to boredom, but the strength and genuineness of that faith in the eponymous hero is murky and questionable. *Moby-Dick* certainly grapples with crises of faith, and "Bartleby, the Scrivener," *Clarel*, and *Billy Budd* are the most complex and penetrating of Melville's preoccupations with religion and boredom. The ecclesiastical student Clarel has detached himself from life and faith, and unsuccessfully seeks friendship and God to fill the void. *Billy Budd* is a final settlement with Melville's lifelong struggles.

Melville's understanding and artistic rendering of boredom demonstrate an evolving thematic foundation, a strategy that reflects and renders boredom as a moral and spiritual crisis rather than a historical or political question. As Melville sheds the limiting and indistinct catchwords for boredom, he defines what boredom truly means to him: a life-robbing malaise. He abandons the various inexact and indistinctive terms for boredom, and begins to dramatize boredom in order to grasp its meaning. In order to do justice to Melville's material, I accept and appreciate Melville's disregard for a terminological understanding of boredom, and focus on the various artistic interpretations Melville develops over his career. Melville was a moral thinker and his art reflects this fact. Joseph Brodsky's observations about boredom reveal similar concerns that boredom is a problem of great moral concern that is not a result of issues of terminology: "Known under several aliases — anguish, ennui, tedium, doldrums, humdrum, the blahs, apathy, listlessness, stolidity, lethargy, languor, accidie, etc.— boredom is a complex phenomenon" (104). For Melville, the problem of boredom is the problem of life.

Crises of the Self

Although the *Oxford English Dictionary* insists that the word *boredom* first appears in Charles Dickens' *Bleak House* (1852), there are antecedents that predate it. Also cited in the *Oxford English Dictionary*, Lord Byron uses *Bores* and *Bored* in *Don Juan* (1823) to differentiate between those who bore, meaning to weary by being dull, and those who are bored by them. Also, it is worth repeating that Melville (1847 and 1850) himself uses variants of *boredom* prior to Dickens: *bore, bored to death*, and *to kill time*. It seems as if the concept was not formalized until 1852, but before this date, people clearly would have been familiar with being bored, dying from being bored, and killing time to avoid being bored. I do not share the conviction defended by Spacks (1995) and Goodstein (2005) that the reason people did not experience boredom prior to 1852 is because they were not bored; after all, if they were not feeling boredom, as these commentators assert, there would have been no need for the word. The examples of Byron and Melville show that boredom did exist and was recognized as such. Furthermore, *Oxford English Dictionary* defines boredom as "the state of being bored; tedium, ennui," and quotes Dickens to exemplify this exact meaning; it does not differentiate boredom from ennui. Because *boredom* or its derivatives did not appear in Webster's 1828 dictionary, it did not mean that boredom did not exist in the United States; Americans reading Byron's poetry (1823) would have understood what the poet meant.

Ennui does appear in Webster's 1828 dictionary, meaning "weariness; lassitude or fastidiousness"; however, the definition is opaque and unsatisfactory. It hedges the fullness of the problem. Emerson's own hesitation concerning the adoption of *ennui* into the American lexicon illustrates the exotic birthmark of "this word of France." Other foreign terminology eased its way into the American dialect; however, *ennui* was seen as unsuitable to the American vernacular. In the October 1886 edition of *The Century*, Benjamin E. Smith acknowledges:

> The language-makers have not transformed every familiar foreign word into English, and hence, while we, for example, with right, use the English pronunciation of Galileo and Luther, we must use the German of *Hegel, Fichte,* and *Jacobi,* and the French of *rendez-vous* and *ennui.* Whether *Simplon* should be pronounced as English or French is probably a matter of taste, since the English pronunciation of it is hardly established; but *employee* is a good English word, preferred by the "Imperial" to *employe,* and admitted by "Webster" to be "perfectly conformable to analogy" though it is not given a place in his vocabulary [967].

Even in 1886, the problem of accuracy still was debated. Pronunciation was one barrier; to know the proper French pronunciation one would require an education, a kind that only the American bourgeois would have access to. Early American literacy was low, and so how would an average farmer or poor city dweller know *ennui*? In "The American Scholar" (1837), Emerson gives a defiant cry for a dignity in American letters; he wants the American to become truly American by rejecting all things European. This would include foreign words such as *ennui*.

Most serious attention to boredom involves the British and European, while American articulations of this problem virtually have gone unnoticed. The general absence of any attention to the centrality of boredom in the American imagination can be understood because it was never considered an American problem. As Ralph Waldo Emerson points out in an October-November 1841 journal entry: "This discontent — this Ennui for which we Saxons had no name, this word of France — has become a word of terrific significance, a disease which shortens life & bereaves the day of its light"

(143–44). Although ennui sometimes was seen as a foreign malady, it still menaced American victims. If Americans struggled to diagnose and name this illness, it certainly did not mean they did not experience it. Emerson may have believed, no matter how untrue, that ennui had no American equivalent, but has realized that it has become "a word of terrific significance" for Americans. There may be no accurate word to represent or define ennui for Emerson and other Americans; a problem of translation should not hinder one's understanding of the concept.

Like Emerson, Walt Whitman in "Democratic Vistas" (1870) is annoyed concerning the infiltration of "ennui" in America. Whitman begrudgingly admits that ennui is in America, but shares Emerson's conviction that "ennui" is an émigré; for Whitman, there is something un–American about ennui. Whitman writes:

> What is the reason our time, our lands, that we see no fresh local courage, sanity, of our own — the Mississippi, stalwart Western men, real mental and physical facts, Southerners, &c., in the body of our literature? especially the poetic part of it. But always, instead, a parcel of dandies and ennuyees, dapper little gentlemen from abroad, who flood us with their thin sentiment of parlors, parasols, piano-songs, tinkling rhymes, the five-hundredth importation — or whimpering and crying about something, chasing one aborted conceit after another, and forever occupied in dyspeptic amours with dyspeptic women [242].

"Ennuyees" are effete, affected, and blasé; everything about them is the opposite of the rough, direct, and plain American. "Ennuyees" seemed to be too delicate, refined, and irritable; they apparently were part of the European leisure class who led overindulgent lives, had limitless time, and needed constant diversions from their petty annoyances. American men, especially its leading cultural spokesmen, simply did not want to admit that they had experienced ennui. The condition suggested unmanliness, a problem best avoided. Thomas Jefferson partly shares Whitman's sentiment that ennui is mainly an idler's problem, and he blames the individual for experiencing it. In a 21 May 1787 letter to his daughter Martha, he insists on enterprise and activity as ways to curb ennui, "the most dangerous poison of life"; however, he is unsympathetic with those actually corrupted by it. He writes, "The idle are the only wretched. In a world which furnishes so many employments which are useful, and so many which are amusing, it is our own fault if we ever know what ennui is" (41).

A lack of understanding and unwillingness to face the seriousness of ennui restrained any efforts by Americans to tackle this unfortunate but American problem. In the January 1879 issue of *Atlantic Monthly*, Charles Dudley

Warner forces Americans to accept ennui as an aspect of American life. Horrified by the trends in the country's youth, Warner writes:

> This unusual phenomenon of a conservative youth may be due to want of faith, to the spread of the scientific spirit, to the *ennui* of wealth and culture. Probably it is less marked in America than in Europe. We like to believe that it is less here. For the country in the future is to be not so much what the young men think they will make it — if they trouble themselves with the problem — as what they themselves are.
> We cannot believe that the American people are about to succumb to the gospel of indifference [1].

Even European artists were not able to describe clearly the nature of this moral and spiritual disease. "This word of France" that frustrated Emerson also bedeviled the French; just because ennui was a part of the French vocabulary, it did not guarantee eloquence or precision in usage. Reinhard Kuhn even admits that the French themselves used "ennui" to poeticize the intense, soul-deadening condition, and at the same time used "ennui" to whine about a minor, petty annoyance (6). Overriding his own strict distinctions between boredom and ennui, Kuhn seems to admit, if unconsciously, that language is unreliable or, at the very least, limits, intermingles, and obfuscates what ennui and boredom supposedly are. If Kuhn insists that boredom represents a superficial and temporary state and ennui signifies a profound and deadly condition, he seems not to take into account translation. No matter how common the experience, observation, or emotion, something always is lost when rendering a foreign saying into a native equivalent. Kuhn also overlooks the fact that the French appear to have one term to encapsulate both the seemingly transient and less harmful form and the drawn out and lethal malady. The interchange of *ennui* in French points to the fluidity of the term; there is no absolute term, but a relative understanding that the individual felt weary, uninterested, and discontent because life seems to be unremittingly the same. "Metaphysical dignity" and "commonplace inflictions" are but the examples of the usual and narrow approach of discussing boredom/ennui.

Czeslaw Milosz argues that meaning loses clarity when foreign words are ushered into a different language. In "Salagia," Milosz describes his childhood catechism lessons, focusing on the seven deadly sins. Surveying each transgression against God, Milosz discusses *acedia*, another foreign word connoting boredom which plagued monks during the Middle Ages. *Acedia* is another word of contention, and is just as inapt as *ennui* for an adopted idiom. Milosz writes, "*Lenistwo* (laziness) instead of *acedia*. Polish is not responsible for the comical misunderstanding. The word is not Latin but was borrowed via the Latin directly from the Greek *akedia*, and should have been translated as *obo-*

jetnosc (indifference)" (291). Part of the problem is that sloth replaced acedia as a deadly sin, and although sloth has some attributes of *acedia*, it is vastly different. Adding to this conflation is the problem of rendering a word which itself is a translation from a different language. This series of dilutions weakens any attempt for integrity. Milosz is far more interested in the concept these words stand for than the terms themselves. If one were to be literal, no one but monks would ever feel *acedia*; however, how many people have experienced *acedia* while attending church service or reflecting upon spiritual matters during the Middle Ages or even today?

Milosz suggests the literary transmission of *acedia* into linguistically diverse and unrelated languages blurred and misrepresented the concept that translators tried to convey. This may be the root of the problem, but we must also consider the scabrous history of *acedia*. The term itself is a point of contention. The word comes from the Greek, meaning "lack of care," but Siegfried Wenzel indicates that it was used infrequently and was "vague and often even ambivalent" (6). Its roots spring beyond Greece, reaching into Jewish and Christian soils (3). Hippocrates, Cicero, Lucian and other various classical philosophers utilized the term, and even the Jewish Psalmist applied its meaning to signify soul weariness, tedium of the spirit, and metaphysical exhaustion and apathy. Because of the relative fluidity of the meaning and inchoate nature of *acedia*, it did not mean that the concept the word represented did not exist. Evelyn Waugh stresses, "There is no true classical term for this state, not because it was unknown to the ancients, but because it was too commonplace to require identification" (60). *Acedia* as a concept would attain clarity during the fourth century in the Egyptian desert monasteries near Alexandria.

Acedia represented the most threatening peril facing a Christian, particularly the ascetic. It was hazardous due to its effect of drawing the monk away from religious zeal. Wenzel characterizes *acedia* as boredom, and by defining acedia as boredom, Wenzel sees no ideological or formalistic distinctions between a classical-medieval term and the modern condition; he is interested in the concept the term represents (5). This boredom is a serious and arduous predicament that pulls away the Christian from his God. In *Pensées*, Blaise Pascal categorizes boredom as a distraction. Its Latin root, *distrahere*, indicates the drawing away that boredom does to an individual. Boredom undermines religion, and also by examining religion's Latin root, one sees that boredom cuts the bindings of religion on the soul (*religio*, *religare* to tie fast). Boredom leads the monk astray from God, and without God, he is to wander alone, return to the city, to fornication, secularization, and chaos. Having abandoned God, he faces death alone and the likelihood of hell.

Siegfried Wenzel has shown that the monks did not themselves name this form of boredom. Citing Hebrew biblical sources of acedia in the Septuagint, Wenzel notes the particular Greek rendition of acedia in the holy text as "noonday devil" or "noonday demon" (7), and quotes from a scholium to a passage from *Psalms* 90:6. The association of acedia with Satan undoubtedly pinpoints the source of acedia's danger; falling under the spell of boredom is submitting to the devil. Acedia was the lure and weapon that Satan used to destroy man; and by dismantling God's creation, the devil also struck God Himself. Acedia is violence against life itself. It is an admission of failure. Man's connections to life and God are cut. The world cannot give the monk what he needs, and God cannot provide spiritual sustenance. To withstand acedia is to resist the devil. On the other hand, the devil is not the sole cause of acedia. The monk himself is to blame as well. Free will and man's flaws allow acedia to infiltrate. Acedia is a choice. Man decides to accept or reject God's grace. Man is not completely powerless; in spite of the devil, man can control his destiny. Acedia then is a measure of humanity's volition and love for God.

Seigfried Wenzel explains that the disappearance of acedia from the finalized list of cardinal sins is a result of Gregory the Great's vision of the catalogue (26–28). The change to the series reflects the attitudes and different monastic orders influencing the papacy. The Egyptian desert monks were of the Eastern tradition, a harsher and more isolated brotherhood. Acedia was perceived as a problem encountered frequently in the solitariness of the desert and separation from other monks, despite living within the same compound. The desert environment was bleaker and less conducive to physical sustenance than its European or Western counterparts. The western monasteries did not confront deadly heat or the unforgiving desert. The Eastern monasteries were not as structured as the West's, with its regulations dictating the spiritual exercises and physical labors of every hour of the day. Even attitudes toward sleep distinguished the two orders. More importantly, acedia was considered an Eastern, desert problem, one not encountered as often or as severely in the West.

Nonetheless, this foreign ailment, this word of Egypt, did afflict the Latin Church. Thomas Aquinas wrestled with this demon in his writing. The noonday demon was too important and deadly to ignore and underrate by its omission from the list. Morphing acedia into sloth obscured the danger. Aquinas therefore needed to qualify this serious problem. Wenzel recalls that "the exalted position of *acedia* indicates that to Scholastic theologians the vice meant more than simple laziness" (58). *Acedia* is not sloth, the sin that replaced the desert torment on the list.

Trying to distinguish boredom and ennui along sharp lines, Reinhard Kuhn in his attempt to categorize ennui inadvertently concedes that precursors of ennui existed; Kuhn's adamant insistence that victims of ennui differ from bored suburbanites because "the former suffers from a metaphysical malady, and the latter only feels a superficial and vague disquiet" (9) buckles due to his own interchange of the two terms and equivocation. Offering a history of ennui in Western literature, Kuhn starts with the ancient Greeks and Romans. If his working thesis regarding ennui hinges on so-called modern tendencies and the modern period, why go back so far? If his concentration is on so-called modern ennui, why lose precision by calling his work *The Demon of Noontide*? The demon of noontide was a synonym for *acedia*, not *ennui*. Kuhn traces certain untranslatable Greek terms that lead to monotony. He admits that Plato thought deeply about the idea of monotony. He also characterizes Aristotle's concept of "black gall" as ennui. Plutarch and Horace's concepts of *horror loci* also bear similarities with Kuhn's rigid constructs of ennui. Before long, having traced ennui from the ancient to modern times, Kuhn seems to say that the concept, not the name itself, of ennui has existed for a long time.

Obviously the ancient world would not have used "ennui" or "boredom"; however, the concept of boredom would have been familiar to both lower and upper classes. And just as important is the idea that boredom was part of the human condition, that everyone, from servant to senator, would have experienced it; ever since the individual was aware of his surroundings, limitations, and moods, he was conscious of boredom. The very fact that Kuhn traces ennui/boredom to ancient times underscores the fact that boredom was around before 1750, and all types of people suffered it. However, at other times in his study, a lower-class member or factory worker's wretched, demeaning, and grim existence choked by endless routine and monotony is not considered to have "metaphysical dignity." What then are we to call it? Do these social classes fail to meet unstated, clandestine prerequisites? Are their existential crises to be ignored and undermined? Should their problems even be called existential? Are Baudelaire, Nietzsche, and Wilde's representations of ennui/boredom more genuine — ennui of the idle, educated, or affluent class — than the "boredom" of an illiterate, poor, and unrepresented proletariat? Simone Weil does consider this type of boredom to be serious and dangerous; moreover, it is appropriate to study boredom in all of its expressions. In "Factory Work" (1936, 1949), Weil recognizes and characterizes factory workers' deep unhappiness and hopelessness as soul killing brought about by the numbing and tedious monotony. "Factory Work" is important because Weil includes the common laborer as an individual who also wrestles with boredom. She debunks the false, class-based notion of boredom. A common worker also faces the abyss; the terrible heart of boredom's darkness as described by Nietzsche and Baudelaire also is encountered by the factory worker. That void produced by boredom pulls all; there is no discrimination. Rich and poor are dealt the same fate. That inner emptiness bored by the tedium, routine, and monotony punctures outward. The internal void becomes external. Weil writes, "This loathing for their work colors their whole view of life all their life" (71). There is no future, and the present is only the past repeating itself. The factory worker has no hope or joy; he has no life. He feels a kind of *acedia*, secularized, but the concept is the same. He can find no joy in his life.

Unlike Reinhard Kuhn and other cultural critics, Czeslaw Milosz considers boredom in democratic terms. For Milosz, boredom is a modern existential crisis afflicting all. Knowing firsthand the abuses and crimes committed in the name of ideology and "the people," Milosz is deeply suspicious of any categorization along class lines. Boredom does not segregate, favor, or exclude some over another; it attacks unmercifully. Going into greater detail about the sin of *acedia* in "Saligia," Milosz prefers *acedia* to signify boredom. *Acedia* is the void. As Milosz says, it is a "grappling with the nothingness that encircles us; man has been faced with these trials for a millennium" (307). It uproots the self and its values; there is no "metaphysical dignity," while experiencing this terror. Milosz's acedia is not the petty and dandified annoyances and "ennui" (the source of Modern French *ennuyer*, "to annoy, bore") of selfish/egocentric and mean-spirited gentility. This acedia is powerful; this acedia is demoniac. In *Roadside Dog* (1998), Milosz calls acedia "a demon of boredom" (157).

Although not calling it by name, colonial American thinkers and artists also wrestled with boredom. The Great Awakening is the defining monumental event that marks a Puritan's birth of consciousness, a moment that ushers in for the first time a vision of divine beauty that brings forth the joy of salvation. Within a Puritan context, jeremiads were designed to awaken a spiritually lethargic congregation who felt no joy in God. Jonathan Edwards can be seen as describing his spiritual/religious crisis in terms of *acedia*, and his doubts and physical illnesses exacerbate his feelings of joylessness of God. In "Personal Narrative" (posthumous, 1765), "Letter to Rev. Dr. Benjamin Colman" (posthumous, 1935), and selections from "A Faithful Narrative of the Surprising Work of God" (1736) and "Religious Affections" (1746), there are features of *acedia*, a joylessness of God, in Edwards' writings. This identification of Edwards' spiritual upheaval as boredom grounds the fact that it was on these shores long before anyone wanted to admit it.

Mary Rowlandson uses language in her captivity narrative that is highly suggestive of boredom. Like Edwards after her, Rowlandson experienced an acedia-like condition during her imprisonment. Feeling like she had lost interest in things God, she describes a poignant moment in which she appears like a medieval desert monk; she writes, "Then also I took my Bible to read, but I found no comfort here neither, which many times I was wont to find: So easie a thing it is with God to dry up the Streames of Scripture–comfort from us" (442). Her boredom was understood by Rowlandson as a test of faith, an emotion or lack thereof that was not necessarily hopeless or sinful; if overcome, it would and did strengthen her piety. Edward Taylor also wrestled with bouts of acedia.

In "Christ's Reply," he confesses that prayer has become unengaging, sermons unstimulating, and faith and zeal cold. The American Puritan's affection for God has slackened. By writing this poem, he chides himself, trying to neutralize the deadening effects of his spiritual dryness. Because he is aware that this boredom-like condition has caused him to grow distant from God, Taylor is not in immediate spiritual danger. At the same time, he must be ever-vigilant; the devil of boredom is omnipresent. Boredom and joylessness with/in God are unending threats. This war continues in "Meditation. Col. 2.17 Which are Shaddows of things to come and the body is Christs" of *Second Series*. The devil of boredom does not rest. Taylor's faith always is in question. For Edwards and Taylor's generations, pious passion was the mark of a true believer; without it, hell awaited. Spiritual joy for God was to be sought and husbanded.

By the nineteenth century it was clear that the "demon of boredom" had emigrated to persecute Americans. Whitman wanted to trivialize and suppress expressions of boredom in American letters, but Emerson conceded that it had arrived. Boredom was here long before Emerson ever admitted to it. Underneath its bustle and restless energy, boredom resided in America. Although not describing America's problem as boredom per se, Alexis de Tocqueville is suspicious of the unwavering sameness in American culture; he warns, "In modern society, everything threatens to become so much alike, that the peculiar characteristics of each individual will soon be entirely lost in the general aspect of the world" (312).

Melville read Pascal, Montaigne, and Voltaire, all who focused on boredom as a malaise, causing great spiritual harm. They did not dissect or over-intellectualize the condition. In *Pensées* (1662), Blaise Pascal writes, "*Man's condition.* Inconstancy, boredom, anxiety" (6). In Voltaire's *Candide, ou l'Optimisme* (1759), the Turk notes, "Our labor keeps us from those three great evils: boredom, sin, and want" (129). Melville's art supports these statements;

like his French influences, Melville sees boredom as part of life, which affects every aspect of life. There is no escaping it; one can deny, repress, or divert it, but as Pascal notes, "But take away their diversion and you will see them bored to extinction [death]. Then they feel their nullity without recognizing it, for nothing could be more wretched than to be intolerably depressed as soon as one is reduced to introspection with no means of diversion" (8). The body is fixed here, desiring to be somewhere else, while the mind flees its disappointments and vexations, dreaming of over there. It is a short-term coping mechanism that proves dependable for Melville's protagonists; however, when this daydreaming becomes ineffective, boring in and of itself, then what had seemed to be harmless, pleasant, and superficial truly reveals itself to be a horrifying and lethal problem.

Like his contemporaries Ralph Waldo Emerson and Henry David Thoreau, Melville was most concerned about deeper and higher questions of life. Emerson started as a minister, and when he became a man of letters, he continued examining those questions. Angered by the period's commercialism, materialism, complacency, and shallowness, Emerson demanded more out of his country. Thoreau too condemned his neighbors for sleeping through life, leading superficial lives. The soul was what mattered, and Transcendentalism, with its blend of the religious and metaphysical, emphasized the importance of the inner life. In *Walden* (1854), Thoreau writes, "If they had not been overcome with drowsiness they would have performed something. The millions are awake enough for physical labor; but only one in a million is awake enough for effective intellectual exertion, only one in a hundred millions to a poetic or divine life. To be awake is to be alive. I have never yet met a man who was quite awake" (61). To be alive is to experience the joy of life, to be attuned to the sources of life; to be alive is to unleash the soul. Boredom is that drowsiness that inhibits individuals from reaching their potential and forestalls them from their inner selves. Boredom is so pervasive in people's lives and yet so obscure that, as Pascal has identified and Thoreau as well believes, they do not know what and when it is afflicting them. Thoreau adds, "If we were always indeed getting our living, and regulating our lives according to the last and best mode we had learned, we should never be troubled with ennui" (76).

Trials of Faith

Drawing upon medieval religious notions of acedia as boredom, I understand Melville's treatment of boredom and religion as a kind of joylessness in/of God. Considered broadly, Melville's concern with boredom emphasizes a growing tendency toward a modern sensibility: joylessness with life itself. This interdisciplinary approach enables a significant reinterpretation of Melville's literary ambitions and insights. It also offers a different way of understanding the relations of boredom to ennui, psychology to religion, and American Romanticism to Modernism. Ultimately, this study adds to the important but largely ignored subject of boredom in American literature and culture.

My interpretive method is based upon close textual analysis that incorporates ethical criticism, questioning the meaning, influences, and outcomes of individual conduct, evaluating Melville's assumptions and contexts. My study rests on the conviction that literature illuminates, dramatizes, and renders profound psychological and philosophical questions and the insights literature offers deserve critical attention. Many currents in academia reject the moral approach as apolitical, elitist, and old-fashioned. In response, Todd F. Davis and Kenneth Womack say:

> Yet to pretend that the ethical or moral dimensions of the human condition were abandoned or obliterated in the shift to postmodernity certainly seems naïve. Part of being human involves the daily struggle with the meanings and consequences of our actions, a struggle most often understood in narrative structures as we tell others and ourselves about what has transpired.... As creatures driven by story, we find ourselves immersed in narrative in almost every aspect of our lives. The act of telling stories ... grounds and distinguishes human activity. Thus, it would be ludicrous to imagine that readers of literature over the past several decades somehow disengaged their ethical faculties as they encountered their culture's grand narratives [ix–x].

Lawrence Buell questions the suspicions surrounding the ethical dimensions of literature, and welcomes a reexamination of ethical criticism. Buell states that ethical criticism had not disappeared and resurfaced lately in the so-called "return to ethics." Foucault, Levinas, Nussbaum, Eldridge, and Rorty have been focusing on ethical issues along with political ones, despite the "coeval perturbations of the theory revolution and canonical revisionism of the 1970s" (2). Buell shows that the hesitation and mistrust with which some theorists regard ethical criticism stems from a misunderstanding of what ethical criticism is. Echoing some of this argument in his 1999 *PMLA* introduction of the special issue on ethical criticism, Buell traces how poorly defined the practice has been since the nineteenth century and still is. He emphasizes how the academy and its dominant theorists fully embraced without reservation Clifford Geertz and Hayden White despite their outdated approaches: "we responded enthusiastically even though [Geertz's] model of ethnography as reading was based on an already obsolescent new critical formalism ... when

Hayden White gave us history as discourse, we cheered him in even though his model of metahistory was based on Northrop Frye's obsolete archetypalism" (6). He adds:

> but when Rorty and Nussbaum try to give us literature as ethical reflection, we are more reluctant to be pulled back to what looks suspiciously like old-fashioned thematics: the "pre-modern strategy" of making "aesthetic sensibility ultimately subservient to the goal of moral improvement." Perhaps the key difference between this and the previous two cases [Geertz and White] is not so much the specter of rampant moralism as such as it is longstanding reluctance on the part of many if not most literary scholars to allow the central disciplinary referent or value to be located in anything but language [6–7].

Even Terry Eagleton, a critic known for his mistrust of the moral or ethical approach to literature, has begun to recant some of his harsh critiques of this kind of literary practice.

The academy's skepticism toward close reading, a crucial component of ethical criticism, restricts the significance of Melville. Lifelong Melville scholar, Edgar A. Dryden counters the attack on textual analysis, arguing that the skills required are "necessary in order to understand Melville's work properly, but [also] because he himself valued and employed them" (4). I agree with Dryden's position. To be historically true to Melville and his art, one must adopt the same interpretative systems as Melville did (5). Dryden appreciates, demands, and practices ethical criticism. Melville too was an ethical critic, closely reading and writing about Hawthorne's tales. If one does not penetrate Hawthorne's "blackness of darkness," his literary/artistic moral dilemmas, one instead, as John Gardner believes, debases and reinvents art in order to fit a prescribed view. What makes this form of criticism dangerous is that it can prove to be censorious and self-righteous. Gardner points out, "True art is too complex to reflect the party line" (15). For Gardner, art is alive; he notes, "Art is not philosophy but, as R. G. Collingwood said, 'the cutting edge of philosophy'" (9–10). This view of art as "the cutting edge of philosophy" is a tenet of ethical criticism, one developed by Martha C. Nussbaum, Wayne C. Booth, and others.

Another disregarded and misconceived analytical approach is the philosophy of religion. Jacques Derrida defends the so-called "return of religions" (45) as a worthwhile and timely endeavor in literary analysis. Derrida challenges us:

> How "to talk religion"? Of religion? Singularly of religion, today? How dare we speak of it in the singular without fear and trembling, this very day? And so briefly and so quickly? Who would be so imprudent as to

claim that the issue here is both identifiable and new? Who would be so presumptuous as to rely on a few aphorisms? To give oneself the necessary courage, arrogance or serenity, therefore, perhaps one must pretend for an instant to abstract from everything or almost everything, in a certain way. Perhaps one must take one's chance in resorting to the most concrete and most accessible, but also the most barren and desert-like, of all abstractions [42].

Stanley Fish agrees with Derrida's claim that the critical study of religion shows signs of ambitious development; Fish says in the 7 January 2005 issue of *The Chronicle of Higher Education*, "[it] is now where the action is," and "the academy is finally catching up." Fish insists, "it is one thing to take religion as an object of study and another to take religion seriously. To take religion seriously would be to regard it not as a phenomenon to be analyzed at arm's length, but as a candidate for the truth."

In order to better understand Melville's complicated, hard-to-define attitudes toward religion, one can compare him to another religiously troubled doubter-believer, Czeslaw Milosz. Milosz's range of Christianity — disbelief, agnosticism, faith, and countless qualifications — puts into perspective Melville's own knotty and idiosyncratic system of religion. As did Melville, the 1980 Nobel Laureate fought to attain certainty, hope, and God in a world that subverted and ruined those values. Having stared into the twentieth century's heart of darkness, the poet varies in his responses to faith in God and pessimism over the world. He can speak intensely, passionately, and piously about both religion and atheism; however, finding a sliver of a hard-won hope, one, which, until his death in August 2004, proved to be always within reach, but somehow elusive, he ventures to answer "Why Religion?" in *Roadside Dog* (1998). Sounding more like an attempt toward self-enlightenment than a response to public critique, "Why Religion?" is a profession of Milosz's obligation, one that he cannot explain or understand adequately, to mull over the role of religion in his life. He does not want to pass this duty over to theologians; it would be too easy to do so. Feeling as if he must answer the most vexing questions of life for himself, by himself, he embraces this most uncertain project confidently.

Melville's own religious crisis was to settle artistically the question of how to bind back man's connections to life and of how to find affirmation in the face of boredom. The attempt to re-align Melville's protagonists with life and God is best exemplified in *Moby-Dick*, "Bartleby," *Clarel*, and *Billy Budd*. Neglecting the materiality that is intertwined with man's metaphysicality, God, it seems, has abandoned himself. This conflict between doctrine and personal feeling, letter of the Law versus spirit of the Law, complacency against scrutiny, and stagnation contra energy found within the death-of-God theology is an expression of the problem of boredom. How is one obligated and capable of praying to and obeying an indifferent God? How can one feel the joy of God within if one feels apathetic about God, about an emotionless God? In *After Religion*, Mark C. Taylor develops these dilemmas when he states, "But what if God is indifferent? Or, more precisely, what if God is Indifference? What if binding ["Religion: *re* + *ligare* — to bind back"] back does not bind together but binds us to abandonment? What if there is no turning away from that which turns away and turns itself away" (253). Unable to answer these vexing questions himself, Taylor also adds, "Whether Melville is urging confidence or no confidence, belief or disbelief, trust or mistrust remains completely undecidable" (11). How is Melville's protagonist to define himself if he is staring into the abyss?

The death-of-God movement within contemporary theology may help shed light upon Melville's own unorthodox and idiosyncratic religious beliefs, as expressed in his art. What at first seems to fly in the face of reason — how can Christianity exist without a belief and foundation in God — the death-of-God movement is rooted within a strong faith in Jesus Christ. In his seminal *The Gospel of Christian Atheism*, Thomas Altizer challenges the tacit moral assumption of a transcendent God, and asserts that the death of God is really a benediction. Despite being understood in orthodox Christianity as the ultimate creator, God is seen as stagnant, unworldly, and disconnected; God is not an active, engaged, and living god. Altizer sees a Christianity based on a God-inspired model as joyless and dead. Altizer searches for and demands a Christianity that participates in the world; he wants a kind of Christianity that is alive. Mark C. Taylor in *Nots* clarifies these points of the stagnation and negation of life in conventional Christianity; he also highlights the importance of nihilism, a kind of affirmative nihilism — for this movement. He says, "The Christian moralist is inevitably a 'Nay Sayer'" (59). The death of God becomes an act of nihilism, a way to make the believer say yes to life, a life, however, with Jesus. Nihilism in this case is not a complete negation of values, but a necessary cleansing or rejuvenation of values; nihilism is an affirmation.

Mark C. Taylor's response to the troubling problems that arise with the death-of-God theology is deconstruction. In an effort to hold on or bind himself back to a meaningful religion, while fighting off the enthusiasm over the death of God, Taylor asserts in *Erring: A Postmodern A/Theology* that "deconstruction is the '*hermeneutic of the death of God*'" (6). Because deconstruction operates in the realm of the liminal or marginal, Taylor uses this critical approach to reveal and express the complexities of maintaining, regaining, or abandoning faith in God and/or Christ. Deconstruction is not about gaining finality or answers; one is meant to question unceasingly, or, as Taylor understands and labels it, to err. *To err* is to be "forever wavering and wondering, [it is] deconstruction [which] is (re)inscribed betwixt 'n' between the opposites it inverts, perverts, and subverts" (11). The hostile, adverse, and "negative" implications of "erring" are in fact precisely what leads one to illumination and meaning. In a traditional sense, to err means to lose direction, to violate standards of conducts, or to stray. But to err can mean to "drift toward" (11). By deconstructing "errabund," "errand," and other err-based terms, Taylor shows why one should err. In *After Religion* (1999), Taylor says erring is an "of(f)-erring" which is sacred.

The elasticity found in the concept of erring and the refusal to settle for finality provides discourse surrounding the problem of boredom to shed light on Melville's ever intricate system of faith. His art is a lifetime erring. Melville cannot declare, believe he is an atheist, and at the same time he cannot validate, accept that he is a Christian. Language fails him as it does for the critic. The artist only can dramatize this predicament, understanding that there are no settled values to gain hold of. Melville always was suspicious of labels; in 1 June 1851 letter to Hawthorne, he writes, "What 'reputation' H. M. has is horrible. Think of it! To go down to posterity is bad enough, any way; but to go down as a 'man who lived among the cannibals'! When I speak of posterity ... I have come to regard this matter of Fame as the most transparent of all vanities" (*Correspondence*, 193).

The emotional strains of sifting through the fragments of faith are magnified by the boredom Melville has discovered, which in turn determines his art. Boredom is a judgment of the world and of God. Civilization and God fail, cannot bring joy into man's life. The stronger of Melville's characters wrestle with boredom to rediscover faith in life, no matter how delicate and slender; those who do not engage in this battle remain joyless and lost. If faith and joy are ever to be attained, they are hard won. Melville never finalized his position on these vexing issues, and that *Billy Budd* remained unfinished suggests the attitude one must take toward Melville. Although Billy must die, there is a muted hope that joy can be had for a moment, and that art endures.

Explorations of Changing Conditions

Melville's realization of his theme of boredom proves to be a toilsome and slow process. The problem of boredom does not follow a logical development as Melville matures as an artist; each work does not presage, make groundwork, or enlarge upon preceding artistic struggles, conceits, characterizations, or protagonists. In one sense, his work ramifies or diverges into various flowerings and tributaries, with the theme of boredom functioning as the main artery; however, in another sense, the art, in the early period, lacks a fixed course because Melville has not seized the material. Although the existential crisis of boredom strikes virtually all of Melville's principle figures, there is no essential pattern similar to all. Indistinct parallels do exist between his earlier mariners and later characters, and reveal the recklessness, immaturity, and escapist attitudes that diagram rather than penetrate the crisis of meaning. His more outstanding and therefore more penetrating work demonstrates the influences, affiliations, and integrations of complementary issues such as friendships, work, faith, and selfhood to highlight boredom's deadly influence. Melville's romantic urges to end his work on hopeful notes determine whether the art can withstand or collapse under such pressures. Not all of his work can tolerate this weight, and therefore functions as a kind of index of artistic integrity, thus measuring the strength of his art. There is no major resolution of the theme of boredom toward the end of his writing career; one cannot say that *Billy Budd* is the culmination of his lifelong artistic struggle with boredom. There is no "final" statement.

Only when Melville abandons his pretensions and crude conceptions of evil, renounces his irresolution concerning the darker implications of his material, and forsakes his own reliance on ill-defined and illusory expressions for boredom, does he then arrive at maturity as artist, becoming more philosophic and artistic in his creative representations of boredom's devastating effects. The uncertainties in his early art — execution, coherence, and impact — suggest hesitation, skepticism, and unconsciousness concerning how the theme of boredom should function in his art; in his better art, to explore boredom means to confront his worst fears, which is to stare into the abyss, and to articulate a tragic vision — to go against his own romantic impulses. This staggering not only marks his juvenilia but even his more advanced work. His at times optimistic straining and his heartbreaking drive to prevent his beloved heroes from succumbing to tragic insight due to boredom and even death itself will become the artistic (and emotional) tension determining his art. Coming between Melville and his artistic aim for boredom in his earlier career is himself. Melville's "shock of recognition" finally will allow him to contain his self-antagonisms, and give him the confidence no longer to wander about for his theme of boredom, but now to pilot over the difficult course of boredom and to record that harrowing trip in his art.

Typee *and* Omoo
Body Here, Mind Over There

Six months at sea! Yes, reader, as I live, six months out of sight of land; cruising after the sperm-whale beneath the scorching sun of the Line, and tossed on the billows of the wide-rolling Pacific — the sky above, the sea around, and nothing else! Weeks and weeks ago our fresh provisions were all exhausted....

Oh! for a refreshing glimpse of one blade of grass — for a snuff at the fragrance of a handful of the loamy earth! Is there nothing fresh around us? Is there no green thing to be seen?

— Herman Melville, *Typee*

In his opening cry, Tommo exclaims his mental weariness, and reveals a deeper and more dangerous state of mind, one that he is not fully aware of. Having no adequate or rejuvenating outlet for his repressed energy and imagination, he suffers from boredom. He easily gives into the atmosphere of idleness and dreariness that plagues the crew of the whaling ship *Dolly*; "Even the officers aft, whose duty required them never to be seated while keeping a deck watch, vainly endeavored to keep on their pins" (9). "The lofty jet of the whale might be seen" (10) in the distance, but the crew remains comfortable in their languor rather than chase after the animal. The peril brought by the boredom that infects nearly everyone onboard is inertia, the lack of spirit and will. Tommo is eager to reach land to relieve his boredom. As John Seelye says, his "action [is] inspired by boredom" (14), and Ronald Mason adds, "*Typee* and *Omoo* represent inertia" (39). The risk Tommo faces unknowingly is masked by the seemingly innocent wish to return to land, and the recklessness and immaturity he will show clearly later is now hidden from consciousness. As he courts danger and surrenders to the impulse — anything to escape the dullness that threatens to overwhelm him — Tommo reveals the extent of his boredom.

Tommo's exclamation of mental fatigue and discontent is at the same time an appeal for sympathy. His complaint almost seems justified. The tropical heat exhausts and the unforgiving Pacific sun scourges an individual both physically and mentally; the vastness of the ocean reflects the spiritual waste-land within. Waiting for the appearance of whales in the face of past failures heightens the reality of nothing to do, and the excessive free time that it brings negates the novelty and excitement of being out to sea. At this moment, for Tommo, John Bryant says, "The sea is a barrier to self-awareness" (135). The lack of any sustaining camaraderie together with the confinement iso-lates rather than consolidates the crew. Life onboard the *Dolly* is stale and monotonous.

Job position seems to be related to the level of boredom in the crewmem-bers. Those with crucial positions, like the helmsman, can work while bored despite poor job performance. Boredom strikes first those who do not work, like Tommo, and then attacks those who do work, like the helmsman. Due to boredom, work becomes highly inefficient or a failure. For the few who actually perform their duty after Captain Vangs sets course for the Marque-sas, work is tolerated because they will reach the island within weeks. The steersman no longer must "coax her to the work" (4), but lets her "jog" (9) while he sleeps at the tiller. Boredom affects the crew like a drug, and no one, including the ship's officers, can ward off its drowsy effects. Work like "squar[ing] in the yards" (9) has been replaced by "spreading an awning over the forecastle" (9), and the men give in to their listlessness. Less work — and eventually no work — serves to intensify their boredom. The crew's aversion to work is not caused by the physical demands of labor — if they did work, despite the lack of whales — but by the episodes of inaction. From these peri-ods of no work, boredom naturally sets in and adds to the monotony.

The land is seen as the only remedy to boredom. Similarly, Alfred, Lord Tennyson, writes in "The Lotos-Eaters" (1832, 1842) about how ancient mariners had grown bored with sailing, and think only of the nearby land for retreat. He writes:

> We have had enough of action, and of motion we,
> Roll'd to starboard, roll'd to larboard, when the surge was seething free,
> Where the wallowing monster spouted his foam-fountains in the sea.
> Let us swear an oath, and keep it with an equal mind,
> In the hollow Lotos-land to lived and lie reclined
> On the hills like Gods together, careless of mankind....
> Resting weary limbs at last on beds of asphodel.
> Surely, surely, slumber is more sweet than toil, the shore
> Than labor in the deep mid-ocean, wind and wave and oar;
> O, rest ye, brother mariners, we will not wander more [150–73].

Melville's seamen give in to the same overwhelming and penetrating forces of lethargy found at sea as Tennyson's ocean-roaming Greek warriors. The sailors of the *Dolly* do not experiment with drugs, but they do partake in similar and dangerous pleasures as Tennyson's seafarers.

Boredom weakens morale and morality. Jack the helmsman is one of few who can work through his boredom; an important position like helmsman requires mental strength. Although a key member of the crew, Jack has difficulty keeping the ship on course; he personifies the ship as a reluctant and tired woman who begrudgingly does her job, much like himself. The helmsman has projected his own boredom upon the ship. He still is able to steer the ship, but as he says of the ship, "[She] won't take it kindly" (4). The apparent lethargy of the *Dolly* noticed by Jack symbolizes the languor of the crew; as John Seelye says, "The whaler ... is here an ark of boredom" (15). The news of reaching the Pacific islands has not motivated all of them to work; rather, it makes some of the crew more sluggish. The new course only intensifies their boredom. With little or strenuous work to occupy or invigorate them, the crew becomes more indolent and bored. Boredom has intoxicated the crew; Tommo says:

> What a delightful, lazy, languid time we had whilst we were thus gliding along! There was nothing to be done; a circumstance that happily suited our disinclination to do anything. We abandoned the fore-peak altogether, and spreading an awning over the forecastle, slept, ate, and lounged under it the live-long day. Every one seemed to be under the influence of some narcotic. Even the officers aft, whose duty required them never to be seated while keeping a deck watch, vainly endeavored to keep on their pins; and were obliged invariably to compromise the matter by leaning up against the bulwarks, and gazing abstractedly over the side. Reading was out of the questions; take a book in your hand, and you were asleep in an instant [9–10].

Six months of no whales, half a year of nothing to do will cause boredom. What is truly amazing is that the crew has not mutinied. Like Tennyson's bored sailors in "The Lotos-Eaters," Melville's seamen have grown tired of sailing; the land only can save them now.

Tommo offers explanations of why he must jump ship, an act that is criminal and punishable, but his justifications fail to satisfy his own troubled moral sensibility. No matter how much he tries to insist that he had no other option, he is still considered a "run away" (2), an identity that simultaneously repulses and excites him. He defines "run away" as "no way flattering to the individual to whom they are applied, it behoves me, for the sake of my own character, to offer some explanation of my conduct" (20). In order to present himself "as an honest man" (23), he goes out of his way to defend himself. He does not consider himself as a criminal; instead he portrays himself as the abused victim, in the moral right. He creates a self-image that is flattering, and this faux image does not prevent him from further morally questionable behavior. Claiming that running away "[is] no way flattering," and "to be sure it was rather an inglorious thing to steal away" (21–23), he cannot square himself, and these self-admitted truths do not change his behavior.

Using a crude sense of justice to bypass the legality of "binding [himself] to serve in a certain capacity for the period of the voyage" and admitting he "was of course bound to fulfill the agreement" (20) and assuaging a bruised self-image, Tommo believes he "[has] settled the principle" (20) of his case by shifting focus off himself and blaming the captain: "in all contracts, if one party fail to perform his share of the compact, is not the other virtually absolved from his liability? Who is there who will not answer in the affirmative?" (20). There is no equality between sailor and captain, and the contract also is a ship registry. I cannot accept Bruce A. Harvey's thesis that "there is too little rather than too much law aboard the *Dolly*.... Tommo explains that he jumped ship because he lacked hope of 'apply[ing] for redress' against such tyranny ... because they [Tommo and the crew] cannot turn to a court of appeal that could enforce the written contractual obligation between captain and crew" (403); no court would have found in the crew's favor. Whaling is a precarious and unpredictable business; how then could a captain be guilty of not providing suitable hunting grounds, filled with numerous whales for the picking? Tommo does not consider the seriousness of his decision to jump; as narrator, he does not point out the real criminal consequences that await him when he returns to the ship's domestic port, where all involved in the ship trade know who joined what ship. He claims the captain is an inhuman, neglectful, abusive, and violent tyrant, but these accusations can be exaggerated. Authority figures such as captains are usually presented unfavorably in Melville's art. And there is no clear or firm consensus among the crew to support Tommo's claims of Captain Vangs' mistreatment. Tommo says:

> With a very few exceptions, our crew was composed of a parcel of dastardly and mean-spirited wretches, divided among themselves, and only united in enduring without resistance the unmitigated tyranny of the captain. It would have been mere madness for any two or three of the number, unassisted by the rest, to attempt making a stand against his ill usage. They would only have called down upon themselves the particular vengeance of this "Lord of the Plank," and subjected their shipmates to additional hardships [21].

No camaraderie is presented favorably but a general desire to reach a harbor is voiced by the helmsman (4). Having no patience and endurance to complete his services, Tommo believes he is legally and morally justified to disobey and breach his contract. His reasons seem clever, and there is a sense of enjoyment in reliving these moments and getting away with it. Any qualms he may have experienced are undermined, but he conceals his real name, a slight indication that he feels guilt.

Suppressing moral misgivings can undo integrity; however, Tommo's ability to offset his sense of doom, confront his spiritual discomfort, and nurse his low spirits in order to realize high spirits are his means to curb boredom. There is nothing he can do realistically to change his fate while bored at sea but wait for the new opportunity to arrive — landing in the Marquesas. As Alan Lebowitz remarks, "The alternative to the potential dangers of the unknown is the continued boredom of a lengthy whaling voyage" (27). Tommo's boredom produces a level of anxiety that forces him to seek change, no matter how drastic or dangerous. He has had enough; the boredom of six months is too much for him. I disagree with Christopher Sten when he says, "Certainly boredom with his life at sea is a factor in Tommo's decision to desert ship at Nukuhiva, and so too is what he calls the 'unmitigated tyranny' of the *Dolly*'s captain. But such things, Melville's narrator asserts, 'could have been endured awhile, had we entertained the hope of being speedily delivered from them'" (31); Sten minimizes boredom's insidiousness, and accepts too readily Tommo's own lack of consciousness. Tommo has not thought about what that span of time actually meant; despite his articulateness, he is not a deep thinker. He is not philosophical or metaphysical. He clearly has an education, but higher questions of life do not interest him. He does not see the hidden dangers of boredom awaiting him, nor can he imagine what they may be. He is no Ishmael; he is not even close to Taji. His youth, naiveté, and recklessness occlude consciousness. It takes a level of sensitivity and experience to make sense of boredom. His thrill for life seems to offset his way of living life unconsciously. The reader has no access to Tommo's past or what drove him to the sea, but he has managed to avoid disaster so far. In short, nothing is known of him.

Tommo may not be able to spot "Descartian vortices" in the waves like Ishmael, but his appreciation for beauty and his political awareness help him to avoid the full force of boredom. He manages to shake off the spell of boredom to be in awe of nature "and to appreciate the beauty of the scene around me" (10). He describes the scenery as if he were describing his own boredom: "pale clouds which never varied," "long, measured, dirge-like swell of the Pacific," "some shapeless monster of the deep ... would ... sink slowly," and "the almost unbroken silence." At the same time, he notes the sky's "clear expanse of the most delicate blue," or how a "shoal of flying fish ... would leap into air, and fall the next moment like a shower of silver into the sea," or "the occasional breathing of the grampus" (20). Such moments break the unbearable silence and point to the life and beauty that exist in the relative void. Tommo's imagination and eye for beauty keep at bay the full onslaught of boredom; it is a kind of strength of mind, which he shares with Ishmael of *Moby-Dick*. Tommo's poetic sensibility for nature helps him maintain his good spirits when he is a Typee captive.

Just as acute as his appreciation for beauty is his social and political commentary. Anticipating Sigmund Freud's critique of civilization, Tommo says, "A high degree of refinement, however, does not seem to subdue our wicked propensities so much after all; and were civilization itself to be estimated by some of its results, it would seem perhaps better for what we call the barbarous part of the world to remain unchanged" (17). He also observes, "What has he [the Polynesian] to desire, at the hands of Civilization? She may 'cultivate his mind,' — may 'elevate his thoughts,' — these I believe are the established phrases — but will he be the happier?" (124). He adds, "Civilization for every advantage she imparts, holds a hundred evils in reserve" (124). His social and political observations reveal a kind of moral consciousness. His insights into the abuses of Christian missionaries and European colonists are scathing, and anticipate Joseph Conrad's disapproving commentary on European colonial criminality in the Congo.

Tommo may be politically aware, but these astute and mature observations fail to keep boredom at bay for long. Distractions of any kind soon falter and render the self unprotected. Diversion causes a loss of vision which weakens consciousness, thus increasing Tommo's recklessness; limited consciousness leaves him uncritical of himself, which also intensifies his self-complacency. Tommo may want to believe he is preserving himself by jumping ship, restoring health and vitality to a flagging spirit, but he is a shallow man; his immaturity goes to the core of his nature. Blaise Pascal notes, "What people want is not the easy peaceful life that allows us to think of our unhappy condition, nor the dangers of war, nor the burdens of office, but the agitation that takes our mind off it and diverts us.... That is why the pleasures of solitude are so incomprehensible" (38). Tommo will become in Melville's canon a major prototype because of these traits. He may at times be reflective but is essentially impulsive and daring. Overlooking rightly so the superficial affirmations of Tommo's character, John Bryant also finds Tommo to be a highly fickle and dangerous individual whose recklessness demonstrates a "failure of conscience" (134). Tommo thinks he has thought through every detail to hide out on the island so that he can stop feeling bored. Why did he sign up on the whaler in the first place? Living life in the extreme seems to be a tendency in Melville's art; Tommo has difficulty coping with humdrum existence. Perhaps he expects too much and risks everything to offset monotony. For a man with relative sophistication and learning to join a ship is as wildly impractical and risky as to live among the "cannibals." His reasons, if one is to take them as such, are outrageous and indicative of his character.

Tommo does not comprehend the predicaments his boredom places him in. He is aware that he must nip this developing problem, but his approach to combating this malady is unsound; he acts without safety or results in mind. He avoids any serious, deep, and honest self-analysis. His attempts to escape boredom simply extend his feelings of nothingness, masking them with initiative and action. He seduces himself into believing all will be well, while instead he is losing more of his self-control and self-identity. He may think he is running away from boredom, but it follows him; boredom is an inner, not an outward, problem.

Tommo's world is lonely and bleak. Boredom compounds the dreariness. Tommo is solitary and does not bond with the other men; the spirit of brotherhood does not exist on the ship. Isolation deepens his boredom and the crew's perception of him as different — higher education and other class biases — further alienates him. Being at sea at such close quarters would suggest camaraderie, but circumstances hamper friendships from developing. Living and working together should promote intimacy, but it does not. A whaler's life does not require men to know one another by personal name. Sailors and most officers, except for Captain Vangs and Jack Lewis, the helmsman, are anonymous. Only on land does the reader discover Tommo's "name" (72), and even then, Tommo's real name is not known on either land or sea.

The use of an alias may signify an uncertainty of one's identity. A nom de guerre may be used to gain an advantage such as power over another and as self-protection. But going by a false name can suggest a person's difficulty with social relations. The reader never learns Tommo's true name; the narrator of *Typee* adopts and uses "Tommo" after more than a third of the novel. Given that Tommo does not mention that he has any friends onboard the *Dolly* and does not interact with any of the sailors or reveal much about himself, his anonymity casts doubt on his identity and social skills. Although Tommo does say that he participates in the lackadaisical "activities" — sleeping, eating, and lounging with other sailors — he and the other men nap, feed, and loaf separately.

When Toby joins Tommo in the escape, it is indeed surprising. They are not really friends; Tommo only knows him from afar. Tommo has not mentioned him at all to this point. Friendship requires more than mere acquaintance; it demands close intimacy. These men are mysterious to each other and never reveal their real names and identities to one another. The strength of Tommo and Toby's friendship is uncertain; however, the real-life friendship between Herman Melville and Richard Tobias Greene, or "Toby," whom Melville used as the source for the literary Toby, was viable. Greene, upon reading Melville's *Typee*, wrote a letter to the *Buffalo Commercial Advertiser*, a newspaper, to help locate Melville, but also to authenticate Melville's so-called narrative of facts. A year later after their first correspondence, Greene demanded, and later recanted on, royalties from the sales of *Typee*. Melville forgave Greene the insult, and a life-long friendship flourished. Green named a son after Melville, Herman Melville Greene, and had a nephew named Richard Melville Hair (*Correspondence*, 579, 681). Melville sent both Herman Melville Greene and Richard Melville Hair engraved spoons (*Correspondence*, 681). Apparently Melville and Greene visited one another, as Greene writes, in one letter dated 4 January 1860 to Melville, "I would be delighted to see you and 'freshen the nip' while you would be spinning a yarn as long as the Main top bowline" (*Correspondence*, 679), and in another letter dated 20 October 1863, he writes, "When I get out of this Army which will be in June next, I shall certainly make you a visit" (*Correspondence*, 694). The brief encounter between Melville and Greene enabled these men to forge a long-lasting friendship. Robert K. Martin believes that Toby is far more than an ordinary "companion" Melville befriended. Martin considers important the fact that because Melville held on to a daguerreotype of Toby and versed a poem about Toby. As a result, he assumes a more serious, homosexual relationship between the two. Martin's rather strong emphasis of the homoerotic in Melville's art sometimes blurs the line between heterosexual closeness/friendship with homosexual fantasy. Although Tommo holds Toby in "great regard" (31), he at the same time is wary of him.

Tommo's decision to include Toby in his plan to jump ship is rash, impractical, unwise, and even unsafe. Toby is a mysterious and gloomy man who is volatile and wayward. Tommo identifies with Toby; they are almost doubles. Adopting Conrad–like analogies, Nicholas L. Nownes says, "Toby is Melville's furtive secret sharer, a shadow cast from the unconscious promising future disorder and the liberation from rationality that serves as the quest's implicit goal" (329). Just as Tommo's true name is never revealed, Toby too would not give his real name (31). The similarity in the sound of their names suggests a strong recognition of self with the other. The men are both outsiders; they are loners who seem miscast, out of place on the whaler. They appear to have an education and have airs that alienate them from the rest of the crew. This demeanor is however misleading. Like Tommo, Toby is intimidating, pugnacious, and cranky. Toby seems also to suffer from boredom: "leaning over the bulwarks, [he] apparently [was] plunged in a profound reverie" (31), and Tommo "had observed that Toby's melancholy had greatly increased, and I had frequently seen him since our arrival at the island gazing wistfully upon the shore" (32). Tommo also says, "I supposed myself the only individual on board the ship who was sufficiently reckless to think of [jumping ship]. In this, however, I was mistaken" (33). How true.

Once on shore, the paradise the two men envisioned is not there. The dangers no longer are romanticized. They are real. The most menacing threats, however, come from themselves, not the so-called man-eaters. The difficulties encountered while Tommo and Toby are climbing the mountainous regions of the island are the dangers of boredom made concrete. The land is not a cure for boredom; the land induces its own kind of despair. Short bursts of willpower offset desperation as they surge through thick masses of tall, yellow reeds, but the elasticity of the reeds "caused them to spring back to their original position; so that they closed in upon us" (38). As the landscape encases them, "a sort of dogged apathy" (38) sets in. Tommo has overestimated the health and strength of his mind and body, and the entrapment in the reeds not only represents symbolic death, but also underscores how close to death he actually is. The danger of boredom is death in the reeds. They gradually escape, but setbacks become more dangerous, and their romantic notions of easy living are slowly shattered.

Tommo's leg injury symbolically represents his encounter with the abyss of boredom; the ravines he descends represent the abyss. One recurrent element in Melville scholarship concerning the meaning of Tommo's leg injury is that it is an index of consciousness. Although the work of explicators have uncovered important insights into Tommo, there is a strong tendency to separate the implications of the injury from larger concerns, ones that go straight to the heart of selfhood. Often a discussion on the leg injury is short and not given the importance it deserves. What critics fail to recognize is how the leg injury is symbolic of the damage sustained to Tommo's integrity, and wholeness, and that boredom is unraveling him. The physical pain is a manifestation of deeper psychological/spiritual damage. As most critics would agree, the injury is much more than Tommo realizes. I agree with those critics who say the "nameless malady"—an expression that Renhard Kuhn has shown captures the elusive nature of ennui (boredom)—is an index of consciousness; however, I emphasize it, setting a standard in my work by which I evaluate all other Melville figures afflicted with boredom. The abyss is the spiritual emptiness felt when the forces of boredom are unleashed. His narrow escape from the reeds was a precursor to the dangers of the ravines' profound emptiness and danger. Rowland A. Sherrill (1979) understands this episode of the reeds differently, suggesting that "the hazards are appropriately associated with civilization and the difficulties of freeing themselves from it (13). Tommo's description of the tall grasses as "rods of steel" does intimate a critical assessment of the industrial West; however, I believe Tommo is admitting to the psychological impediments he has been facing: their paralyzing rigidity and stubbornness.

Tommo uses humor to help him climb down the ravine, and this joking screens the jeopardy he faces. He succeeds in lightening the mood, yet at a cost; he hurts his leg. His injury is inexplicable. He wants to believe a "venomous reptile" bit him, but learns later when he writes this novel that no snakes exist on the island (48). What accounts for the painful swelling? Psychic damage is rendered physically. Tommo comes onboard the ship unready to confront the hazards of existence. His immaturity and recklessness testify to his unpreparedness for life. His good spirits have managed to protect him from disaster, yet this dodging ends when he faces the abyss. The dangers always have been there, but Tommo has been blind to those forces. He admits to the physical risks he faces while in the ravine, but he speaks with more than irony when he says, "the accumulated horrors of that night ... almost unmanned me" (46). I disagree with Alan Lebowitz's claim that "the descent into the valley is ... the necessary struggle ... toward hard manhood" (29); such an attitude has placed both Tommo and Toby in danger. Their strong sense of masculine pride and strength is a primary cause of their predicament. Testing their might, endurance, zest, and audacity may be an indication of "hard" manhood, but not of selfhood. The more difficult struggle is to attain a manhood that can resist such endurance races, thrill-seeking, and machismo flaunting.

Consciousness can be selective and deceptive; the unconscious is uninhibited. Repression for Tommo is the choice to ignore, bury, and shield present reality and substitute a more pleasing one, despite the jeopardy involved. Only when he writes of his experiences from the distance of time and security of home does Tommo acknowledge the extreme precariousness of his situation as he must face another ravine. He notes:

> with an insensibility to danger which I cannot call to mind without shuddering, we threw ourselves down the depths of the ravine, startling its savage solitudes with the echoes produced by the falling fragments of rock we every moment dislodged from their places, careless of the insecurity of our footing, and reckless whether the slight roots and twigs we clutched at sustained us for the while, or treacherously yielded to our grasp. For my own part, I scarcely knew whether I was helplessly falling from the heights above, or whether the fearful rapidity with which I descended was an act of my own volition [53].

Only as a writer does he begin to see what mindlessness and daring cost; emerging inchoately is consciousness. This second encounter in the ravine is more dangerous than the first, and it reveals the terrifying blankness, uncertainty, and instability that his entire adventure represents. Uprooted is his confidence in appearance, faith in nature, belief that all will be well; every footstep is taken for granted and the stability of the environment is believed sound, but every second reveals more danger. The very notion of agency and direction is questioned. It has taken three years after the publication of this novel for Tommo, as narrator, to see the disaster he narrowly averted; however, his unconscious felt it from the beginning. His body responded to it; along with the mysterious leg infection, "a single drop of the cold fluid seemed to freeze every drop of blood in my body; the fever ... to death-like chills" (53–54).

Climbing the ravines becomes a test of the self facing the extreme. Boredom has lulled and seduced Tommo into believing he can become king of the mountain. His boredom on ship made him feel so desperate that he overlooked any possibility of failure or danger; anything but the boredom of the ship was acceptable, so he believed. Overcoming the second ravine, Tommo finds himself in front of another. Futility sets in, but a determined stubbornness pushes him on. He does not want to appear unmanly in front of Toby. For Tommo, masculinity is unrestraint and heedlessness; physical threats are calls to prove one's virility: "we ought manfully to face the consequences, whatever they might be" (67). Manliness also drives the stereotypical refusal to turn back and insistence on moving forward. Tommo says:

> It was unendurable the thought of retracing our steps and rendering all our painful exertions of no avail.
> There is scarcely anything when a man is in difficulties that he is more disposed to look upon with abhorrence than a right-about retrograde movement — a systematic going over of the already trodden ground; and especially if he has a love of adventure, such a course appears indescribably repulsive, so long as there remains the least hope to be derived from braving untried difficulties [54].

The geography is trapping them, and every step brings them closer to disaster. "A love of adventure" for Tommo is excitement and a display of successful effort. His belief in adventure produces a recklessness that is inconsistent with good sense. He is injured already. Tommo and Toby do not know if they are in Typee or Happar territory: supposedly cannibal or non-cannibal. Even if they reach the Happars, how will they know? " 'Typee or Happar, Toby?' asked I as we walked after them [male and female Polynesians]. 'Of course Happar,' he replied with a show of confidence which was intended to disguise his doubts'" (69). Trying to avoid hostility is good sense, but unreflective decisions, unreliable intuition, and wishing for the best do not compensate for lack of judgment or neutralize danger. "'Faith, I didn't think of that,' said Toby" (56).

Tommo thinks it is an advantage having Toby along because "nothing indeed appeared to depress or intimidate this fellow. Typees or Niagaras, he was as ready to engage one as the other, and I could not avoid a thousand times congratulating myself upon having such a companion in an enterprise like the present" (62). Tommo slights his own despair and misgivings because of Toby's assumed fearlessness. Tommo cannot hold his own, which indicates a vague self. His identity is ill-defined and precarious; he is too dependent on the will of Toby. Tommo's boredom brings to light more than just restlessness; it points out his lack of self-confidence and self-identity. I agree with Alan Lebowitz's observation that Tommo "is essentially without character" (34). Moreover, Tommo's poor state of moral excellence and firmness is further eroded when events, not personal volition, determine who he is, or not. Boredom has blurred his identity.

Tommo's leg injury represents psychic damage sustained while facing the abyss; moreover, it also intimates the harm endured by his relationship with Toby. Tommo is a sturdy, well-built individual (61), unlike the thin and slender Toby (32). If Tommo is vigorous and has a strong frame, why would he become injured, or be more susceptible to bodily harm than Toby? Tommo's association with Toby is unhealthy, and his body is unconsciously warning him. Tommo sacrifices too much of himself, and his actions are shaped and decided more by Toby than himself. Selfhood is one of the major themes of *Typee*. The novel shows how difficult it is for a young man to forge and maintain his self. Boredom weakens the self: its integrity, defenses, and volition.

Tommo's hurt limb also illustrates the fact that he cannot stand on his own. The wound shows how weak his manhood and selfhood are, and when the Typees adopt him, the debilitation seems like a regression to infancy. Kory-Kory, the special attendant/caretaker for Tommo, carries, feeds, and washes Tommo; Tommo, in effect, is an infant. "[Kory-Kory] brought us various kinds of food; and, as if I were an infant, insisted upon feeding me with his own hands. To this procedure I, of course, most earnestly objected, but in vain" (88). He protests but enjoys the treatment. Nicholas L. Nownes suggestively notes, "Tommo is spared once and for all the agony of action.... Absolved of his identity ... Tommo, forfeiting his agency, forfeits also his role as protagonist, and ... has, for the time being, essentially disappeared from the narrative" (331). The Typees treat Tommo's leg using their herbal remedies, a form of medical attention, but are unsuccessful, which could indicate that the leg injury is not simply a physical ailment. It is interesting to note that in the beginning chapters of *Omoo*, amid scenes of chaos, near mutiny, and the lack of medical supplies and a proper physician, Tommo's leg heals quickly and without any lingering effects. In *Typee* the herbal applications ease the pain, but "did not remove the disorder" (98).

Tommo changes his outward appearance only when Toby leaves for good. Toby's presence deters the emergence of Tommo's own selfhood. Once Toby is gone, Tommo's "limb suddenly healed, the swelling went down, the pain subsided, and I had every reason to suppose I should soon completely recover from the affliction that had so long tormented me" (123). He overstates this almost miraculous recovery because the injury does not entirely heal (144); the swelling and pain return toward the end of the novel, which suggests again the psychic dimensions of the lameness. Nonetheless he feels healthier, and the bleakness of his boredom subsides; he begins to "experience an elasticity of mind" (123), carefree enjoyment, and "a new interest to everything around [him]" (131).

Health and wholeness both serve to offset boredom, and, in Tommo's opinion, the Typees are free from boredom because of their great merriment, lack of strife or concern, and variety in their lives. The Typees have the joy of life. Believing in Rousseau's concept of the noble savage, Tommo credits the Typees' "buoyant sense of a healthy physical existence" (127) as their reason for not experiencing the soul-draining and body-depleting effects of boredom. Typees enjoy simplicity; they take pleasure and feel satisfaction from "the little trifling incidents of the passing hour" (144). This attitude toward life is a kind of Transcendentalism in the Pacific. Typees appreciate the higher life long before *Walden* (1854) was published; even Thoreau acknowledged and praised the Typee way of life. The Typees are not "sleepers in life" (Thoreau); they "derive the utmost delight from circumstances which would have passed unnoticed in more intelligent communities" (144). They live life fully, and the world is filled with wonder and joy. They have a deep regard for life, which means careful attention to the world and self. Much earlier than Thoreau, Tommo notes, "with these unsophisticated savages the history of a day is the history of a life" (149). Life on this South Seas island is cherished; nothing is taken for granted. Tommo learns through their example that "the fresh morning air and the cool flowing waters put both soul and body in a glow" (149). Sexuality is uninhibited; in fact, nudity is nothing of which to be ashamed. The alluring eyes and swaying hips of the female Typee dancers are "almost too much for a quiet, sober-minded, modest young man like myself" (152), but Tommo continues to watch and partake in the sexual freedom of the island; he certainly does not say no to Fayaway. For the Typees sex and the human body are natural, and a ménage a trois is ordinary.

It seems that boredom is a cultural construct and an existential crisis of the West. Life in the South Seas is the opposite of the white "civilized" hemisphere. Tommo argues that Polynesians are happier than Europeans because "the heart burnings, the jealousies, the social rivalries, the family dissensions, and the thousand self-inflicted discomforts of refined life, which make up in units the swelling aggregate of human misery, are unknown among these unsophisticated people" (124–25). Occidental civilization creates and fosters the conditions necessary for uncertainty, sadness, discontent, and chaos, all the elements of boredom. The forces that shape existence and identity in the Euro-American world unbrace and negate the self. Civilization debilitates health and ruins wholeness; it foments discontent and disunion. Life in the West compels some to sign up on a whaler to escape, but Tommo cannot run away from it. The social ills that infect the soul are so entrenched in his identity that sailing thousands of nautical miles does not heal the spirit. Society constrains and fractures; it censures and limits. Not only do social forces work against the individual; man blunts and frustrates himself. Nothing in society supports or promotes humanity. Tommo has not acquired or received the essentials he needs to live in oneness, and what he needs he cannot gain from civilization. What he needs is stability. He has suffered near collapse, and his romantic impulses have averted it narrowly. Tommo knows that society is unsupportive and antagonistic toward individuals. The ills of society have contributed to the predicament Tommo faces; boredom is the prime detriment in civilization.

Indeed, the Marquesas is a paradise, a haven free from all forms of Western corruption. Without money on the island, "all was mirth, fun, and high good humor. Blue devils, hypochondria, and doleful dumps, went and hid themselves among the nooks and crannies of the rocks" (126). Believing in the conventional moralistic adage that money is the root of all evil, he admires and almost envies the Typee way of life. He admires the Typees' joy of life. This kind of existence provides "almost always some matter of diversion or business on hand that afforded a constant variety of enjoyment" (127). Of course, Tommo is romanticizing his perception of the Typees and his nearly four-month stay does not necessarily render him an authority, but his observations do reveal an important distinction between two cultures and how one suffers as a result of his culture.

The joie de vivre is a joy to witness; Tommo cannot get over the fact that the Typee way of life is so nourishing to the self. It does not limit, withdraw, humiliate, or negate the self. Typee identity is based on the joy of life.

Health, vitality, and freedom are the foundation of their life. For Tommo, who is spiritually infirm, existence in the valley is both shocking and inviting. Western morality and prejudice color some of his assessments, but it is difficult for the white man not to exaggerate either praising worthily or moralistically. The Typees are decent people. Their only inhibitions are taboos, which do not conflict with their joie de vivre; rather, they serve to protect it.

However, people living in the Pacific remain healthy only if they are untouched or have no contact with European colonization and missionaries and the international whaling industry. The beauty, strength, and integral wellness that had existed on other Polynesian islands have disappeared; these admirable traits unattainable for the white explorers and visitors are lost forever to the indigenous people and they too become like their white oppressors: miserable, corrupt, and sick. The discontents of white civilization are foreign problems that the people of the South Seas never had to grapple with. It is through Western contact that this metaphysical ailment — boredom — becomes universal. With the arrival of the French fleet beginning to consolidate their presence and authority on the Marquesas Islands, home of the Typees and Happars, this place too will follow the fate of the Sandwich Islands, modern-day Hawaii. Tommo wishes for the Typees to be exempt from the foreign curse of boredom because:

> Better will it be for them for ever to remain the happy and innocent heathens and barbarians that they now are, than, like the wretched inhabitants of the Sandwich Islands, to enjoy the mere name of Christians without experiencing any of the vital operations of true religion, whilst, at the same time, they are made the victims of the worst vices and evils of civilized life [181–2].

In *Omoo*, the Tahitians exhibit the effects "of the worst vices and evils of civilized life"; one particular vice and evil they suffer is the effects of boredom. During a poignant scene in *Omoo* describing the spiritual collapse of the Tahitians, Tommo/Typee quotes one of the natives in despair: "Lies, lies! you tell us of salvation; and, behold, we are dying. We want no other salvation, than to live in this world. Where are there any saved through your speech? Pomaree is dead; and we are all dying with your cursed diseases. When will you give over" (191)? As Tommo points out in *Typee*:

> How little do some of these poor islanders comprehend when they look around them, that no inconsiderable part of their disasters originate in certain tea-party excitements, under the influence of which benevolent-looking gentlemen in white cravats solicit alms, and old ladies in spectacles, and young ladies in sober russet low gowns, contribute sixpences towards the creation of a fund, the object of which is to ameliorate the

spiritual condition of the Polynesians, but whose end has almost invariably been to accomplish their temporal destruction! [195].

The destructive nature of boredom ultimately attacks all.

It is through western eyes that Tommo, no matter how much he enjoys the novelty and pleasures of island living, can call the Typees lazy and indolent. He insists that he has not observed them farm or work; instead, "nature has planted the bread-fruit and the banana, and in her own good time she brings them to maturity, when the idle savage stretches forth his hand, and satisfies his appetite" (195). In Christianity, idle hands lead to sin and Satan, but the Typees, who supposedly have nothing to do, are not plagued by boredom or vice. Tommo's culture is an obstacle, and its prejudices color his interpretations. Tommo himself was lazy and indolent on the *Dolly*; moreover, he avoided any moral responsibility and felt no guilt when he did not carry out his duties, and, now on the island, does not object to the coddling he receives from Kory-Kory. As a sailor, he gave into his listlessness and enjoyed the narcotic-like effects; boredom on ship had benefits — no work — even if it undermined his integrity. There is little meaning when Tommo describes the Typees as indolent because their culture has no concept of indolence or boredom. Given the absence of crime (201), and that a general sense of brotherhood exists (203), and "a perfect tumult of hilarity prevailed" (203), how could boredom emerge here without Western influence? Typees live satisfied lives, and this point is truly beyond Tommo's comprehension. There seems to be no complacency, envy, or strife. The narrator expresses envy of this way of life and entitles a sub-section of Chapter 27 as "Jealousy of Europeans"; indeed, how do these people in paradise live so happily, without any of the discontents found in Tommo's civilization? Perhaps European colonial aggression is more than just acquiring land; it may be an unconscious urge to kill what they cannot be. To bring Western ideas, practices, and beliefs to the indigenous tribes of the Pacific is to bring death and despair; there is no enlightenment or improvement on the islanders' behalf. Tommo notes:

> The depopulated land is then recruited from the rapacious hordes of enlightened individuals who settle themselves within its borders, and clamorously announce the progress of the Truth. Neat villas, trim gardens, shaven lawn, spires, and cupolas arise, while the poor savage soon finds himself an interloper in the country of his fathers, and that too on the very site of the hut where he was born. The spontaneous fruits of the earth, which God in his wisdom had ordained for the support of the indolent natives, remorselessly seized upon and appropriated by the stranger, are devoured before the eyes of the starving inhabitants, or sent on board the numerous vessels which now touch at their shores [195–96].

The façade of order, purpose, and industry hides the turmoil that will develop into boredom's heart of darkness; the superficial appearance of progress is an inner nihilism projected outward. Melville is pointing to Joseph Conrad, who also witnessed the outrages done to "announce the progress of the Truth" in the Congo. The Truth for both Melville and Conrad was hollowness, having no redeeming values. Melville is beginning to anticipate modernist tendencies, such as radical skepticism, moral ambiguity, and the critique of unreliable institutions. Corruption is everywhere, including the missionaries. Such a trenchant denunciation of society would be unwelcome anywhere and anytime, as both Melville and Conrad could testify.

Two worldviews, peoples, and concepts of reality are colliding, and the doubts Tommo raises against Christian civilization and Pacific Ocean cultures compound his own loss of the self. His first feeling of settling into the tropics and living with the native population is newness; romanticism, the friendliness of the Typees, and the status of being a castaway underscore his perceptions. He learns to make adjustments to his worldview; he learns about Typee culture and admires it. He has unlimited sexual access to Fayaway. Pleasure warms his heart, and prejudice melts away. He is able to defend the Typee practice of cannibalism by observing: "this only enormity in their character is not half so horrible as it is usually described.... It is upon the bodies of slain enemies alone; and horrible and fearful as the custom is, immeasurably as it is to be abhorred and condemned, still I assert that those who indulge in it are in other respects humane and virtuous" (205). His tone is calm, rational, and objective; he is not horrified, and somewhat accepts this Typee way of life. He even questions who indeed the true savage is: the Euro-American or Polynesian? He notes:

> The hospitality of the wild Arab, the courage of the North American Indian, and the faithful friendships of some of the Polynesian nations, far surpass any thing of a similar kind among the polished communities of Europe.... How are we to account for the social condition of the Typees? So pure and upright were they in all the relations of life, that entering their valley, as I did, under the most erroneous impressions of their character, I was soon led to exclaim in amazement: "Are these the ferocious savages, the blood-thirsty cannibals of whom I have heard such frightful tales!" [202–3].

The alleged cannibals are more civilized, neighborly, and generous than the Europeans. He undergoes a moral reevaluation, a first step in correcting the image of the man-eating Typees; he is re-forming who they are, and, as a result, is reviving his own self-image. He cannot embrace and accept what he once believed; his values are at stake, and he is strong enough to uproot old misconceptions and plant new, more reliable tenets. His consciousness is developing and so is his conscience. Bruce L. Grenberg understands this potential growth of selfhood to be a kind of test of "allegiance" (11), whereby Tommo is not choosing between the Polynesian and Western worlds, but exploring some new, unknown identity. Grenberg also believes that critics have been focusing wrongly on the supposed binary competition between white man and Polynesian and nature/paganism and Christianity; instead, Grenberg thinks Melville is striving for a coalition. This alliance would be complimentary; it would be founded on equal terms. Tommo has a first-hand account of how misleading his home civilization is. His crisis of identity has exfoliated some of the discontents of civilization.

Tommo is undergoing a healthy and necessary nihilism of values; his radical skepticism illuminates the falseness and superstition of European culture, and he discovers new values. He sees classical beauty in the profiles of the Typees; they "were in every respect models of beauty" (184); the joy of life is easily recognizable. Fayaway and her fellow maidens possess natural, graceful, and unconcealed beauty; they are free of the artificiality that marks the women of Europe and America. Typee way of life naturally would produce such stunning and genuine beauty. The women suffering the discontents of European civilization must camouflage and prop in order to create the illusion of beauty. The disguises poison any innate beauty. Island life promotes health, and so the men and women of Typee glow. Their simple ways allow this beauty to exist; beauty is health and happiness. Tommo does not find it completely ugly when Fayaway eats whole, uncleaned raw fish: "I soon accustomed myself to the sight" (208). He tries to romanticize and soften this image of the lovely Fayaway eating fish this way, but is unconvincing. He too eats raw fish, occasionally (209).

Tommo participates and takes great pleasure in the Typee way of life; he shares in their joy of life. Tommo adopts their way of dress, not merely to preserve his western clothing; it suggests a loosening of his prejudices and mores. During the Feast of Calabashes, the chiefs appreciate that he completely adopts their dress. Wearing a robe of tappa and short tunic allows him to become more sensual. He becomes less ashamed appearing so and feels comfortable being among semi-nude women; now when Kory-Kory bathes him, there is no fear or guilt. Although the language at times is guarded, he enjoys the immense sexual freedom; he pursues and gratifies his sexual wants. He manages to break a taboo, a restriction against women riding in canoes with men (133); "many a time afterwards was this feat repeated" (134) with Fayaway. He does not condemn or sound shocked that the Typees practice ménage a trois; he only questions how a man "can consent to give up a corner in the thing he loves" (120). Tommo notes that no infidelities occur, and jealousy and strife do not darken marriages.

Despite his growing acceptance of Typee ways and his developing consciousness, Tommo eventually grows bored. Chapter 29 is important because it symbolically depicts his anxiety at the prospect of remaining on the island and "turning native." The chapter deceives the reader in that it reports the natural history of the Typees' homeland: animals, vegetation, and weather. One can easily skim through or pay less attention to this part of the novel. The dogs, cat, lizards, and birds instead represent aspects of his identity and psyche. Each animal uncovers how Tommo sees himself. They each represent an aspect of Tommo's spirit and identity. "Like one of those monstruous imps that torment some of Teniers' saints" (211), these animals are figments of the sailor's boredom. Before this chapter, Tommo has grown into his position on the island, accepting the pleasures and customs of his hosts; he feels comfortable, and conforms to island living.

However, from chapter 30 to the end, Tommo quickly undergoes a radical change. He may admit that he fears that he will be tattooed or be a victim of cannibalism, but that anxiety is a subtle disguise for his boredom. From the beginning of his adventures, boredom has weakened his selfhood and compromised his consciousness. The potential physical threat posed by the Typees wanting to tattoo him is similar to Tommo's own harrowing experience in the reeds: only when a tangible and imminent danger intimidates him does the psychological harm become explicit. He has been repressing his unconscious and its portents, and boredom has been occluding his consciousness. I agree with Christopher Sten's assessment that the real threat is Tommo's losing his selfhood (31). And so chapter 29 bridges Tommo's acceptance of being with Typees with his need to escape; this part of the novel does appear clearly to be a bridge or transition. I believe it helps to explain the sudden and seemingly inexplicable urge to escape; it touches upon the very essence of Tommo's identity and struggles with boredom.

The first of these animals, the Marquesan dog, is an unusual breed, and Tommo strongly doubts whether it is a canine; it is more rodent-like than dog. Its appearance is frightening and disgusting. He is convinced that this animal is not indigenous, and believes that the rat-dog knows it is a meddler, a thing that should not be there. What Tommo says of the animal is revealing: "Indeed they seemed aware of their being interlopers, looking fairly ashamed, and always trying to hide themselves in some dark corner. It was plain enough they did not feel at home in the vale — that they wished themselves well out of it, and back to the ugly country from which they must have come" (210). Disputing the dog's identity and recognizing the animal's intrusive manner, its self-awareness of shame and its urge to return home, Tommo seems to be describing himself, too. He is a foreigner and out of place, and feels repulsed with himself for being there. "Scury cur," he says of the dog. Not quite comfortable ever with his hosts, like the dogs, he longs to return home. He is confessing that he no longer can fool himself that he can adopt Typee ways and remain with them. This section is a heavy-handed self-criticism. He is the dog; both he and the dogs are taboos. His call to exterminate the dog, his declaration for a "canine crusade," which Mehevi the chief refuses to allow, is on the unconscious level an urge to kill or do away with those offensive qualities in him. His stay on the island has endangered the very essence of himself; his previous bouts with boredom has undermined him, and the longer he stays, the more his psychic health is in danger. His complacency with island living has weakened his selfhood.

Like the dog, a single cat terrifies Tommo; the cat too seems to be an alien on the island. What heightens his state of alarm is the fact that he alone sees the feline. He guesses that the cat had to have escaped from a ship, and so he identifies himself with a fellow runaway. He could have imagined the animal, and this situation suggests that this animal is a manifestation of his unconscious. He compares the cat to the monstrous beasts in the painting "Temptation of Saint Anthony" by David Teniers the Younger (211). Tommo is not steadfast or stalwart like the saint, but is tormented by his self-image. Like the dogs, the cat is an unconscious warning from his troubled soul. The demons persecuting Saint Anthony in Teniers' painting can be understood as demons of noontide, the medieval incarnation of boredom. As seen by Tommo, the island's animals are as real and demonic as Saint Anthony's harassers of the soul. They torment and drive Tommo off the Eden-like island in similar fashion as the medieval diabolic torturers afflicted and prodded monks out of their desert cells. In a secularized version, Tommo wrestles with his own kind of acedia.

At the same time, he likens himself to both the "beautiful golden-hued species of lizard" (211) and the birds that populate the island. The reptile's appearance pleases him; he also admires its tameness. Tommo has become tame as well. The birds are also beautiful and tame. He admires their flight through the valley, which connotes freedom and movement. But these birds lack the power of song or voice, alluding to Tommo's own unformed consciousness. Island living indeed is beautiful and gratifying, but it does not promote his individual growth; it domesticates, silences, and imprisons. Tommo feels melancholy looking at the birds, and their muteness lowers his spirits. Echoing the alien status of the dogs and cat, Tommo says, "I was almost inclined to fancy that they [the birds] knew they were gazing upon a stranger, and that they commiserated his fate" (216). He is both stranger and prisoner. Melville is beginning his study of the Ishmael type here. These allusions to animals reveal the hidden effects of Tommo's boredom.

Whatever security Tommo felt living with the Typees was artificial; his demons of boredom awaken by Chapter 29 and undermine his happiness. The perils encountered in the ravines were only diverted and suspended. No serious reflection has taken place, and his experiences have not breached the surface of consciousness. His unconscious only sensed the damage, and it has been repressed until Chapter 29. Chapter 30 turns Tommo's raw and concealed apprehensions into more tangible forms; just as the vague feelings of boredom experienced on the ship were transformed into the palpable leg injury. The real threat facing Tommo now is the Typees wanting to tattoo his face.

The integrity of Tommo's self is at stake once more. I share Rowland A. Sherrill's (1979) observation that Tommo's genuine plight, which becomes more and more undeniable to his unconscious, is the complete destruction of his selfhood if he remains on the island (31). His despair and feelings of entrapment increase as the islanders pressure him to be tattooed. The uneasiness created by the potential to be tattooed is a larger expression for Tommo's compromised sense of selfhood; he always lacked integrity of the self, and any attack upon the self, already weakened by the corrosive action of boredom, demonstrates how at risk he is for a breakdown. The Marquesans' relentlessness and Tommo's emerging despondency exacerbate the pain in his leg. He has not complained about his leg injury until now. In order for this malady to heal, Tommo must face his demons of boredom; not doing so will keep him a psychological cripple. As Tommo had said about his encounter with the elements of boredom in the ravine, he now says again: "This added calamity nearly unmanned me" (232). He is in danger of losing himself. He always has had a limp hold on his identity, and with each challenge to his manhood, he loses his grip ever so slightly. Will he have enough of a personality to retain it?

Marnoo unknowingly focuses on the very heart of Tommo's boredom when Tommo pleads with him to help him escape. Marnoo says, "You taboo. Why you no like to stay? Plenty moee-moee (sleep)—plenty ki-ki (eat)— plenty whihenee (young girls)—Oh, very good place Typee! Suppose you no like this bay, why you come? You no hear about Typee? All white men afraid Typee, so no white man come" (241). Tommo is taboo, meaning that he is set apart or untouchable; in effect, he cannot be cannibalized or mistreated. Marnoo cannot begin to realize what is bothering the runaway or grasp that his boredom is driving him to run away again. Tommo does not work, has no responsibility; he should be carefree and happy. He is living a fantasy: he sleeps and eats whenever he wants. How could Marnoo understand that Tommo is bored? How could he understand that his very existence is in peril, and that no amount of pleasurable activities can relieve Tommo's fate?

The more Tommo suffers psychologically, the more he becomes enfeebled, and Kory-Kory once again must carry him. His selfhood has regressed; again he has become, in effect, a baby. He cannot stand on his own; his legs give out. His leg injury is an unconscious remainder of the threats to his integrity. He tries to repress any serious self-examination, and distracts himself. Blaise Pascal makes a keen insight into the problem facing Tommo; he says:

> When men are reproached for pursuing so eagerly something that could never satisfy them, their proper answer, if they really thought about it, ought to be that they simply want a violent and vigorous occupation to take their minds off themselves, and that is why they choose some attractive object to entice them in ardent pursuit. Their opponents could find no answer to that, (Vanity, pleasure of showing off. Dancing, you must think where to put your feet.) but they do not answer like that because they do not know themselves [39].

Tommo lacks self-knowledge; he does not understand what is happening to him. He has gone through his South Sea adventures blindly, and when confronted with death, he still remains blind. A limited mind whose unthinking, uncritical nature only magnifies its dangerous complacency and purposelessness is the exact weakness that boredom exploits; boredom neutralizes and then erases the self. Boredom renders the self impotent and annulled. A weak self has little chance surviving the full onslaught of boredom.

Tommo sees three bread-fruit trees and believes that they soothe him spiritually (244), uplifting a bruised self-image. Given the spiritual and physical agony he goes through now, those three trees suggest the Crucifixion scene: in order to ensure a spiritual life, one must suffer physically. Many chiefs and Tommo's faithful friends follow him to shore, and some try to prevent him leaving. Mow-Mow, a chief who is resistant to Tommo returning to the white world, forbids anyone to carry the maimed sailor. This order demonstrates that Tommo must act on his own, taking his own steps for freedom. But Tommo does not go far, indicating weakness of his selfhood, and Marheyo, a sympathetic chief who has looked after Tommo, orders Kory-Kory to carry him. Tommo cannot mature and remains a child; his boredom has made him dependent and powerless. He truly is unmanned by his experiences with boredom. Fortunately, he has good friends to avert disaster and help him. Tommo may equate the sea now with escape and freedom, but he does not earn this independence; boredom has incapacitated his will. He attempts to author his freedom when he strikes Mow-Mow with a boat hook, thus ensuring a successful escape. Exhausted, he collapses into the arms of his rescuer. It becomes difficult to accept Alan Lebowitz's assertion that one sees in Tommo's escape the shadow of Ahab (33). There is none of the greatness, energy, and force of Ahab in Tommo. They are crippled, more so Ahab than Tommo, but, given Tommo's ambivalent escape attempt, he shrivels next to the mighty Ahab. Bruce L. Grenberg's reading of the ending is more convincing than Lebowitz's because Grenberg sees equivocation (15), not the stirrings of Ahab. The ending captures the very ambiguity that defines Tommo's self. Questioning the soundness of Tommo's identity, John Bryant understands Mehevi's mistrust of Tommo as a reaction to the unsoundness of Tommo's identity. Mehevi has come to realize that Tommo cannot honestly choose one culture over the other; Tommo cannot be a part of both. Mehevi concludes that Tommo is unable to commit all or nothing (164). Tommo "chooses" nothing because he lacks any firm, mature, or decisive stand on the position; he flees because he is scared.

Tommo escapes the Typees and is rescued by the crew of an Australian whaler. The sea now is the location of freedom, security, and life; the land represents bondage, vulnerability, and death. Actually, neither the land nor sea is a place of boredom; boredom is everywhere and nowhere. His need to change geography governs the amount of time he spends in a particular location. His need to roam suggests that the problem is in him, not in the sea or land; he carries his dissatisfaction, restlessness, and boredom with him. Running away from boredom will not lose it; evasion increases the intensity and severity of boredom. Tommo's relief upon returning to the sea at the end of *Typee* and the beginning of *Omoo* (1847) quickly regresses to boredom in Melville's second novel. The marine environment becomes a watery wasteland, and the new whaler, too, becomes a ship of boredom. Repetition, monotony, and illness plague the *Julia*.

Tommo's diplomacy in *Omoo* distinguishes him from his earlier selfish absorption in *Typee*. Bruce L. Grenberg sees a greater humanistic awareness in Melville's second book (20). Even while recovering from the leg wound he received in *Typee*, Tommo participates in shipboard politics in *Omoo*. He is a member of a special group summoned by Jeremin, the first mate, to decide the fate of the ship (50). Tommo is successful, along with Long Ghost, the ship doctor, in tempering the crew's frustrations and thoughts of mutiny (70–74). Tommo proposes that a "round robin" or a statement of grievances be written to the consul in Tahiti (74); the round robin is a way to "arrange the signatures in such a way, that, although they are all found in a ring, no man can be picked out as the leader of it" (74). Tommo has developed a deeper social conscience that helps keep him from being further weakened by the boredom that surrounds him.

Another possible reason Tommo does not succumb to the hopelessness of the *Julia* is his friendship with Long Ghost. Impressed with the ship doctor's "good-will" (36) and his ease with the crew, Tommo — also known by a new name, Typee — becomes Long Ghost's best friend. Of his new mate, Typee says, "Aside from the pleasure of his society, my intimacy with Long Ghost was of great service to me in other respects. His disgrace in the cabin [the fight with Captain Guy] only confirmed the good-will of the democracy in the forecastle; and they not only treated him in the most friendly manner, but looked up to him with the utmost deference, besides laughing heartily at all his jokes" (36). Explicators of the text often look at Long Ghost suspiciously, considering him to be a morally questionable figure; however, I classify the ship doctor as a relatively decent man who has good cheer, and is free from any elitist tendencies. He blends in well with the crew, and the crew treats him as one of their own; being a doctor — whether he actually is a professional physician — does not alienate him. He understands and shares in their concerns as mistreated men. Loving books, playing chess, sharing quarters with the men, and other traits (36–38) make him a democratic hero. I agree with Christopher Sten's claim that there is a sense of "genuine brotherliness" (51) between Typee and Long Ghost. Friendship prevents boredom from becoming a menacing presence.

Work also provides Typee an escape from boredom. Physical labor seems to be a last resort to control boredom in Typee's Tahiti. Placed in jail for their attempt to mutiny, the crew of the *Julia* becomes lethargic. Their incarceration is a just punishment for the crew's aversion to work, but the men grow bored. Their jailor, Captain Bob — an old Tahitian man — allows the prisoners to do what they want, even to roam the island (131), only to return to the mock prison. The men grow bored with the loosely supervised freedom offered by Captain Bob and resort to taking drugs. Long Ghost arranges for opium to be "prescribed" by Doctor Johnson, a physician caring for some sick sailors (135). Typee notes the effects of the drug on some of the crew:

> An hour or two passed, when Flash Jack directed attention to my long friend, who, since the medicine boy left, had not been noticed till now. With eyes closed, he was lying behind the stocks, and Jack was lifting his arm and letting it fall as if life were extinct. On running up with the rest, I at once connected the phenomenon with the mysterious vial. Searching his pocket, I found it, and holding it up, it proved to be lau-

danum. Flash Jack, snatching it from my hand in a rapture, quickly informed all present, what it was; and with much glee, proposed a nap for the company [136].

Reminiscent of Tennyson's warrior-sailors who were "Eating the Lotos day by day / ... To lend our hearts and spirits wholly / To the influence of mild-melancholy" (105–9), Typee's fellow sailors use opium to numb the boredom. Some of the men think about leaving the island because of "the proverbial restlessness of sailors," and Typee informs that "some of the men began to grow weary of the Calabooza Beretanee [the prison]" (159). Alan Lebowitz adds that the world in *Omoo* is "flabby, decadent" (45). The consul eventually releases the men. Finding jobs as plantation workers (199), Typee and Long Ghost soon grow bored with their tedious physical jobs and their powerful aversion to work drives them to seek royal positions.

The sea has promoted the friendship between Typee and Long Ghost, and the land is able to develop their brotherly union; however, neither the ocean nor the island can sustain the friendship. One does not learn of the fate of Long Ghost or whether Typee and the doctor reunite as Tommo and Toby eventually do in "The Story of Toby, A Sequel to *Typee* by the Author of that Work." Little is known about the real-life relationship after Melville (Typee) and John Troy (Long Ghost) parted in Tahiti. Troy had sent Melville a letter before September 1850, but this letter is lost; however, George Duyckinck, a friend of Melville's, makes reference, in a 23 September 1850 to Joann Miller, to this lost letter. Duyckinck writes, "Do you remember 'Long Ghost' in one of his [Melville's] books? He had a letter from him the other day dated from California" (*Correspondence*, 604). It may be likely that Melville and Troy never met, and there is no known letter from Melville to Troy. The strong relationship the two men had in Tahiti did not survive. Having grown tired, bored, and defeated by their adventures in Tahiti, both Typee and Long Ghost realize it is time to leave, though not together. They must separate because a new whaling captain agrees to accept only Typee as a crewman, and refuses Long Ghost; he denies the doctor because of the gossip the captain of the *Julia* has been spreading.

In order to leave his friend, Typee needs — and receives — Long Ghost's brotherly approval. The world divides the two friends, but Typee still cares for his colleague, and, by sharing his money with the doctor, an act which Christopher Sten admires (51), he shows great character here. I fail to see any Judas-like betrayal committed against Long Ghost, as John Samson maintains (77). Rather, their friendship ends on good terms, and Typee returns once again to the sea. The sea has become an ambivalent force; it may offer freedom from the perils and boredom of land, but it too fatigues and annoys, causing men to dream of the land. Tommo/Typee changes locations frequently, but never entirely escapes the effects of boredom. Long Ghost's companionship provided only a temporary antidote.

Yet, having grown bored with life on a whaler in both *Typee* and *Omoo*, Tommo/Typee returns to another whaler at the end of each novel. His pattern of escape from and return to the sea reveals a spiritual uncertainty, a crisis of the self. The calling of the ocean is both invigorating and benumbing; mariner life is ambivalent, and that equivocal dynamic gnaws at his integrity of the self. The sea's animating powers can boost health, confidence, and the joie de vivre, but this same exhilaration can fade quickly, leaving the sorry tar empty. His ability to brace both the fresh salty air and the stale brackish water is measured by his endurance of boredom. Even the most hale and industrious sailors — Jack, the helmsman — fall under its spell. Tommo tries to fathom the effects of boredom on his soul, but evades any real confrontation with boredom; rather than any personal action or responsibility, circumstances largely save him from despair and death.

At this early point in his artistic career, Melville's romantic impulses are predominant forces shaping his literary vision. By "romantic" I mean a strain in Melville which a buoyant faith in action dictates favorable outcomes in his art. In general, *Typee* and *Omoo* are lighthearted adventure stories that promote further perils, boldness, and heedlessness in *Mardi*. Boredom functions simultaneously as both a deterrent to and impetus for action, and, at the same time, screens and concentrates one's attention. Tommo experiences these varying and dual impulses, demonstrating that boredom is a complicated and overlapping state. Unconscious forces may try to coax Tommo into a more contemplative mood, obliging him to face boredom, but his larger and more developed emotional appeals of what is heroic, adventurous, remote, mysterious, and idealized suppress any affirmative attempt at well-being and consciousness. Boredom tests Tommo's strength of mind and reveals his ineptitude.

Even though Tommo is the primary protagonist in these two novels, in many ways he recedes from the plot. He does not reveal much of himself, causing a strained, obscure, and aloof relationship with the reader. This hesitation to disclose himself helps to explain why Tommo may avoid deep self-reflection, thus evading existential pressures to find self-meaning and to curb the growing sense of meaninglessness triggered by his boredom. His constant movement and comfort in distraction and the exotic prevent earnest character development. Political, social, and historical commentary prevails over the personal in *Typee* and *Omoo*; in spite of Tommo's sexual and other episodic adventures, these two novels are more about the South Pacific than about a bored and reckless mariner. It can be said that Tommo/Typee is more of a secondary character, if one is to call him one. Melville eventually will gain artistic control of this sketchiness in rendering characters, which can be seen in Bartleby.

On the other hand, Tommo/Typee does inaugurate the problem of boredom in Melville's art, notwithstanding the cursory introduction. Part of the reason for the shallow treatment of boredom in these early works is Melville has yet to embrace the implications toward which his art is leading him. First, boredom is an indistinct and unrealized concept for Melville. There are no fully realized artistic models for Melville to study, and at this point, he does not understand fully what boredom means. I would even say that boredom is not a conscious theme in Melville's mind; boredom will become a dominating force shaping his art, but will grow into one rather haphazardly. It is not that Melville chose this theme deliberately; the material arose as he explored other and related motifs. Questions of manhood and selfhood: consciousness and conscience, and the dualities between the land and sea, activity and abeyance, the physical and psychological, hedonism and responsibility, and faith and skepticism are the motifs he begins his career working with; these recurring, salient, and eventual supportive thematic elements, which, in their diluted forms, do not anticipate necessarily the theme of boredom in Melville, will become vital components of it. Nonetheless, as Melville searches for the exact expressions and dramatic depictions for what he has sensed as a sailor himself and is about to discover as artist, these ancillary topics will influence each other, allowing Melville to discover boredom, becoming conscious of it in his art. Gradually, these disparate subjects become integrated, refined, and elaborate, and then boredom emerges as a unified, potent, and multivalent force. As of now, boredom is mainly an unconscious and divided concept in Melville's art.

Second, the burgeoning sense of evil in Melville's art at first checks his artistic progress, causing him to take refuge in conventionalism and romanticism. This reluctance to grasp the role of evil obscures and delays the unfolding of boredom as a serious theme in his art. The relationship between boredom and evil is complicated, one that Melville learns firsthand as a naval seaman, but terrifies him as artist. In *Typee*, Melville writes, "I formed a higher estimate of human nature than I had ever before entertained. But alas! since then I have been one of the crew of a man-of-war, and the pent-up wickedness of five hundred men has nearly overturned all my previous theories" (203). Through his narrator, Melville admits that his stay among the Polynesians uplifted his view of humanity, but that affirmation becomes negated quickly through his military service; *White-Jacket* dramatizes that process. At some level, Melville is trying to regain that preliminary vision, despite the world's "power of blackness." The blackness of boredom is rooted in evil, and in *Either/Or*, Søren Kierkegaard observes:

> A person needs only to ponder how corrupting boredom is for people, tempering his reflections more or less according to his desire to diminish or increase his *impetus*, and if he wants to press the speed of the motion to the highest point, almost with danger to the locomotive, he needs only to say to himself: Boredom is the root of all evil. It is very curious that boredom, which itself has such a calm and sedate nature, can have such a capacity to initiate motion. The effect that boredom brings about is absolutely magical, but this effect is one not of attraction but of repulsion [285].

Kierkegaard adds, "What consequences this boredom had: humankind stood tall and fell far, first through Eve, then from the Babylonian tower" (286). Bertrand Russell also notices the juncture between evil and boredom: "Boredom is therefore a vital problem for the moralist, since at least half the sins of mankind are caused by the fear of it" (51). In order for the theme of boredom to become self-perceived and controlled for Melville, he must realize that there is no way back to Eden, that evil disfigured man (Billy's stutter), and that idle hands and restless spirits make for boredom, and entice the Devil.

Omoo *and* Mardi
Searching for a Theme

In *Omoo* and *Mardi* Melville develops the religious themes that will increasingly shape his understanding of boredom. Melville may have been a disapproving critic of the South Pacific missionaries, but his censure did not limit or prevent him from exploring religious belief. Because religion, in one sense, is a search for meaning, Melville was drawn to it because of his own uncertain relationship with God. And since boredom undermines meaning, religion becomes a prevailing means in Melville's art to resist the subversion of meaning; at the same time, religion is a target of Melville's most exacting skepticism. Exploring religious matters is also a way for Melville to find the poetic and philosophic language necessary to articulate boredom's effects on the self. Losing one's self certainly has religious overtones, and so Melville is pairing unconsciously the psychological with the spiritual, which could be understood as an extension of the moral. Boredom has had roots in religious soil ever since medieval times and then through Pascal, whom Melville read. As he describes the destruction of the Polynesian soul and dramatizes the spiritual crisis of the Tahitians, Melville comes to apprehend his own religious sensibilities through his artistic exploration of boredom.

Like his early treatment of the theme of boredom, Melville's initial artistic explorations of religion are ill-defined. By "ill-defined" I mean Melville has not yet gained full artistic perception of his material; even though Melville ultimately will remain ambivalent about God, the nature of his contradictory attitudes toward God is extremely complicated. Melville's exploration of religious motifs is not a deliberate attempt to lay the groundwork for his prolonged examination of the problem of boredom. The theme of boredom is not a conscious subject matter for Melville at this time; given the fragmentary and rudimentary nature of the subject of boredom in the beginning of his career, Melville is still searching for a theme. As he reaches the limits of his early material, the themes and motifs he is working remain irritatingly ambiguous, but these minor annoyances, if one is even to call them such, really are the birthing pains of Melville the artist. The topic of boredom will become a conscious one, and will change, deepen, and darken only when he masters his fear of evil.

Moby-Dick becomes possible only when Melville unleashes his unconscious realization that evil indeed is formidable, a mighty force that tests the integrity of virtue and character; Melville's Manichean tendencies keep in check an all-out nihilism. Evil is not a completely overwhelming power in Melville's art, although at times it seems that way; a fragile balance does exist. The scholarly belief that Melville's mother's severe Christianity formed the foundation for Melville's own may, in some ways, be true; however, Melville set out to separate, define, and determine religion for himself. Even later, while composing *Clarel*, he would grow sympathetic toward Roman Catholicism, a heresy for strict Protestants, like his mother.

A central problem for Melville is God: yes or no, to believe or not to believe, salvation or damnation; it is a mystery that he cannot resolve. This conflict between belief and nonbelief— meaning and meaninglessness — is the main tension determining his art, and as Melville matures as artist, this crisis grows exponentially, heightening his existential concerns, which he exemplifies through boredom. There is no artistic decline. The initial creative process is slow and uncertain because Melville cannot choose either/or; it is a dichotomy that haunts his art. There are masterpieces even after *Moby-Dick*. Given his inevitable tragic vision, he will know that Billy Budd must die, a sign that Adam must grow up. The emotionally and existentially significant convergence of faith and the lack of conviction in God ingrains the equally dire clash between a meaningful life and one marked by boredom. How is the Melville protagonist to find self-confidence and pious certitude when worldly pursuits and distractions and religious skepticism lure him into the spiritual wasteland, much like the noontide demon did with the desert monks? Melville is yet to explore this crisis focusing on an individual protagonist; however, he does delve into the problem by examining the spiritual plight of the Tahitians in *Omoo*.

Omoo: The South Pacific Great Awakening and Nightmare

Melville's study of the spiritual crisis of the Tahitians is brief, uneven, and fleeting. It is not comprehensive, but nonetheless is a vital sketch of Melville's linking together spiritual and cultural emptiness — the loss of faith, identity, and selfhood. Even in its cursory and rapid depiction of this soul killing in *Omoo*, Melville's artistic gaze upon religion points to the consequences of this cultural and spiritual problem, going beyond the simple and obvious criticism of missionary imperial religious indoctrination, and begins to lay the artistic foundation for the joining of religious doubt and the state of boredom, demonstrating that boredom is not simply a superficial and temporary problem of attention span. Because the native populations lack serious piety toward Western Christianity, and their conversions are insincere, their despair and resulting spiritual emptiness creates a harrowing form of boredom, one that dispossesses them of self-meaning and the will to live. The boredom Melville dramatizes here is similar to the medieval version of boredom or acedia. All spiritual values are negated, made hopelessly void, leaving the individual with himself, that is, alone in the universe with nothing; with no cultural identity, no stable self, and no reliance upon a divinity, the Tahitian is in his own hell. If *Typee* is a scathing philosophical attack of missionary abuse, *Omoo* is the heartbreaking and emotional depiction of it. The "power of blackness" in *Omoo* is the nightmare of boredom.

Melville depicts the missionaries as both praising and condemning the Tahitian's "constitutional indolence" (189), and ultimately revealing a gross misunderstanding of the Tahitian's soul. On the one hand, they believe it to be malleable for their purposes, and on the other the Tahitian's supposed impulsiveness makes him a poor candidate for Christianity. The missionaries [and Typee, too] believe that the native's mind is excited too quickly, but also quickly loses interest, and Typee also understands the Tahitian's conversion in this way. The Tahitian is perceived as unindustrious; he wastes his land by not developing it, and kills his time doing nothing. His "constitutional indolence" implies a temperamental disinclination to labor or activity, verging on apathy — in a religious sense, not doing what God expects of one because one is not moved to, or does not care about one's duty to God.

Also, the Tahitian's alleged simultaneous excitability and disinterest recalls a similar accusation against the New Lights and Jonathan Edwards. Powerful orthodox religious leaders doubted the sincerity of the "awakening," or a highly intense religious experience that transforms the individual into a truly devout, "affected" believer. The "great awakening" is the unprecedented, definitive, and soul- (and life-) changing conversion that elicits the greatest spiritual transformation, and the event that causes the individual's eyes to be fully opened to see the light of God and the soul to be emptied so that God may enter. Acknowledging the controversy, Jonathan Edwards notes in "A Faithful Narrative of the Surprising Work of God" (1736): "Some have been too ready to be impressed with fear, that instead of becoming better, they are grown much worse"; he also points out, "When they hear of the signs of grace laid down for 'em to try themselves by, they are often so clouded that they don't know how to apply them" (628). Even Edwards himself admits in "Personal Narrative" (posthumous, 1765) that initially his "affections seemed to be lively and easily moved, and I seemed to be in my element, when engaged in religious duties. And I am ready to think, many are deceived with such affections, and such a kind of delight, as I then had in religion, and mistake it for grace" (631). Edwards had several awakenings, all of which had fooled him, until he truly knew he was awake. His final awakening, in essence his first and only conversion, was unambiguous; he writes:

> I felt withal, an ardency of soul to be, what I know not otherwise how to express, than to be emptied and annihilated; to lie in the dust, and to be full of Christ alone; to love Him with a holy and pure love; to trust in Him; to live upon Him; to serve and follow Him, and to be totally wrapt up in the fullness of Christ; and to be perfectly sanctified and made pure, with a divine and heavenly purity [639].

Although his description here is restrained, his accounts of becoming awake are filled with emotion and sensuality, almost bordering on the erotic; as he admits, "the whole Book of Canticles [*Song of Solomon*] used to be pleasant to me" (633), noting that one can be impassioned with God. As long as the burning in his heart and soul was for God, then his passion was sanctioned, or at least tolerated.

No such tolerance was offered to the Tahitian; even Typee misunderstands the Tahitian's good-natured, warm, friendly, and sensual character. Carol Colatrella notes that Typee is quick to denounce the Tahitian for his supposed fickleness, impetuous, and nonresistance, but his censures fail to uplift or dignify the religious and political authorities who are not morally better (112). The missionaries apply a strict Victorian, perhaps puritanical, code of conduct upon the native people. What may be seen as spontaneity in the Tahitian, Westerners interpret as impulsive; the Tahitian's sensual nature is viewed as lewdness. Nudity has become nakedness, and shame, indecency, and sinfulness replace the Tahitian system of values; instead of morality, there is moralism. Even their sexuality has been tampered with; "kannakippers," or the so-called native "religious police," prowl "round the houses, and in the daytime hun[t] amorous couples in the groves" (180). Sex is the barometer measuring the Tahitian acceptance of missionary Christianity; Typee recalls an episode with Ideea, a young Tahitian woman:

> "Mickonaree *ena*" (church member *here*), expressed she, laying her hand upon her mouth, and a strong emphasis on the adverb. In the same way, and with similar exclamations, she touched her eyes and hands. This done, her whole air changed in an instant; and she gave me to under-

stand, by unmistakable gestures, that in certain other respects she was
not exactly a "mickonaree." In short, Ideea was
> "A sad good Christian at the heart —
> A very heathen in the carnal part" [178].

This index of faithfulness, or rather adherence to Christian morality, is a
telling sign that the Tahitians are not embracing Christianity or committing
themselves fully to it. Typee considers this situation as "hypocrisy" (178)
because the Tahitians have been coerced into religion. The Tahitians are not
openly, willingly seeking out faith in Christ; "They pretended" a religious
enthusiasm "by the preaching which they heard" (175). Describing them as
fickle and interested in novelty, Typee notes, "It leads them to assume the
most passionate interest, in matters for which they really feel little or none
whatever" (175). The consensus is that the Tahitians "can hardly ever be said
to reflect: they are all impulse; and so, instead of expounding dogmas, the
missionaries give them the large type, pleasing cuts, and short, and easy lessons of the primer. Hence, anything like a permanent religious impression,
is seldom or never produced" (174). Typee's observation exactly fulfills what
the Old Lights suspected would happen to those people claiming the so-called
"Great Awakening." Viewed as simpleminded, unthoughtful, and distracted,
the Tahitians are caught in the middle of a metaphysical disaster.

In *Typee* lovemaking outside the Polynesian marriage is a common and
approved practice; it is not an insult or considered infidelity. In *Omoo* a similar habit exists; however, the kannakippers view it as a sinful crime. Once
caught, would-be adulterers are punished and called "Tootai Owree" which
means "a bad person or disbeliever in Christianity" (180), a stigma much like
Hester Prynne's scarlet letter. Passion is misunderstood both by the religious
zealots in Hawthorne's work and the religious police in Melville's. Sex is associated with sin, and the religious establishments in the two fictions make it
their mission to control, suppress sex. For the Tahitians sex is not sinful and
is a major part of their identity. What the missionaries see as promiscuity and
fornication, the Tahitians view as an instinctive, joyful meeting, which
involves more than just the physical. Sex sometimes can be seen, by the missionary moralists, as an activity for the idle; those who have nothing to do,
who have sex to fill the time, can be seen as bored. Characterized by the missionaries and others as indolent, listless, unproductive, and irrational, the
Tahitians are the example of lust, sin, and corruption; idleness breeds sin.
Their idleness ultimately is not sinful nor is it boredom. However, once the
missionaries tampered with this element of Tahitian life, it brought out boredom because not only was there nothing left for them to do, but also their
lives became meaningless.

The Old Lights of eighteenth-century New England were skeptical of Jonathan Edwards and the supporters of the Great Awakening because it appeared too emotional, rash, and groundless; converts were passionate, too demonstrative, and perhaps uncontrollable. Typee's own suspicions concerning the Tahitians' comparable Great Awakening bear striking resemblances to the Old Lights. The core of Typee's disbelief in genuine Polynesian conversions has been their supposed impulsiveness, a characteristic the Old Lights perceived in the conversion of the New Lights. Spiritual conversions are personal, but critics found them to be overly and suspiciously subjective. Typee believes the moral tenets of Christianity do not take hold because:

> It is a noteworthy fact, that those very traits in the Tahitians, which induced the London Missionary Society to regard them as the most promising subjects for conversion; and which led, moreover, to the selection of their island as the very first field for missionary labor, eventually proved the most serious obstruction. An air of softness in their manners, great apparent ingeniousness and docility, at first misled; but these were the mere accompaniments of an indolence, bodily and mental; a constitutional voluptuousness and an aversion to the least restraint [175].

Typee supports this claim of Polynesian "ingeniousness," of the native's ability to deceive the missionaries of his adoption of the Christian faith:

> At one of the Society Islands — Raiatair, I believe — the natives, for special reasons, desired to commend themselves particularly to the favor of the missionaries. Accordingly, during divine service, many of them behaved in a manner, otherwise unaccountable, and precisely similar to their behavior as heathens. They pretended to be wrought up to madness by the preaching which they heard. They rolled their eyes; foamed at the mouth; fell down in fits; and so, were carried home. Yet, strange to relate, all this was deemed the evidence of the power of the Most High; and, as such, was heralded abroad [175].

Implying an obvious falseness that fools only the gullible, Typee discredits the conversions in Old Light fashion: instead of heartfelt and genuine rebirths, these were examples of emotional, irrational, and crazed behavior feigned in order to gain approval and, most likely, food. The enthusiasm or "religious affections" that moved the people of Raiatair motivated the missionaries to call the conversions the "Great Revival at the Sandwich Islands"; by calling it "Great Revival" the missionaries suggest that they viewed the conversions in Edwards' terms. But this seemingly decisive adoption of Christianity brought about no sober moral convictions, as the "almost instantaneous relapse into every kind of licentiousness" (174) revealed. This "almost instantaneous relapse" was the exact fear of the Old Lights: conversions were fits, mere emotional outbursts, and the likely work of Satan.

Starvation, superstition, and missionary fanaticism motivated many to convert during the Sandwich Islands Revival; in fact, missionaries there seemed to play upon the Polynesians' emotions by making them believe a divine curse was placed on them for not converting. Interpreting the devastating spiritual circumstances suffered by the Tahitians as an illustration of God's disfavor sounds like Puritan typology, the practice of making sense of natural events and disasters as the work of God. Instilling fear is playing on the emotions, which technically would offend Old Light sensibility, and the missionaries are leading Polynesians to Christianity not out of genuine conviction, but fear.

Typee's critique of Polynesian conversions is a tacit critique of missionary methods; Polynesians are not coming to Christianity willingly. As testimony to many personal narratives, conversion experiences are not always gradual; they are uneven, arduous, lengthy, and ultimately earned. The moment of true awakening is prefaced by struggle, doubt, and hopelessness. It is never easy. Jonathan Edwards himself went through a series of awakenings before achieving the true "Great Awakening." Emotional and spiritual maturity seems necessary in order for a true awakening to occur, and so time is needed along with the desire to find God within. The period of time prior to the awakening is a kind of sleep, an unconscious state where the soul's feelings toward God are unformed. When the awakening occurs, it truly is an awakening; one breaks out of unconsciousness and can see God everywhere. The mass conversions are happening much too quickly in Polynesia; converts are not experiencing a spiritual transformation. They are in an unfortunate position produced by imperialism, starvation, disease, and death. Their motives are of another kind — survival. Physical existence is at stake. Typee sees this problem, but fails to understand it fully; the unsoundness of their religious lives offends him, but he fails to see how quickly their conversions become true problems. Angered by their hypocritical intentions, he says, "[They] assumed the most passionate interest [in Christianity], in matters for which they really feel little or none whatever" (175). He blames them for fickleness, but points out a common problem even the successive Puritan children wrestled with: genuine faith. How many young Puritans felt like the Polynesians? Unable to proclaim their conversion experiences, the young Puritans created an atmosphere that influenced their fathers to become less demanding concerning church membership. And what of Typee's own beliefs? Carol Colatrella says, "Polynesian indolence parallels the laziness of Typee, the doctor, and the other sailors from the Julia, who resist and prefer intoxication and indulgence" (111). Typee admits to attending Tahitian church services, but it seems that he is spotting attractive female attendees rather than fulfilling his Sunday obligation.

If Tahitian spiritual matters initially appeared illusory, rushed, and shallow, eventually they become horrifyingly deadly. Along with spiritual concerns, the missionaries propose to instill a Western work ethic into the South Pacific people; they see islanders as lazy and idle. No systematized agriculture and manufacturing exists on the islands. These people seem bored; with nothing to do, they seem to have too much unoccupied time and unused land. For Westerners, what a waste! Polynesian culture seems to support such idleness, and the missionaries outlaw all forms of Polynesian art and custom. All forms of expression, practices that identify Polynesians as a people have become "punishable offenses" (183). The missionaries believe that if a productive-minded culture could replace a slack one, an alert and occupied state could be exchanged for a drowsy and free way of life, the islanders would become more Western-like and acceptable. Manufacturing centers had sprung and quickly faded because the native peoples were too "indolent."

Without any legal ways to express their authentic cultural identity, the Tahitian soul despaired. What before looked like torpor now really is a crisis, and Typee realizes it, too. Typee observes:

> Doubtless, in thus denationalizing the Tahitians, as it were, the missionaries were prompted by a sincere desire for good; but the effect has been lamentable. Supplied with no amusements, in place of those forbidden, the Tahitians, who require more recreation than other people, have sunk into a listlessness, or indulge in sensualities, a hundred times more pernicious, than all the games ever celebrated in the Temple of Tanee [183].

The listlessness that Typee and countless other white observers have always faulted the Polynesians for has now become boredom. Was it ever listlessness, and not lightheartedness, a life filled with contentment, joy, and self-meaning? If they seemed inactive and shiftless, traits superficially associated with the Tahitians, the missionaries, who have destroyed the very essence Tahitian cultural identity, have made them numb, soul weary, and lifeless. Left with nothing to do, the islanders are struggling with the meaninglessness of their lives; their boredom is the result of the "denationalizing" by the missionaries. Christianity, a form of spirituality meant to improve the soul and provide ultimate meaning, through the thoughtlessness and ineptness of the missionaries, has ruined the Polynesian spirit. The Tahitian was not prepared to contend with the metaphysical difficulties — despair, godlessness, and meaningless — that arose as a result of the boredom plaguing them and is unable to overcome them. Perhaps his prohibited dance, song, sports, festivals, tattoos, taboos, or clothing would have eased the loss of hope. Without them, he faces the yawning mouth of boredom.

The listlessness that now truly plagues the Tahitians is "a hundred times more pernicious" because it sterilizes the soul. The native people ultimately give in, and the diseases of Western civilization — psychological and moral — inflict the people of the South Pacific. *Typee* only alludes to these spiritual ailments; in *Omoo* Melville documents the fate of the Tahitians in detail. Typee notes, "The depravity among the Polynesians ... was in a measure unknown before their intercourse with the whites" (188). Venereal and other diseases decimated the local population, but a far deadlier killer exacted more destruction: boredom. Typee becomes sympathetic to their plight because he sees first-hand the death toll due to boredom. Citing "the good old Quaker Wheeler," Typee recounts, "There is scarcely anything ... so striking or pitiable, as their aimless, nerveless mode of spending life" (190). Typee also cites Kotzebue, the Russian navigator, as saying, "A religion like this, which forbids every innocent pleasure, and cramps and annihilates every mental power, is a libel on the divine founder of Christianity" (186). Indoctrination has domesticated and sapped the Tahitian spirit, and conservatism has eradicated their culture.

A religion that was meant to liberate has enslaved the tropical islanders. Oppression rather than salvation is what they find; death instead of the promise of eternal life is what they must cope with. Joyce Sparer Adler describes this crisis as "nothing less than a charge of genocide" (9). Typee cites a Tahitian: "Lies, lies! you tell us of salvation; and behold, we are dying. We want no other salvation, than to live in this world. Where are there any saved through your speech? Pomaree is dead; and we are all dying with your cursed diseases. When will you give over" (191)? The Tahitians indeed are dying of Western diseases, but their complete loss of hope, both as a symptom and effect of boredom, also is killing their souls; their destruction is not simply a physical one: it is a psychological, spiritual one. Missionary speeches were empty, false, and insincere; their promises of salvation, of coming closer to God, turned out to be damnation. Tahitian boredom is similar to medieval acedia in its complete absence of joy in life, but more importantly, the joy of spiritual matters. Whether Tahitian conversions were genuine is irrelevant at this point; the spiritual toll, which takes on massive metaphysical implications (one's sense of place in the universe), is more deadly than the venereal diseases wiping them out. The Tahitians are dying without peace; the horror of their deaths is that they are dying with their souls already dead.

This account of the Tahitian spiritual nightmare casts a dark shadow on the novel. Convinced by D.H. Lawrence's claim that *Omoo* is a "literary romp," John Wenke insists that Melville "avoids symbolic dark forests" (4). If the cries and corpses of the Tahitians are not trees of gloom, then what are they? William Braswell writes that Melville "showed when he wrote *Typee* and

Omoo that what he had seen had convinced him that some people would have been better off if they had never heard of Jesus Christ" (8). Many years later in his literary career, Melville will make a similar statement in *Clarel* (1876):

> Unvexed by Europe's grieving doubt
> Which asks *And can the Father be?*
> Those children of the climes devout,
> On festival in fame installed,
> Happily ignorant, make glee
> Like orphans in the play-ground walled [1.3.135–40].

Boredom, as Melville imagines it, is not a Western problem; it is an universal crisis. Once the conditions are there, it affects everyone; no one is spared, not even the so-called savages presumed to have no soul. It does not discriminate. It shows that the Tahitians can and do undergo serious, complex, and deadly moral and psychological development and injury. They are not simpleminded or child-like; they suffer from the same despair as Americans and Europeans. When the foundations of the self deteriorate, boredom attacks and completes the annihilation. Annihilation — to destroy until nothing is left — is the endpoint of boredom. The Tahitians now understand what has happened to them; their ancestor, high-priest Teearmoar, notes in song their fate:

> *A harree ta fow,*
> *A toro ta farraro,*
> *A mow ta tararta.*
>
> The palm-tree shall grow,
> The coral shall spread,
> But man shall cease [192].

Their once Edenic paradise now no longer is. Seeing Melville develop as an ethically minded writer, Sten stresses that Melville "is willing to take a stand on principle, on his inherent sense of what is right and just" (49). I would add that Melville the artist has gained moral stature because he wants to be a moral thinker, he wants his art to be shaped by principle. *Omoo* is not a simple sea adventure story; instead it promotes the human rights of the Tahitians. Melville is deconstructing not only the myth of the "Noble Savage," but also the suggestion that they are primitive. By focusing on the spiritual matters that plague the Tahitians, Melville at the same time demonstrates that these people are sophisticated.

Melville's illustration of Tahitian boredom is not thorough; however, it is far more indicative of the creative direction Melville eventually will take in his pursuit of his theme of boredom. He has come by chance on something vaguely important, unaware that he even is drawing out its hidden, dark, and weighty fragments, trying to locate its source, and searching for the means both to define and dramatize the significance of boredom. As a sailor, Melville would have experienced periods of having nothing to do, of whiling away the time, and of staring into the boundless horizon, as do his whaler protagonists; but as a budding artist, unsure of himself and the material, Melville lacks the clarity, comprehension, and control of this emerging yet raw, scattered, and unconscious theme. His growing interest in religion will provide him with the body and system to articulate precisely what are the sources, symptoms, and dangers of boredom. The oftentimes mysterious nature of boredom makes it difficult to fix the exact causes and relevance of this spiritual dis-ease. Since religion deals with the mystical and the higher questions of life, religious discourse and its relation to metaphysics will provide Melville with the philosophical and aesthetic tools needed in order to examine the problem that undermines the meaning of life: boredom.

Mardi: Killing Time

Severing himself from the style, content, and genre that made his first two works financially and critically successful, Melville seeks artistry with *Mardi*. He becomes disenchanted with his skimming of important themes in his so-called narratives-of-facts; rather than disclosing merely (semi-)autobiographical anecdotes of beachcombing and jumping ships, he feels compelled to be more than just the lover of Fayaway. Art, not nonfiction, motivates him now, and thereby this transformation of his creative identity alienates his reading public. Specifically, his sudden, unexpected, and radical change in artistic course, disposition, and ambition confuse and tax his audience; sales of *Mardi* are comparatively much lower than his previous works. He does not have the imaginative reach in *Typee* and *Omoo* to handle sensitively the problematic and emotional material he is uncovering now, and given that he still is finding narrative voice and theme in *Mardi*, Melville's discovery of metaphysics is indeed shocking. Even with his growing concern with religion, nothing in the first two novels anticipates this development. His unusual turn to the transcendent, visionary, conceptual, and unconventional supplies him nonetheless with the necessary revelation and dialect to get ever closer to his theme of boredom.

Mardi is an attempt to grapple with this menacing artistic problem, and his treatment of boredom begins to take on a more existential tone due to its metaphysical articulations. In some ways, *Mardi* is a hybrid of *Typee*. Melville's third novel is a kind of rewriting of his first but with metaphysical flourishes. Nonetheless, *Mardi* is a breakthrough. John Evelev argues, "Given Melville's new commitment to authorship as a profession, it is not surprising that the early parts of *Mardi* show the imprimatur of the popular Irvingesque male sentimentalist.... Melville's new ambitions required that *Mardi*'s narrator be genteel, rather than a regular sailor [as in the earlier sea novels]" (309). I accept the standard view that Melville's art improves and is marked by the introduction of his metaphysical strain in this third novel. As a result of the pronounced philosophical and poetic inflections echoing in the work, Melville now is able to locate his theme with more confidence; through his use of intricate and deep phrasings, he is beginning to acknowledge artistically the emergence of boredom as a formidable, undeniable, and now recurring feature in his art. Boredom is not a short, ambiguous, and passing phase experienced by the Melville protagonist, just as it is no longer an unconscious, underdeveloped, and inconsiderable aspect in Melville's art. Boredom has become a valid feature in his art, and Melville unfolds this key theme through metaphysics.

The moral universe of *Mardi* is complicated. On the one hand, it praises sensibility and eloquence, and on the other, it subverts them. It marries the life of the mind with the life of action, only to jeopardize this union through Melville's romantic impulses toward daring, excess, and unconsciousness. It points to the artistic successes of later works, but remains bound to its predecessors' inclination toward oblivion. It shows directly the sources of boredom's darkness, but allows itself to get caught in its pull, unable to draw an end for its hero. The narrator warns of boredom's perils only to fall victim to them himself. The enormous structural and thematic instability unleashed by the ambiguity of the story causes Melville still to be unable to subject his literary character to the fullest range of consciousness, which means tragic insight, because Taji evades the guilt of murdering a Polynesian chief, dodges his responsibility toward his friends, and persists in his crazed quest to find Yillah. Melville keeps Taji alive in the story despite everything, and keeps him sailing forever, a kind of curse and unstated punishment.

Melville himself seems to have an answer for this artistic failing in the 24 February 1849 letter to Evert A. Duyckinck in which he relates his belated discovery and immediate admiration of Shakespeare. Melville writes, "Dolt & ass that I am I have lived more than 29 years, & until a few days ago, never made close acquaintance with the divine William" (*Correspondence*, 119). It is by reading Shakespeare and then later discovering Hawthorne that Melville matures as artist, permitting himself to accept the "blackness of the darkness." The "power of blackness" is the insight that there is finality in life; the Melville protagonist cannot continue to evade, ignore, and suppress the dark forces undermining him. Melville's artistic insight into the inner nature of things is a difficult one for him to learn and accept. This advancement materializes in *Moby-Dick* and thereafter. Melville finds Shakespeare two weeks before *Mardi* is published and Hawthorne about four months after that (Melville will meet Hawthorne during the summer of 1850); these major literary figures in his life will prepare him to write *Moby-Dick*. Melville finds Burton and others quite useful, but his desire to be a serious artist inspires him more. The long and challenging process of writing *Mardi* for Melville uncovers difficult material. *Mardi* baffles itself, avoiding resolution of its own oppressive themes, as its unwieldy size and aimless progression testify. It divulges consequential aspects of boredom, but is imprisoned by the very nature of the problem.

The problematic issue of *Mardi* is the concept of time. In *Walden* (1854), Henry David Thoreau notes, "As if you could kill time without injuring eternity" (4). Correcting the popular misconception that one can lighten one's annoyance with boredom by employing senseless, futile activities, Thoreau insists that "killing time" is not an innocent and harmless activity. Time feels drawn out for Taji when his enthusiasm and attention have waned, and then the gaping mouth of boredom sucks him in. The German word for boredom, *langweile*, "long time," captures the essence of boredom. Lars Svendsen explains how dangerous is "killing time," emphasizing that "boredom is linked to a way of *passing the time*, in which time, rather than being a horizon for opportunities, is something that has to be beguiled" (23). Svendsen adds, "The emptiness of time is an emptiness of meaning" (31), and "Boredom is like some sort of death, while death assumes the form of the only state possible — a total break with boredom. Boredom has to do with finitude and nothingness. It is a death within life, a non-life" (40–1). Boredom is a kind of stoppage of time when everything seems the same, and yet is not. This slowing of time or the sensation that time has stopped makes one's boredom feel like prison, even death. To combat boredom, the individual wishes the time to pass, and it is this point of distraction, to deceive not only oneself that time can actually pass by, but time itself. Instead of finding fulfilling ways to combat boredom, Taji of *Mardi* engages in hazardous pursuits that give only the semblance of meaning. He uses pointless, temporary activities and distractions to speed up the sense of time; time has become unbearingly slow, and this murderer of time (and men) believes he can control it. He cannot. Taji's way of passing time actually worsens his problem with boredom. His methods cheapen, belittle, and desecrate life; such mindless retaliation really kills Taji's selfhood.

Michael L. Raposa also understands boredom as a failing of the self. Boredom does not go away by simple diversion or exodus; the meaning not found in the boring situation is really an expression of the lack of meaning within (39). Raposa believes that a kind of "ethics of ennui" (74) exists. The ability to deal with boredom is a measure of the self's integrity. A contemplative or political mind is not enough; Melville's protagonists may be observant and vocal about worldly abuses, like Tommo, but still neglect their own problems. This ethics of ennui encompasses critical judgment on the self, and reveals a serious lack of moral concern of the self. In essence, not only is boredom a caring less of the world, but makes one care less about one's self (Raposa 36). The choice of dealing with or evading one's boredom is a sign of the health of the conscious. It is a question of life or death of the soul. Boredom is a moral failing; it causes Taji to lose sight of everything.

Melville also believes in and institutes his own literary ethics of boredom. No matter how Taji may try to establish good terms with the reader, like Tommo before him, he still is a morally questionable character who places others and himself in jeopardy. Melville again spares another of his characters the fullest consequences of his destructive behavior, and tempers the forces of boredom afflicting him. Boredom's darkness shadows *Mardi*, but Melville's romantic sensibilities circumvent the disaster and bleakness emerging there. Taji has injured eternity and his selfhood when he kills time in the Mardi archipelago. At the same time, Melville struggles to retain his artistic belief in the self-affirming possibilities of action. Only when Melville begins to debunk his mythologies of optimism and embraces a tragic vision do the full implications of boredom become clear. However, this transition is a painful one, and Melville resists it until *Moby-Dick*. He sees the consequences of boredom, but to articulate them requires a strength of mind he did not possess during the compositional period of *Typee* through *White-Jacket*.

Tommo of *Typee* and *Omoo* never was able to understand how his boredom weakened and corrupted him; Taji does not either. Taji clearly is more educated, fluent, and philosophic than Tommo. These qualities would suggest a higher consciousness. Not so. Taji is extremely reckless and impatient; he behaves like a spoiled, impulsive adolescent. His pursuit of wisdom and recognition of aesthetic values only go so far; he lacks the composure to face trouble or the endurance to cope with boredom. Elements of the philosopher shape his artistic sensibilities: he may be penetrating and eloquent, but refuses to criticize himself, even when facing death. His boredom occludes consciousness; it functions like an illusion.

Like *Typee*, *Mardi* also begins with an exclamation, but of excitement and adventure, not boredom. Taji is intensely enthusiastic, having energy that may have erupted out of an unstated but likely previous bout of boredom. He announces, "We are off!" (3), but the ship has been in the Pacific for some time now. His eagerness is suspicious, and he quickly grows bored. Taji notes:

This round-about way did the Arcturion take; and in all conscience a weary one it was. Never before had the ocean appeared so monotonous; thank fate, never since.

But bravo! in two weeks' time, an event. Out of the gray of the morning, and right ahead, as we sailed along, a dark object rose out of the sea; standing dimly before us, mists wreathing and curling aloft, and creamy breakers frothing round its base. — We turned aside, and, at length, when day dawned, passed Massafuero....

A few days more and we "took the trades." Like favors snappishly conferred, they came to us, as is often the case, in a very sharp squall; the shock of which carried away one of our spars; also our fat old cook off his legs; depositing him plump in the scuppers to leeward.

In good time making the desired longitude upon the equator ... we spent several weeks chassezing across the Line, to and fro, in unavailing search for our prey.... So, day after day, daily; and week after week, weekly, we traversed the self-same longitudinal intersection of the self-same Line; till we were almost ready to swear that we felt the ship strike every time her keel crossed that imaginary locality.

At length, dead before the equatorial breeze, we threaded our way straight along the very Line itself. Westward sailing; peering right, and peering left, but seeing naught.

It was during this weary time, that I experienced the first symptoms of that bitter impatience of our monotonous craft, which ultimately led to the adventures herein recounted.

But hold you! Not a word against that rare old ship, nor its crew. The sailors were good fellows all, the half-score of pagans we had shipped at the islands included. Nevertheless, they were not precisely to my mind. There was no soul a magnet to mine; none with whom to mingle sympathies; save in deploring the calms with which we were now and then overtaken [4].

The shifts in mood are so erratic and demoralizing that he fastens upon any change that arouses interest to keep boredom at bay. He is so profuse in his gaiety about the marooned convicts, in his despair over the squall and subsequent calms that hit them, and in his isolation from the other crewmen that he does not tolerate any spells of boredom. His only defense against boredom, which is unsafe, haphazard, and grievous, is his mania; in fact, mania can be perceived as an expression of boredom. Orrin E. Klapp understands boredom as a manifestation of an overload of information, citing the redundancy, repetitiveness, and deluge of information. With so much information to process, one becomes overwhelmed, and boredom is one's response to this flood of information. Unable to decipher what is relevant, meaningful information and not, modern man loses all sense of meaning. An overload of sensations, appetites, and stimuli is as detrimental as the lack of excitement or absorption; for Klapp, gluttony and starvation are not so different. In a sim-

ilar vein, Taji cannot appreciate good fortune and enjoyment. He does not
know when to stop.

Even the prose in *Mardi* is far livelier, more effervescent, than in Melville's
first two novels. The paragraphs are short, concentrated bursts of poetic imagination that demonstrate the range of his mind, but Taji's attention zigs and
zags, which suggests his need for new and intense stimuli. Taji's boredom is
much more deadly than that of his literary predecessor: it is a violent, intense,
and unceasing boredom. He convinces Jarl, the voice of reason, experience,
and seeming maturity, to jump ship in the middle of the ocean because the
boredom onboard is too much for him cope with; Jarl's willingness to join
him indicates that Jarl's qualities are not enough to counter and dissuade
Taji's wilder impulses. Taji is willing to die stranded in the vastness of the
Pacific rather than cope with the tedium, drowsiness, and uneventfulness
found on *Arcturion*. He intentionally places others in danger in order to keep
boredom from numbing him. He resists it by forcing it out of his consciousness; he needs constant distractions of the mind and circumstances that will
keep him moving to avoid feeling his spiritual emptiness. Ultimately, this
evasion leads him to his wildly absurd quest for Yillah, the maiden. His mania
is only exceeded by Ahab's. I disagree with Alan Lebowitz's casual rejection
of this comparison between Taji and Ahab. Taji directly and indirectly is
responsible for many deaths, and places many individuals in harm's way. He
also neglects reason, and insists on the impossible. His monomaniac tendencies strongly suggest to me Taji is a strong precursor of Ahab.

Boredom does not slow or restrain Taji's momentum. He is self-moti-
vating; his intellect propels him out of the calms of boredom. He is too emotionally stimulated to let boredom paralyze him, but it is not to say that he
does not experience boredom. Rather, he feels boredom acutely. He cries out:

> Ay, ay Arcturion! I say it in no malice, but thou wast exceedingly dull.
> Not only at sailing: hard though it was, that I could have borne; but in
> every other aspect. The days went slowly round and round, endless and
> uneventful as cycles in space. Time, and time-pieces! How many cen-
> turies did my hammock tell, as pendulum-like it swung to the ship's dull
> roll, and ticked the hours and ages. Sacred forever be the Arcturion's
> fore-hatch — alas! seamoss is over it now — and rusty forever the bolts that
> held together that old sea hearth-stone, about which we so often lounged.
> Nevertheless, ye lost and leaden hours, I will rail at ye while life lasts [5].

Because he is so demanding, particular, and pampered, he is never satisfied.
Boredom entraps him severely, limiting him. This physical and emotional
exertion that Taji forces upon himself is an attempt, which Christopher Sten
believes, to liberate himself from the confines of his social class and position

in life (78); however, what is the cost of this illusory freedom? Is Taji really oppressed? Or is he a self-absorbed hedonist? Like Tommo, Taji feels an injustice incurred against him by the captain, and decides to jump ship. Unlike Tommo, he jumps ship "a thousand miles from land" (26); he steals a small craft and flees. Taji's boredom is the most reckless, crazed, and perhaps irrational of all of Melville's protagonists. To escape the drudgery, monotony, and lethargy of a dry whaler in Taji's manner is to invite death. He even manages to convince Jarl, a respected and seasoned mariner, to join him in the escape. The extent of his unpreparedness and impulsiveness is terrifying: Taji says, "Thoughts of sextants and quadrants were the least of our cares" (19); for him, navigational instruments are unimportant. His disregard for these vital nautical tools anticipates Ahab's; the captain of the Pequod will destroy and throw away all sailing devices to rely solely on his own senses. Like Ahab, nothing can stop Taji.

Unable to find anyone who can quote Burton on Blue Devils, Taji must do it for himself. Who on the *Archturion* can match his ingenuity? Even beloved Jarl is inarticulate; playful yet accurate, the title for Chapter 11 is "Jarl afflicted with the Lockjaw" (35). Calling his boredom "my impatience of the ship" (9), he poetizes and finally gives into his boredom in the masthead. It is up in the main that Taji, White Jacket, and Ishmael all can delve into their boredom; however, there is no safety in isolation. Taji's masthead experiences are indicative of his mania: doom masquerades as euphoria. Unlike the brotherhood on the *United States* in *White-Jacket*, where the men bond through shared experiences of boredom, Taji isolates himself more by making his bouts of boredom more personal. In fact, he is aggravating his condition through self-quarantine. It is the same problem Tommo and White Jacket face.

Taji's masthead experiences with boredom reveal existing patterns that set the course for the entire romance. As wild and dangerous as he is awake deflecting boredom, his boredom-induced trances are just as treacherous and frantic. Taji's imagination is rapid, intense, and concentrated, and even while lulled to numbness, his creative mind dreams. He stays awake by thinking artistically; his concentration does not allow him to rest or admire the scene or mood. He must be consistently distracted. His eyes must constantly roam, and when all possibilities to entertain his mind are exhausted, his duty on the watch demonstrates the same crazed psychological activity when he falls under the spell of boredom. He says:

> I cast my eyes downward to the brown planks of the dull, plodding ship, silent from stem to stern, then abroad.
>
> In the distance what visions were spread! The entire western horizon high piled with gold and crimson clouds; airy arches, domes, and minarets;

as if the yellow, Moorish sun were setting behind some vast Alhambra. Vistas seemed leading to worlds beyond. To and fro, and all over the towers of this Nineveh in the sky, flew troops of birds. Watching them long, one crossed my sight, flew through a low arch, and was lost to view. My spirit must have sailed in with it [7–8].

It is a kind of sensory overload. Vivid colors and images of exotic locales blend with his imagination; he really thinks he can fly and touch the sky. Needing more and more stimuli, Taji taxes himself to the brink of mental and physical collapse. Just as seductive as his sublime musings are, his narrations describing his boredom atop the ship are as voluptuous and pleasurable. Catastrophe looms behind this narcotic-like high. Is he even aware that he could fall? Reality is not just what we make of it; the mundane, predictable, and the bland also compose and shape existence. Taji filters out this part of his life, forever objecting to its joy-killing power. As in his conscious state, in his dream-like state up in the crow's nest, he tries to suppress all undesirable, stale, and prosaic aspects of life. For Taji, life must be robust, glistening, sparkling, and savory. But life cannot be exciting and vivacious all the time. Comparing his concept of boredom as overload to eating, Orrin E. Klapp observes that any initial satisfaction one gets from mass consumption is misleading. Likewise, Taji has a deep hunger for life; however, does he truly appreciate it as he claims? Could his palate have become dull and insensitive, given the immensity of his appetite? Can an epicurean enjoy a simple meal, or must he, like Taji, constantly search for something new? His "impatience of the ship" is disappointment, a letdown, but more importantly is confirmation of his unreadiness to live. Life inevitably consists of boredom, and he does not cope well with it.

Even in a state of boredom, Taji's mania strangely emerges. It is strange in the sense that boredom suggests slowing down, cooling off; instead, his imagination becomes frenzied. Taji is a man who lives consciously and unconsciously at breakneck speed. Depressed that the ship is leaving the warm, sunny water near the equator "for cold, fierce squalls, and all the horrors of northern voyaging" and "the brown planks of the dull, prodding ship" (7) only emphasize his condition, he immediately fastens his attention to the brilliance, wonder, and glow of dusk that hypnotizes him. He is all too willing to exchange the boredom of dullness to one that is pleasing in its narcotic-like effect. Weary of the ship, he finds the masthead as his gateway to blissful oblivion. He says:

> [It] came upon me the cadence of mild billows laving a beach of shells, the waving of boughs, and the voices of maidens, and the lulled beatings of my own dissolved heart, all blended together.

Now, all this, to be plain, was but one of the many visions one has up aloft. But coming upon me at this time, it wrought upon me so, that thenceforth my desire to quit the Arcturion became little short of a frenzy [8].

Like Tennyson's Lotos-Eaters, Taji longs for a numbness that comforts; Taji will point the way for White-Jacket and Ishmael, both of whom lose themselves to boredom while in the masthead. Boredom is escapism for Taji, White Jacket, and Ishmael.

Taji's next recorded episode of boredom is during a calm; he demythologizes the utter sensualness of experiencing the nothingness found in boredom. I totally disagree with Cindy Weinstein's interpretation of the calm section. Weinstein completely ignores the monumental perils of the calm; these forces ruthlessly assault the individual. There is nothing beneficial, pleasing, or attractive to be found during a calm. It is a living death. Weinstein ignores many key passages, noting only moments where Taji alludes to literature or work. Weinstein misinterprets the calm, believing that "the calm constitutes that interstitial moment in which he will choose either the sweetness of leisure or the path of Industry.... Although one may look idle while experiencing a calm, a great deal of work is going on" (246). Taji does not describe any kind of work that he performs. No amount of work can save Taji or anyone else during a calm; nature is against man. A calm is a nautical weather pattern that is free from winds and rough activity of water; the ocean is completely still and quiet. Such tranquility is terrifying. It traps the ship: no wind, no sailing. A calm can last for days. A calm is not something to be enjoyed, or a time to give in to the narcotic-like atmosphere. The calm unsettles everything; the calm strips the sailor naked. The calm does not offer a choice whether to be industrious or slothful; one is lucky to be alive. A calm desensitizes the individual; it does not, as Weinstein thinks, make one become "keenly attentive to the interpretation of books as well as the meaning of the world" (245). As Taji notes, "To a landsman a calm is no joke. It not only revolutionizes his abdomen, but unsettles his mind; tempts him to recant his belief in the eternal fitness of things; in short, almost makes an infidel of him" (9).

A calm is the complete stillness of the ocean and weather; tranquility is overwhelming. He says:

The stillness of the calm is awful. His voice begins to grow strange and portentous. He feels it in him like something swallowed too big for the esophagus. It keeps up a sort of involuntary interior humming in him, like a live beetle. His cranium is a dome full of reverberations. The hollows of his very bones are as whispering galleries. He is afraid to speak loud, lest he be stunned; like the man in the bass drum.

But more than all else is the consciousness of his utter helplessness. Succor or sympathy there is none. Penitence for embarking avails not. The final satisfaction of despairing may not be his with a relish. Vain the idea of idling out the calm. He may sleep if he can, or purposely delude himself into a crazy fancy, that he is merely at leisure. All this he may compass; but he may not lounge; for to lounge is to be idle; to be idle implies an absence of any thing to do; whereas there is a calm to be endured: enough to attend to, Heaven knows.

His physical organization, obviously intended for locomotion, becomes a fixture; for where the calm leaves him, there he remains. Even his undoubted vested rights, comprised in his glorious liberty of volition, become as naught. For of what use? He wills to go: to get away from the calm: as ashore he would avoid the plague. But he can not; and how foolish to revolve expedients. It is more hopeless than a bad marriage in a land where there is no Doctors' Commons. He has taken the ship to wife, for better or for worse, for calm or for gale; and she is not to be shuffled off. With yards akimbo, she says unto him scornfully, as the old bedlam said to the little dwarf:—"Help yourself."

And all this, and more than this, is a calm [10].

Taji's warning is a model for Ishmael's own admonition of the perils of giving into external nothingness that serves to intensify the one inside. It is a lesson Taji does not heed himself: nothing can be done to abate the nothingness. The horrifying calmness is so unsettling and merciless that it can annihilate one's soul. Taji's ceaseless drive to occupy his mind — his fear that an emotional calm will enshroud him — is as destructive as a physical calm. There is no way out of a calm; one must have patience and wait it out. Taji does not have patience. The calm exposes his sense of futility when confronting the calm within. It debunks the false security of action. The experience with the calm evaporates those vivid and incredible golds and crimsons found in the western horizon that had so intoxicated him while in the masthead; this feeling of complete still erases those mystical cities he had imagined beyond "the yellow, Moorish sun" (8). The pantheistic oneness with the universe gives way to spiritual fallout. The effect, "in short, almost makes an infidel of him" (9). The calm is choking the life right out of Taji.

The calm of boredom attacks the very foundations of the self. I concur with John Evelev's explanation of the perilous nature of a calm; Evelev describes the calm as existential stagnation, a condition in which all conventions are undermined. This weather pattern does not bring peace or calm to the sailor; instead, it forces him to "exist" (312). Alan Lebowitz also supports this line of reading by emphasizing the existential state of neither joy nor misery (61). All things fall apart. All values are made baseless, and nothing can be trusted. Melville writes, "It is a calm, and he grows madly skeptical" (9).

Any effort to assure the soundness, permanence, and empiricism of reality is negated. He adds:

> At first he is taken by surprise, never having dreamt of a state of existence where existence itself seems suspended. He shakes himself in his coat to see whether it be empty or no. He closes his eyes, to test the reality of the glassy expanse. He fetches a deep breath, by way of experiment, and for the sake of witnessing the effect. If a reader of books, Priestley on Necessity occurs to him; and he believes in that old Sir Anthony Absolute for the geography, which from boyhood he had implicitly confided in, always assured him, that though expatiating all over the globe, the sea was at least margined by land [9].

Science, art, philosophy, religion, in short, all of man's faculties that bring order, reason, and knowledge are illusions. He says, "To his alarmed fancy, parallels and meridians become emphatically what they are merely designated as being: imaginary lines drawn round the earth's surface" (9–10). When facing the calm, man loses his sense of place, direction, and time — he confronts the meaninglessness of boredom. What is man when a calm creeps on him? Melville writes, "His physical organization, obviously intended for locomotion, becomes a fixture; for where the calm leaves him, there he remains" (10). Man is hollowed by this experience.

The danger always is there. The calm — boredom — can occur whenever, wherever. One cannot avoid it, and it is out of man's control. It gnaws Taji. Even when the calm has subsided, there is "so much blankness to be sailed over" (11). The blankness of the ocean is a reflection of what lies beneath man's mask of purpose, confidence, and wisdom: the terrifying emptiness within. Ignoring his own experience with the serenity of the nothingness, does Taji think he can survive the countless leagues facing him? There are exotic lands on the horizon, and there is Mardi and even Yillah, but did he ever imagine the misfortune that lies ahead for him, too? His willfulness is self-destructive. Even Ishmael commits the same faults as Taji, which shows the awesome power of boredom.

The profundity of the silence, the terror of the paralysis, and the unexpectedness of the calm are the specter of death. Even "the final satisfaction of despairing may not be his with a relish" (10); prayer and patience help not (10). Man must go through it, but it is not out of volition (10). The experience of the clam is nihilism. Melville notes, "Vain the idea of idling out of the calm. He may sleep if he can, or purposely delude himself into a crazy fancy, that he is merely at leisure. All this he may compass; but he may not lounge; for to lounge is to be idle; to be idle implies an absence of any thing to do" (10). To be idle is to lack substance. It is to be without value. Melville is rejecting the notion of self-reliance and Emerson's faith that man has endless possibility. Melville is describing the wasting away of selfhood. Can man really exist? The metaphysical dilemmas that Melville raises here are complex and emasculating. The American public in 1848, steeped in Emersonian optimism, naturally rejected Melville's Polynesian romance. No wonder his readers, reviewers, and family thought him insane.

In his efforts to kill time — to curb his boredom — Taji in effect is responsible for several deaths that take place in *Mardi*. Due to the immoderate degree to which he relieves himself of boredom (jumping ship in the middle of the ocean with Jarl) Taji murders a Polynesian priest, which subsequently causes the deaths of Jarl and Samoa, chaos in Mardi, and the disappearance of Yillah, the virgin whom he rescued from sacrifice. Knowing he has committed a serious crime and that he should be punished, he nonetheless evades feeling guilt for any of these actions. He believes he has virtuous motives for killing the priest, who is about to immolate Yillah, but sexual and metaphysical arousal provokes him to deadly action. Carol Colatrella also sees Taji's motives in morally questionable terms (113). He is not motivated ethically. In spite of his seeming heroism, he is troubled by guilt and must suppress it, and his subsequent adventures are ways to elude responsibility and punishment. I have mixed feelings toward James Duban's (1983) reading of Taji's victorious attitude toward saving Yillah. Duban ignores Taji's overt repression of guilt, which at times, surfaces and attacks him. During these moments, Taji is not the jingoistic American parading with his native lover Duban makes him out to be. At the same time, Duban does make an important point that Taji's arrogance and disregard of native cultural practices is typical of chauvinistic nationalism.

He has sailed over many miles, encountered numerous devastating calms, and grown annoyed (French root for "ennui") with Jarl and Anatoo (Samoa's wife), so that anything that promises adventure, anything to stir him out of boredom, is welcomed; these prior episodes worsened his condition, any relief, even murder, is better than having the nothingness gnawing at one's self. This feeling is similar to the thrill of the hunt, of killing game and feeling exhilarated by it.

Not only does Taji repress any sense of culpability for his criminality, which in turn makes him suffer more guilt — in essence, he is not successfully repressing it — he becomes more relentless in his pursuit of Yillah. It may appear that Melville loses control in composing Taji's quest to reunite with his love; however, Taji's pursuit for his lover is a digression and an avoidance of dealing with his misdeed. Moreover, Melville's unwieldy treatment of Taji's adventures is an extension and expression of Taji's mania and failure to grapple with his boredom. Each failing episode that further distances Taji from his love is symbolic of his unwillingness to accept that Yillah is lost forever. A member of Yillah's rescue party, Babbalanja, rebukes Taji: "'Tis true, then, Taji, that an evil deed gained you your Yillah; no wonder she is lost" (423). Canvassing the hundreds of islands in Mardi to find Yillah, Taji disregards the wastefulness and futility involving the time, resources, and men that he has used; he has killed time — killed life. He is willing to risk life for such a doomed cause. Melville writes:

> But fiery yearnings their own phantom-future make, and deem it present. So, if after all these fearful, fainting trances, the verdict be, the golden haven was gained;— yet, in bold quest thereof, better to sink in boundless deeps, than float on vulgar shoals; and give me, ye god, an utter wreck, if wreck I do [557].

Island after island and new experience after new experience are not enough. Taji at the end of the novel (ironically, there is no end for Taji) faces the same predicament that annoyed him at the start of the romance: dissatisfaction and boredom. It is a cycle of failure. The rescue attempt has become monotonous and meaningless for all except Taji; his mania blinds him to the inherent senselessness, madness, and peril his adventure represents. Instead of Yillah, he encounters the void, and as he resumes his frenzied chase, his friends are horrified to witness the extent of his embrace with death. Taji cannot accept failure, and magnifies the risks to his life by going alone.

Taji's boredom is the driving force that impels him to his own doom. From beginning to end, *Mardi* documents how lethal boredom is, especially for a man like Taji who cannot tolerate it for long. *Mardi* reveals more than *Typee* the underpinning of evil lurking in boredom; however, it will become more pronounced as Melville excels in his art. Taji is an advance in Melville's conception of boredom and he will become another prototype in his art. Taji's disregard for the safety of others along with his refusal to heed sound advice and curb his excesses point to Ahab. Melville's treatment of Taji is ambivalent in the sense that Taji at many points in the novel is not the center of attention; he often does not behave like a protagonist, even disappearing from the narrative despite being in the plot. Like Tommo, who often narrates about Typee history, geography, and culture and not himself, Taji, at times, does very little. Bruce L. Grenberg also perceives this sense that Taji is an invisible protagonist in the sense that not only does his sense of self deteriorates by the end of the novel, moreover, the other characters seem to represent Taji as "composite sketches" (53). This awkward rendering of characters eventually will become a strength in Melville's art, particularly with Bartleby. In his quest to kill time, Taji has murdered more than his boredom; he has done great harm to others, himself, and life.

Clearly, Melville is drawn now to the theme of boredom and seems to have realized its importance and scope; however, he has not found the sensibility and control of the subject to join his auxiliary themes to dramatize and articulate the range and depth of the problem of boredom. His gathering of themes, almost by mistake, allows him now to see more clearly how pervasive this fundamental attack on self is. Melville has begun linking the crisis of boredom with the struggle to maintain self-meaning; this battle to protect selfhood is the trial to attain a higher meaning in life. However, because of the hostile response to *Mardi*, Melville reevaluated his position as artist (both as commercial and serious novelist), and his art altered somewhat, too. Although Melville cursed his next two works (*Redburn* and *White-Jacket*), he made significant breakthroughs nonetheless. He became more interested in psychology and philosophy. Paul McCarthy says, "Wellingborough Redburn [of *Redburn*] is the first Melville narrator vitally concerned with the nature of his own psychology" (36). Taji may be seen as concerned, too, about his psyche, but Redburn is a decent, honest, and grounded individual. He tries to avoid dangerous situations, unlike Taji, and more importantly, Redburn seeks sound remedies to aid his spirit. Although the figure Redburn is not afflicted by boredom, he does feel estranged and suffers frequently from despair. Perhaps he is too young and inexperienced to succumb to this psychological malady. Nevertheless, he admits "a boy can feel all that, and much more, when upon his young soul the mildew has fallen" (11). Melville may have believed he watered down his art, and perhaps in some way ways he did, but at the same time he continued to focus on deep issues; despite writing with a conventional and fickle audience in mind, he did not abandon his dark themes. In fact, this restriction may have even disciplined him as an artist.

In *Typee* and *Omoo* evil forces are identified primarily with political institutions. *Mardi* begins to expand those boundaries by searching out the wickedness within. In the earlier novels, immorality often is concealed by an adventuresome spirit, and any activity that diminishes boredom is seen as a tolerable good. Self-harm is ignored, just as long as the only thing that is murdered is time. *Mardi*, in contrast, demonstrates how self-deception and egoism obstruct consciousness and conscience, and how severe, unrelieved boredom leads to disaster. The self now is the seat of iniquity in Melville's art; if Melville is squeamish in presenting morally questionable characters who do not show any remorse for their actions, *Mardi* initiates an artistic liberation. He begins to consider aspects of life that go beyond merely offending reader propriety; man's heart of darkness offers richer possibilities for his art. His treatment of boredom as a result also becomes darker. As his concentration focuses on the metaphysical and psychological, Melville sees boredom more as a serious problem; he sees boredom as a judgment on the world. The world cannot provide contentment, peace, and joy; instead the world aggravates the joylessness the Melville figure already feels. This insight is a crucial watershed in Melville's literary vision.

White-Jacket attempts to sketch most of these artistic problems. Even if *Mardi* eventually will serve as a kind of poetic-philosophic model for drafting his metaphysical concerns, *White-Jacket* is a better conceived and structured novel than its predecessor. It is not as deep and ranging as *Mardi*, but Melville has arrived at an impasse where he has exhausted his potential as a middling artist. Constricted by market demands and the American reading public's distaste for metaphysics, what is he do? Until he overcomes his philosophic reluctance concerning evil, Melville will remain indecisive as an artist.

White-Jacket
The Devil Loves Idle Hands

I formed a higher estimate of human nature than I had ever before enter-
tained. But alas! since then I have been one of the crew of a man-of-war,
and the pent-up wickedness of five hundred men has nearly overturned all
my previous theories.

— Herman Melville, *Typee*

Through his narrator Tommo in *Typee*, Melville opposes the immorality and corruption of the whalers, missionaries, and imperialistic forces occu-
pying Polynesia with the unexpectedly humane, decent, and altruistic
attributes of the so-called savage Typees. Living with the Typees for nearly
four months, Tommo affirms his belief in humanity. This favorable and benevolent judgment of mankind, however, is transient. Western civilization made
him fearful, suspicious, ill, and bored; he found health in the South Seas.
With his return to Western civilization, those problems returned full force
and attacked his newfound values. In *White-Jacket* (1850), it seems evil is too
strong, and good cannot balance it; Melville depicts the world in Manichean
terms. There is little good in the world of *White-Jacket*, and boredom is a
serious threat. Boredom undermines and threatens White Jacket, the protagonist. Boredom tests the resources of the navy and the character of its men.
Boredom spawns the "pent-up wickedness" of sailor and officer. White Jacket
responds to boredom in many ways — friendship, imagination, and religion —
but none of these ultimately provides relief.

Examining the devastating outcomes of the *Neversink*'s "pent-up wickedness," White Jacket notes that the expression of this evil is "a general social
condition which is the precise reverse of what any Christian could desire"
(375). For Melville this disposition is a painful and telling depiction of the
nature of man. This insight is the source of Melville's disillusionment, which
he expresses flinchingly; in *White-Jacket* he hesitates, qualifies, and retreats,
but he writes nonetheless. Cesare Casarino observes, "Much of this novel is
spent in the paradoxical process of recording exactly what one continually
claims to want to forget, of jotting down for future memory all that one wants

never to have existed — and it is then clear that the desire to forget is here shot through with the unfulfillable dream of retroactive excision" (46). Melville's composition about his naval service shaped him into a tragic artist, and, as Bruce L. Grenberg notes, *White-Jacket* is "indicative of Melville's ever-darkening vision" (78). The struggle to achieve this sensibility took him years, and this moment in his life and art testifies to the artistic inevitability that he would incorporate this biographic material in his art. I agree with Howard P. Vincent who says, "*White-Jacket* is an excellent book.... [Melville] sought out some of the meanings of his experiences, and the experiences of others, he touched truths which he would not have done had he written to the prescription of such sailor-authors as Selfridge, or Langhorne. He was an artist, not a tape recorder and a camera" (4–5). And I also concur with John Wenke when he observes, "Melville's reductive descriptions of these literary 'jobs' [*Redburn* and *White-Jacket*] do not describe his achievement" (76). *White-Jacket* is a crucial work in Melville's oeuvre because it can be seen as the first determined exploration of religious faith as a response to boredom, but the strength and genuineness of that faith in *White-Jacket* is murky and at the very least questionable. This work of art also examines in greater detail than his three earlier Pacific novels the powerful and lethal effects of boredom, and looks forward to the much more complex studies of boredom in later works. As Kathleen E. Kier states, "*White-Jacket* is a seedbed for later Melville works" (Abstract). More importantly *White-Jacket* inaugurates a pattern concerning Melville's struggle to come to a conclusion in his art. He either forces an optimistically religious ending which is unearned, as he does in *White-Jacket* and *Clarel* (1876), or succeeds in earning affirmation as he does in *Moby-Dick* (1851), "Bartleby, the Scrivener" (1853), and *Billy Budd* (1924, posthumous). *White-Jacket* then becomes the keystone work of my study; I cannot accept or agree with Melville's own assessment that this work is flawed or unimportant.

Critics who posit that *White-Jacket* was written to pick up sales due to the national debates over naval flogging abuses, or that Melville wrote this work to fill in a niche in mariner literature, or that he resorted to near plagiarism by patterning his art on other books dealing with the sea, all ignore Melville's artistic concerns and growth, minimize his own art, and downplay the fact that he actually experienced life at sea. I agree with John Samson that "*White-Jacket*, more than a preparation for *Moby-Dick*, is a culmination of Melville's early narratives of facts" (130). Experiences can be and are commonly shared; after all, limited movement and confinement, similar shipboard duties, and strict discipline are common on all ships. Unlike his literary sea comrades, Melville spent an entire artistic career surveying these mutual experiences; moreover, his treatments on similar themes and events are strikingly poetic, imaginative, powerful, and original. His focus is complex.

Melville has focused since *Typee* (1846) on the moral nature of boredom, but it is with *White-Jacket* that he analyzes the association between boredom and evil, and is more focused on the dangers of boredom. Ishmael in *Moby-Dick* (1851) depicts how bored Mahattanites line up the shore and pine for the sea. There is a healthy and starry-eyed wholesomeness and appreciation of the sea that Ishmael believes these city men are experiencing while entranced by the ocean. It seems entirely vital for their well-being that they transform their yearning into action; sea life, in their minds, offers the promise of rejuvenation. It is unknown how many of these men actually sign up for a sea voyage. A year earlier, Melville had dramatized in *White-Jacket* a troubling and grim portrait of bored landsmen entering the Navy; absent are the poetical and dreamy impulses to curb boredom, and instead a savage and ominous passion incites a different sort of man to turn to the sea to help ease his boredom. The office workers wile away their boredom, whereas in *White-Jacket* "the skulkers and scoundrels of all sorts in a man-of-war are chiefly composed not of regular seamen, but of these 'dock-lopers' of landsmen, men who enter the Navy to draw their grog and murder their time in the notorious idleness of a frigate" (382). And the key to this different artistic depiction focuses on "who are the men, and of what moral character they are, who, even at the present day, are willing to enlist as full-grown adults in a service so galling to all shore-manhood as the Navy" (382).

The skulkers and scoundrels suffer from an extraordinarily immoderate form of boredom that cannot be curbed; life on land has triggered the worst elements of the soul malady. Not much is known of these men, only that they are violent, and White Jacket dislikes them. Along with a universal bitterness that infects the entire ship, these men contribute to the dreadful and revolting conditions on the *Neversink*. Because the Navy is "a service so galling to all shore-manhood" (382), it attracts many morally questionable men. Life on land has produced destructive and immoral habits in these men in part due to the excessive unoccupied free time they have. These "dock-lopers" (382) apparently mob around the piers and instigate trouble. Throughout Melville's fiction the calling to the sea initially is an affirmative and healthy release of distemper and weariness, but for these men who enlist in the Navy, their boredom stays and only worsens: these sea men "enter the Navy to draw their grog and murder their time in the notorious idleness of a frigate" (382). Warship duties do not counteract the men's restless energy or occupy their time productively; despite the numerous offices to fulfill, they are short-lived and beneficial only to the Navy. After a function is carried out, a seaman is left with nothing to do, and that intolerable ennui sets in (176). Left with only the possibility to murder their time, the skulkers and scoundrels fall deeper into the abyss of boredom, and commit malicious acts. Unrelieved boredom swells to more destructive forms and spawns "other evils, so direful that they will hardly bear even so much as an allusion" (375). Intermittent work, therefore, does not curb the onset of boredom.

"Killing time in a Man-of-war in Harbor," the title of Chapter 42, indicates that life on a naval ship can be boring. Given the violent conditions onboard, the sailors' responses to boredom naturally also are violent; the men are on a warship, an instrument of violence, and spend all day doing nothing but anticipating war. They must wait for war in order to fulfill their highest duty, and waiting is boring; war may never come, and the anticipation only intensifies their boredom. Performing war exercises prepares the crew for future battle, but also occupies their time; these war games quickly become boring, too. The phrase "killing time" connotes killing life itself, a sin against life that is masked by the seemingly innocent and contradictory expression. Boredom murders man's connections with life; instead of "passing time" — another horrifying phrase — by killing it, the protracted time kills man. Killing itself appears exciting in a sense. Strangely, the smell of death heightens the senses and provides a false sense of being alive. Killing time sickens the soul. Killing time is suicide. Contrary to the innocuous connotations often associated with "killing time" — of just passing the time with meaningless activities — it is a terrifying and potentially malicious act. What is perceived as a kind of action is further evasion of time.

White Jacket's catalogue of killing time, of coping with boredom — reading (167), needlework and tattooing (170), cleaning and polishing brass or steel (171), walking around the gundeck (171–2), playing checkers (172), daydreaming and thinking (173), sleeping (174), violent sports and games (274–6), gambling (305), gossiping (386) and smoking and drinking — secures no constructive plan or discharge for boredom. Robert K. Martin has shown that "polishing brass" or masturbation was a key activity to while the time away. These activities gloss the issue and serve as a hastily contrived temporary remedy for a problem that may not have any cure. Diversions allow men to avoid facing the malady seriously and the aggressive contact sports may appear to purge unutilized potency, but such activities do nothing to combat the damaging effects of boredom on the soul. For those who are morally decent, the non-violent strategies may on occasion work to while away the time. But they are ultimately unsuccessful and temporary. And what of the skulkers and scoundrels? Nothing discourages the immoral manifestations of their boredom.

The relatively light responsibilities of the Marines on the *Neversink* make for boredom. White Jacket claims that the marines are "useless as soldiers" (374) and that they "had no other martial duty to perform" (373). He even asks himself, "What, then, were they for?" (373). While bias may color White Jacket's conviction, they are shown to be ineffectual during a naval battle. Their only other official role is to supervise the conduct of the sailors. Aside from this duty, they have little to do, and are left on their own. With nothing to occupy them, and the little power of rank they have, a "mutual contempt, and even hatred" (374) mounts between them and the sailors. Naval authority takes advantage of this joint rancor and considers it as "checks and balances, blood against blood" (374); it insures discipline. White Jacket sees the marines as degrading the common sailor, an abuse which the Navy implicitly endorses. And it is this debasement of the humanity of the sailor and the loathing of the marine by the sailor that precipitates White Jacket's horrified awareness of the relationship between boredom and evil.

Boredom draws out hostile and spiteful interactions among the men on the *Neversink*; boredom creates a mutual, deep-seated, and universal ill will. It causes one to lose the connections with life and with others. It breaks down camaraderie and human rights. It is a spiritual illness of the loner that soon infects and consumes the whole ship; it moves from a personal problem to a social and even political crisis. It eventually becomes a national security issue: a country is at stake when its navy is bored. Even the surgeon, Dr. Cuticle, relieves his boredom through violence; unmoved by the medical opinions of his staff that to amputate the leg of an injured seaman would be unwise and deadly for the patient, he cuts it. Cuticle has not had an "important case of surgery in a nearly three years' cruise" (257), and sees this case as a great relief to his boredom of only prescribing pills to sick seamen. Peaceful times are boring times for surgeons, as he observes when he advises his medical staff:

> At least in these dull times of peace, when the army and navy furnish no inducement for a youth ambitious of rising in our honorable profession. Take an old man's advice, and if the war now threatening between the States and Mexico should break out, exchange your Navy commissions for commissions in the army. From having no military marine herself, Mexico has always been backward in furnishing subjects for the amputation-tables of foreign navies. The cause of science has languished in her hands. The army, young gentlemen, is your best school; depend upon it [257].

Boredom also ironically keeps order, and strangely, even though boredom here seems to tear apart the sense of brotherhood, at the same time it shows that the men all suffer from it and so share something in common. The

Commodore is "so melancholy and forlorn ... [because] of his having so little to do" (22); Captain Claret has nothing to do and harbors vague feelings
of resentment against his subordinates and issues demerits, and in turn these
lieutenants vent their bitterness onto the midshipmen who are bored (25),
and also unleash their desire to see the tars experience pain, injury, or distress. In the March 1873 edition of *Harper's New Monthly Magazine*, Commodore William Gibson, in "Life On Board a Man-of-War," admits to his
own intolerable ennui. He writes:

> The life of the sea, and man-of-war routine, charm us nevertheless, and
> distract our thoughts with occupation. I have traveled in passenger ves-
> sels, and have felt, as wearily as did any landsman, the listlessness of
> nothing to do, the monotony of the blank horizons, the impatience to
> arrive in port. The *dolce far niente* is not sweet on board ship.... Officer
> or man is one of a small community, isolated from all the world. Each
> has his circle of companions and friends, saving always the captain, who,
> even more than the "sacred might" of Homeric kings, is hedged about
> by etiquette and a certain awe and reserve, which exist quite independ-
> ently of the character of the man. He, more than any other human being,
> may be styled monarch of all he surveys, but he is very lonely in his dig-
> nity ... he is far more spaciously and sumptuously lodged than any one
> else. He has his books about him, and his little comforts. And, more than
> all, potent to dispel every shade of *ennui*, is his sleepless and omnipresent
> responsibility [485].

From top to bottom, all the men suffer from boredom.

White Jacket does not confirm whether the activities he mentions, from
reading to dreaming, work effectively against boredom, but he notes that when
all of the crew was "yawning, gaping, and stretching in concert, it was then
that [he] used to feel a certain love and affection for them, grounded, doubt-
less, on a fellow-feeling" (174). The spirit of brotherhood and shared experience seem at times to hold back the worst effects of boredom. That the crewmen
are together indicates that in order to combat boredom, a condition of the loner,
one must be an active member of a group even when the concerted action is
a lack of action. White Jacket chooses his friends wisely, not because he is
elitist, but because "an indiscriminate intimacy with all hands leads to sundry
annoyances and scrapes, too often ending with a dozen at the gang-way" (50).
Christopher Sten also views White Jacket as not an elitist. Sten argues con-
vincingly against the traditional view that White Jacket's attitudes are prob-
lematically anti-democratic despite his anti-flogging stance. He befriends
Nord because he is philosophical, Lemsford because he is poetic, and Williams
because he was "invaluable as a pill against the spleen" (52); a grouping strikingly similar to *Mardi*'s (1848) circle of poet, philosopher, and others.

Being intellectual and highly cultured amongst colleagues seems to curb severe boredom for White Jacket; seizing "the right meaning of Montaigne" (51), writing poetry, and other learned activities help keep the mind engaged and excited, and does more than just "while the time away." In these pursuits these men use time to get something out of it. He says the best way to drive off the spleen is books: "You need never open them; only have the titles in plain sight. For this purpose, Peregrine Pickle is a good book; so is Gil Blas; so is Goldsmith" (46). He insists that the right choice of profession, books, and a lovely wife will ease one's bitterness, but Ahab is rightfully a captain, well-versed, and married family man, but yet is not relieved. Nonetheless, these high-minded exercises raise consciousness, and since White Jacket spends many hours with his group of fellow top sails men, boredom turns out to be a lesser threat than when he is alone; however, he is often alone. Even within his circle, he sometimes is ostracized. Nonetheless this strategy of holding down boredom through poetic and philosophic intellectualism and camaraderie has proven to be an effective one since *Mardi* (1848). In *Typee* (1846) and *Omoo* (1847) the singular pursuit of intellectualism helped Tommo/Typee and Taji to ease their boredom. This pattern of a highly attuned and expressive consciousness will continue with Ishmael in *Moby-Dick*.

As for the friendships Melville made while on the naval warship *United States*, Hershel Parker notes that, "By 1849, when Melville was writing *White-Jacket*, he thought he would hardly be able to recognize many of his shipmates should he happen to meet them in the streets" (272). Melville would have been able to identify Jack Chase, "that 'great heart' whom he never forgot, and to whom he dedicated *Billy Budd*" (Parker 303). There are no letters between Melville and John "Jack" Chase or any mention of Chase in Melville's journals. However, when examined closely, the literary Jack Chase of *White-Jacket* is not a friend of White Jacket. White Jacket praises Jack for his cultivated demeanor, but Jack's outlandish behavior and lofty sensibilities alienate some sailors. For example, "Against all whalers, indeed, he cherished the unmitigated detestation of a true man-of-war's man. Poor Tubbs can testify to that" (15). So could White Jacket, if he ever were to tell of his own whaling days. What would Jack say and do? Would he disown White Jacket? We want to say no because the two have been good acquaintances, if not friends. But are they friends? After an argument between Tubbs the whaler and Jack, White Jacket remarks:

> This outburst [Jack's outcry against whalers] on the part of my noble friend Jack made me shake all over, spite of my padded surtout; and caused me to offer up devout thanksgivings, that in no evil hour had I divulged the fact of having myself served in a whaler; for having previ-

ously marked the prevailing prejudice of men-of-war's-men to that much-maligned class of mariners, I had wisely held my peace concerning stove boats on the coast of Japan [16].

This whaler, White Jacket, would have been "abominated" (15) by Jack, and White Jacket senses it. Jack would forsake White Jacket; White Jacket is a dirty, stinking, and repulsive whaler, not the mannered, gentlemanly, and chummy man-of-war's man he passes himself off to be; he appears as a top main sail man, not a tar like everyone else. Their friendship is based on pretension, and I seriously doubt whether it can be true. Instead of shaking firmly Jack's hand when they depart at the end, White Jacket "kissed that noble hand" (396); friends, equals shake hands, but they are not. Jack does not resist, or find it offensive. White Jacket is lowering himself.

Similarly, in Melville's *Redburn* (1849) Redburn's acquaintanceship with Harry Bolton, although it may seem to be a promising friendship, actually is of questionable moral nature. Redburn is suspicious of Harry from their first meeting. Redburn's uncertainty about Harry rises when Harry, in effect, kidnaps Redburn to London, taking the American youth to what Robert K. Martin believes is "a male brothel" (51). Redburn is infuriated that Harry has taken him on an awkward, dangerous, and mysterious trip. Commenting on the London trip, Redburn says, "But all the time, I felt ill at heart ... [with] my companion" (231). Christopher Sten argues that Harry is not once ever forthright or genuine with Redburn (108). Not only is Harry deceiving Redburn, but quite possibly he is fooling himself. Moreover, therein lies the danger; self-deception which erodes selfhood. Harry's conscious refusal to reveal himself to Redburn causes Redburn to be distant. Redburn no longer feels "charmed with his appearance, and all eagerness to enjoy the society of this incontrovertible son of a gentleman" (216). At first, Harry is what Redburn wants to be; for Redburn, Harry is the wildly romantic, superficial, and dangerous attributes in him. But Redburn wants to keep his distance from him because he is prudent, experienced, and not so eager to grasp his dream of the aristocratic adventurer. Having second thoughts about the life of the aristocrat — Redburn is the son of a failed businessman — Redburn will look out for Harry onboard Captain Riga's vessel, but he will separate himself from Harry in New York. Harry is no friend of Redburn.

White Jacket ultimately fails to stave off boredom through friendship. Lemsford, Nord, Williams, and other top men seem to embrace him, but perhaps insecurities inhibit him fully accepting others. He seems to enjoy these men's company, and often participates in group activities. But he is a loner. Off-duty he wanders about the ship, lurking among the cannons or chains, or climbs the sails, rhapsodizing. He is nearly attacked down below and averts death from above. He probably prefers to be alone; being among others is demanding. White Jacket's behavior reveals a disturbing psychology, one that is cold, impersonal, and unsociable. This demeanor is at odds with his apparent praise of camaraderie. In fact, Wai-Chee S. Dimock argues correctly whether one ever truly gets to know White Jacket (300). Dimock forcefully says he is "a misanthropic spirit" (307). After befriending Queequeg, Ishmael has no such problem, but White Jacket is pointing to Bartleby, a man who seeks out the Lawyer only to evade him. White Jacket also simplifies the virtue of friendship; Jack Chase is not a friend. White Jacket spends time with Lemsford, Nord, and Williams, but idealizes Chase; Chase is the "Handsome Sailor," while the others are not. Even Billy Budd has his flaws. Yes, Chase saves White Jacket from the aggression of other sailors, and White Jacket is grateful. For some unknown reason friendship is insufficient. It is easy to say, "We main-top-men were brothers" (15), but harder to act and feel like brothers.

These strategies to curb boredom do not always work. Boredom is more than just inactivity coupled with melancholy or apathy; boredom at times leads to malice. Of course, the range of abuses varies: the officers endure reprimands and embarrassment, while the sailors are "degraded at the gangway" (375)—flogged. Anything can spark a grudge, but ultimately it is inexplicable. The pretense of rank and discipline does not camouflage the bitterness and spite generated by the boredom hanging over the ship. Senior officers manipulate the system because it is "easy to torture [junior officers] by official treatment, which shall not lay open the superior official to legal rebuke" (375). In *Billy Budd* (posthumous 1926), John Claggart tests how far he can torture Billy Budd, and in fact the master-at-arms can be seen as bored. The "mystery of iniquity" of *Billy Budd* recalls the "pent-up wickedness" of *White-Jacket* intertwined with boredom.

Boredom foments restlessness and spawns the active and profoundly sinister forces that plague the Navy. It sets off a cycle of spitefulness, and the violence it effects really does not expel the men's spleen; instead, it drives the process to repeat itself. It has become so fixed and entrenched that it stuns White Jacket. Although he is able to write down his horrifying revelation into this heart of darkness, he experiences great difficulty committing it on paper. He says, "It were sickening to detail all the paltry irritabilities, jealousies, and cabals, the spiteful detractions and animosities, that lurk far down, and cling to the very kelson of the ship" (375). The evil boredom generates is so shocking that it unsettles and dismantles White Jacket's worldview. This revelation is his harsh introduction to a fuller understanding of human nature; this awakening is similar to that Melville describes in *Typee*: "[It] has nearly overturned all my previous theories" (*Typee*, 203). White Jacket realizes that the intimidation and injustices on the *Neversink* are ruthless, and that there is nothing that can change them. Tradition, ceremony, and discipline remain fixed, and White Jacket uses imagery of steel and military weapons to emphasize that reform is impossible. He confesses, "The immutable ceremonies and iron etiquette of a man-of-war; the spiked barriers separating the various grades of rank, the delegated absolutism of authority on all hands; the impossibility, on the part of the common seaman, of appeal from incidental abuses" (375). The common seaman cannot defend himself; he is so marginalized, he is almost a non-entity. White Jacket notes the impossibility "on the part of the common seaman, of appeal" (375).

White Jacket realizes that boredom is a part of human nature, and the evils generated by boredom are so deeply fixed that he sees the condition in tragic terms; for him, there is no possibility for change, a major element of the tragic. The Navy is too fixed in its ways. It corrodes the very foundations of his selfhood; as he says, "It is unmanning to think of" (375). With slight variation, this phrase is repeated in Melville's art, an expression that reveals how the overwhelming forces of boredom, danger, evil, and death undermine his characters' integrities.

Anticipating the near-death episode stemming from boredom that Ishmael experiences in "The Mast-Head" chapter of *Moby-Dick*, White Jacket too narrowly escapes death due to boredom. His boredom arises unexpectedly, even innocently. The recent death of the cooper has not made him melancholy. On the contrary, he is in good spirits, and is enjoying his duty in the masthead. An indication of emotional strength, he neutralizes the playful mocking by others that he is an astronomer because he spends a lot of time in the main. He transforms their gentle yet direct insults into an identification with the "Chaldean Magi" (76), men seemingly like him who appreciated getting closer to their objects of interest. This comparison also points out his learning and understanding. Bradley A. Johnson says, "Melville associates sailors aloft on the masts with pure exercise of intellect and imagination" (245). It is a self-serving identification and cause of his alienation (Johnson, 247). Being perched two hundred feet up, and so that much closer, in his mind, to the stars, White Jacket can "give loose to reflection" (76), a state of being he prides himself upon doing often and satisfactorily. Routine, however, can give way to complacency. His "meditative humor" (77) is an activity of the loner: to think, one needs to be alone. Furthermore, he is an outcast, despite the occasional companionship of Jack Chase and his crew. The altitude separates him from the hecklers, and draws his attention to the universe; for him it is "divine" (76) to be that close to God. He identifies himself as a thinker, and his mind is acute, sensitive, and poetic, and suggests an education and class difference, which contributes to his alienation from the crew. This divine sensation ushers in the profound, mysterious, and mystical. I call it in part "mystical" because White Jacket undergoes a direct communion with the universe. He commutes his earthbound spiritual reality into a preternatural mode. He disconnects himself from physical manifestations of time and space, and he feels his life melting and commixing with the cosmos; he says, "it is a very fine feeling, and one that fuses us into the universe of things, and makes us a part of the All" (76). No longer are there boundaries detaining the soul's inherent connection with the universe; for a time White Jacket does not feel he is a finite being. He is everything. Such language suggests Melville as a pantheist, a believer in the doctrine that every part of the universe is a manifestation of God or Nature; however, Melville will attack this belief system in *Moby-Dick* (1851). But in *White-Jacket*, Melville is sympathetic and enthusiastic toward pantheism.

Within this pantheistic glow of merging with nature, the shadow of boredom and death lurks. White Jacket seems to be aware of the dangers when one's consciousness is compromised, when one gives into the shift between human spirituality to a supernatural one. What seems to prevent a total collapse of the self and offset death by boredom is the constellation of stars. The stars are his connection between the physical, spiritual, and otherworldly states. The celestial bodies function as a safeguard for White Jacket; while he can see them, he is relatively secure, but when he stays past his maintop duty and fails to mention any stars in his narrative, his boredom nearly kills him. Because of the solitary nature of the duty, he imagines the stars as "circumnavigators ... shipmates and fellow-sailors of ours" (77); he likens them to companions, essential and constant entities that assist sailors and interrupt the lonesomeness that they suffer. Yet at the same time the stars "lur[e] us, by every ray, to die and be glorified with them" (76). The stars can guide and reassure, but lead to disaster as well. Nature cannot be relied upon; nature is neither benevolent nor malevolent. That stars can lure men to death remains a muted threat, but he concentrates on the more pleasant aspects of stargazing.

Perhaps the clouds of boredom obscure those stars on the night White Jacket narrowly avoids death. Choosing not to leave his spot in the mainroyal-yard after fulfilling his duty at eight bells, he readily surrenders to his boredom. Giving into the delusional sense of serenity and assured ease, he tacitly believes this night will be like every other night when he stays past his watch and becomes absorbed in inconclusive thought. Nighttime is especially dangerous, and to remain aloft after one's watch is foolish and reckless. Because he has done it before, he never feels wary about not sleeping in his hammock; he has grown complacent. What at first seems to be a soul-nourishing experience actually is treacherous; White Jacket flatters himself by imagining he is in company with the Chaldean Magi, but to fuse with the universe is deadly. Making himself cozy in the yards, he uses his white jacket as a blanket, which suggests a death shroud. The next watch that replaces White Jacket's is "full of strangers" (77), and are a hundred feet below him and no one notices he is up there. And so the precariousness of his choice to remain increases. Since a mutual dislike exists between most of the crew and White Jacket, the peril only magnifies.

Lapsing into unconsciousness and stirring back to consciousness, these shifts from torpor to awareness are inviting, enveloping, and dangerous. This ebb and tide of the soul erodes his self-possession: "I lay entranced; now dozing, now dreaming; now thinking of things past, and anon of the life to come" (77). Past, present, and future fuse; the natural progression of time is interrupted. A voice from external reality jars him, but this irritation is not strong enough to break the spell of boredom; he is unaware that the sound is around him or who could be speaking to him. "Consciousness glided away from [him], and left [him] in Lethe" (77). This slight interruption from the material world is suppressed, and his inattention to his surroundings becomes more fixed; now he is completely oblivious to what is happening. He is hovering over death and he does not know it: "But when, like lightning, the yard dropped under me, and instinctively I clung with both hands to the '*tie*,' then I came to myself with a rush, and felt something like a choking hand at my throat. For an instant I thought the Gulf Stream in my head was whirling me away to eternity; but the next moment I found myself standing; the yard had descended to the *cap*; and shaking myself in my jacket, I felt that I was unharmed and alive" (77). White Jacket nearly loses his life. Physical reality crashes into his consciousness so suddenly, and his awakening is a godsend at that split second. His boredom has brought him to the edge of death.

White Jacket wants to believe that the proximity of the shore induces a severer form of boredom because "At sea there is more to employ the sailors, and less temptation to violations of law" (160). He seems to have forgotten the episode of boredom in the maintop that nearly killed him. The majority of men are prevented from visiting the port of Rio, and as a result, grow bored and "lead the laziest of lives" (160). In fact, they smuggle alcohol onboard, risking flogging, to dull further their dispirited existences. Boredom has deteriorated these men, and alcohol seems to be their only relief "from the intolerable ennui of nothing to do, and nowhere to go" (176), but the daily allowance of grog is miserably insufficient; it "is not enough to give a sufficient fillip to his listless senses" (176). Intoxication offsets the ever-present threat of boredom, but provides a questionable assurance against it. White Jacket notes, "Take away their grog, and life possesses no further charms for them" (52). Rather than stupefying, the liquor revitalizes; these men feel their élan come rushing back. They are willing to risk the delirium tremens and mania-a-poty rather than suffer the drag of boredom. As White Jacket observes, "'anything that smacks of life is better than to feel Davy Jones's chest-lid on your nose.' He is reckless as an avalanche; and though his fall destroy himself and others, yet a ruinous commotion is better than being frozen in unendurable solitudes" (176–7). For these men physical danger is better than spiritual stagnation. Their drinking arouses exhilaration and emboldens them, but getting drunk is an illusion of liveliness. Their boldness is fatal, consciousness is blurred, and identity is jeopardized; however, they do not see the danger. Employing self-deception which in this case is tantamount to suicide and courting physical death to curb a spiritual one accentuates the disturbing, taxing, and urgent problems of boredom. For these men there is no safety anywhere: to get high from alcohol only camouflages the void of boredom they continually face and to give into their boredom hastens death. The horror of boredom becomes bearable through grog, but the moment they become dry, will they still deny the seriousness of the delirium tremens? How will they cope with boredom sans alcohol?

Alert watchfulness against boredom is tested yet again when the *Neversink* enters Cape Horn's frigid and deadly waters. One cannot let one's guard down especially when arctic blasts can induce an irresistible lack of sensation that resembles boredom. It is unavoidable to slump into boredom: "There was nothing to be done but patiently to await the pleasure of the elements, and 'whistle for a wind,' the usual practice of seamen in a calm. No fire was allowed.... He who possessed the largest stock of vitality, stood the best chance to escape freezing. It was horrifying. In such weather any man could have undergone amputation with great ease, and helped take up the arteries himself" (101). Idleness, fatigue, numbness, and cold thrust the men toward death. In spite of the mounting dangers, the sensation is oddly pleasurable. Languor blurs into sleep which darkens into death; consciousness dims. Narcotic-like in its drowsiness and deadliness, this weather-induced boredom lowers the capacity for action. Why bother? It feels comfortable. White Jacket indicates:

> The severe cold still continued, and one of its worst consequences was the almost incurable drowsiness induced thereby during the long night-watches. All along the deck, huddled between the guns, stretched out on the carronade slides, and in every accessible nook and corner, you would

see the sailors wrapped in their monkey jackets, in a state of half-conscious torpidity, lying still and freezing alive, without the power to rise and shake themselves.

"Up — up, you lazy dogs!" our good-natured Third Lieutenant, a Virginian, would cry, rapping them with his speaking trumpet. "Get up, and stir about."

But in vain. They would rise for an instant, and as soon as his back was turned, down they would drop, as if shot through the heart.

Often I have lain thus [119].

Occasionally huddling together or exercising does not improve conditions. The strict, disciplined, and orderly naval ship is undermined when boredom affects the crew. Melville is beginning to realize that his earlier South Seas responses to boredom — to keep moving and working — are proving to be ineffective, and perhaps never worked at all.

White Jacket also turns to religion to counter the grimness of boredom with a belief that "Life is a voyage that's homeward-bound" (400), meaning, he is looking forward to the Christian afterlife. In its most fundamental and historical sense, Christianity was not concerned with the material and present world; it looked forward to celestial eternity. It fostered and insisted on a disinterest and disconnection with present earthbound reality, and White Jacket's religiosity tends to stress the primacy of immortal existence over a physical one. One can say that Christianity tacitly brings forth a kind of boredom concerning the physical world and time.

To be homeward bound is to be bound toward heaven, the anticipated place of joy and justice. The cruelties committed by bored men are explained away by White Jacket in the hope that all will be forgiven; he is not calling for direct punishment or redress, but understanding or even fortitude. There is no mention of hell, or separating the wicked from the upright. Fortitude, the strength of mind and spirit that makes one endure pain, adversity, or injustice with patience, humility, and nonviolence, is a hallmark of Christianity. White Jacket adopts this virtue in "The Ending," but Melville's narrative is retaliation against inequity, and it can be said that it is White Jacket's counterblow. Instead of issuing a direct call to arms, he asks for an ethical self-examination; however, it is a strained, guilt-ridden, and passive type of existentialism. White Jacket notes, "Yet the worst of our evils we blindly inflict upon ourselves; our officers can not remove them, even if they would. From the last ills no being can save another; therein each man must be his own savior" (399–400). Blame is shifted, and the oppressed, which includes White Jacket, must overlook their mistreatment and focus on myopic, unfair, and misplaced metaphysical matters. It is the individual response to evil that carries weight. It is a classic Christian reply to evil: turn the other cheek. However, Kris Lackey sees White Jacket's use of Christian tenets more favorably: "in White-Jacket's hands the New Testament is more than a guide-book to life; it is a revolutionary manifesto.... The Sermon serves as text for White-Jacket's Bible-thumping polemic" (247–8). White Jacket says, "Oh, ship-mates and world-mates, all round! We the people suffer many abuses. Our gun-deck is full of complaints. In vain from Lieutenants do we appeal to the Captain; in vain — while on board our world-frigate — to the indefinite Navy Commissioners, so far out of sight aloft" (399). Echoes of the *Declaration of Independence* mark White Jacket's plea, but instead of justified rebellion, religious forbearance and conservatism are the appropriate responses. White Jacket is expecting that his and his fellow sailors' passive nonaction will inspire guilt in the corrupt naval system. "Each man must be his own savior" is an appeal to not only heighten personal self-responsibility, but promote it in others. White Jacket may say we cannot save another, but one's action can have a reaction in others. He instructs his mates and readers to "never train our murderous guns inward; let us not mutiny with bloody pikes in our hands. Our Lord High Admiral will yet interpose" (400). God ultimately will right all wrongs.

The ethical response of patience that White Jacket urges in "The Ending" chapter proves impractical and questionable. His eschatological impulses are disguises, expressions that camouflage his repressed and vexing life dilemmas; he uses his religion to voice pessimistic attitudes and observations, which initially appear as statements of anticipation of the afterlife. For example, he says, "the Bible assures us that our life is but a vapor, that quickly passeth away" (130). The line comes from a chapter discussing the gunners who dwell below deck, and White Jacket stresses that, because the ship is filled with explosive material, "the whole earth itself is a vast hogshead, full of inflammable materials, and which we are always bestriding; at the same time, that all good Christians believe that at any minute the last day may come, and the terrible combustion of the entire planet ensue" (129). Christian doctrine glorifies the coming of Judgment Day, but White Jacket may not be as ardent and candid as he wishes to be seen. From the same section quoted above, he declares, "But we are all Fatalists at bottom" (129). Possibly hinting at Calvinistic doctrines, White Jacket admits that events are fixed so that human agency is impossible; if the world is to blow up or injustices hurt him, he is powerless, and if it is God's will, so be it. As naval seaman, there is little if not nothing he can do to make endurable his service time; he must give into fate or fall victim to Naval discipline, which is a kind of death — spiritual — and he almost dies on many occasions.

As Christian spokesman, White Jacket seems resigned to his Christian faith, and yet his confidence in that belief undergoes some damage. He admires the captain of the starboard bow-chaser who finds time to pray; however, this devout sailor's ship position and appearance threatens White Jacket's own core values. He says, "but how, with those hands of his begrimed with powder, could he break that *other* and most peaceful and penitent bread of the Supper" (324). Earlier he challenges warmongers to follow the Christian ethic of turning the other cheek, but also admits that call is doomed: "that passage embodies the soul and substance of the Christian faith; without it, Christianity were like any other faith. And that passage will yet, by the blessing of God, turn the world. But in some things we must turn Quakers first" (320). In White Jacket's worldview the nonviolent response to violence is virtually impossible, and to "turn Quakers first" is an admission of failure and he knows it. To turn Quaker is a radical, arduous, elusive, and ultimately illusive transformation of character and conduct; for a young, aggressive, and expanding country drunk on Manifest Destiny, such a moral demand is hopelessly and sadly absurd. He says:

> Ah! the best righteousness of our man-of-war world seems but an unrealized ideal, after all; and those maxims which, in the hope of bringing about a Millennium, we busily teach to the heathen, we Christians ourselves disregard. In view of the whole present social frame-work of our world, so ill adapted to the practical adoption of the meekness of Christianity, there seems almost some ground for the thought, that although our blessed Savior was full of the wisdom of heaven, yet his gospel seems lacking in the practical wisdom of earth — in a due part appreciation of the necessities of nations at times demanding bloody massacres and wars; in a proper estimation of the value of rank, title, and money [324].

Religion is an honorable and worthy principle to aim for and a concept that inspires men to higher goals, but lacks the possibility of realization. Professions of faith and modeling oneself after Christ are inapplicable to nation-builders; the Christian system of values clashes with the economics and politics of the secular world. To struggle to determine the essential meaning of life and to answer questions outside the physical realm bear no meaning or usefulness for warriors and leaders. How can one be meek and remain so in this world; how can one fulfill the Savior's wisdom and live by his gospel? It seems religion in this world can only exist in the mind and touch the heart, but to transfer that belief into action, an act that White Jacket cannot achieve, is untenable. Spirituality is not a concern and neither is brotherhood in the navy. Realizing the impotence of this model of excellence and perfection, White Jacket salvages religion by insisting, "But all this only the more crowns the divine consistency of Jesus; since Burnet and the best theologians demonstrate, that his nature was not merely human — was not that of a mere man of the world" (324). Even in his defense of Christ's teachings White Jacket admits to the unrealistic and wavering nature of religion. By drawing attention to Christ's ontology, that he was a supernatural being, White Jacket only confirms and strengthens the conviction that Christianity is an impossible, or an extremely difficult, ethic to live by. How convincing is he when he observes, "We must turn Quakers first" now?

White Jacket does not admit defeat concerning his piety here, but in the following chapter when the Assistant Surgeon, who is "full of theological hypoes concerning the state of [his patients'] souls" (329), asks him, "Are you pious?" (329) during an examination, White Jacket cannot answer him. His silence is a stinging and clear testimonial that his recent endorsement of religion is doubtful, that he is not secure with his faith, and dominating forces of the material world unveil his uncertainty, which he can offer no reply to. At best his affirmation of trust in God is ambiguous, and at its worst that confirmation is strained, unconvincing, and contrived. For John Samson, his Christianity is marked by self-satisfaction and a kind of cowardice (149). White Jacket's non-answer negates or seriously undercuts his pronouncements. Melville does not pursue this material. I must disagree with Samson's claim that White Jacket "has not, though, lost his faith" (160). White Jacket is "somewhat staggered" (329) by the question and keeps silent, and the surgeon does not examine any further White Jacket's spiritual illness. Possibly the inconclusiveness is a sign of haste, Melville may not have thought through the possibilities of this highly charged scene. It is an opportunity missed and an artistic flaw, and its unsatisfactory and unfinished status may symbolize White Jacket's coat: like the patches that hold the jacket, Melville has not made whole cloth out of the patches of this scene. However, Judy Logan sees no irony or deception in Melville's use of religion (402). It seems that public declaration is pivotal to verifying the genuineness of White Jacket's religious beliefs; this verbalization has strong similarities to the citizenship and church membership requirements for young Puritans entering the congregation; for some Puritan youths, they too had difficulty acknowledging their faith publicly.

In spite of the severe blow to White Jacket's faith, perhaps Melville, as artist, fighting off the growing tendency in the novel that all things ultimately tend toward evil, prevents the inherent hopelessness from overtaking the work, and creates a scene where White Jacket experiences a kind of resurrection and this rebirth offers a muted hope. Performing a dangerous task at night in the top-mast and injuring himself and falling into the ocean, White Jacket goes in and out of consciousness in the water. The threat of death and the loss of self can place one in danger of boredom; the calming and drawn out empty-ing of his life, a kind of blankness, which is suggestive of nihilism, resembles the draining of the spiritual forces experienced while bored. The similarities between White Jacket's near death drowning and boredom are not pressed further. Succumbing to the "feeling of death" and "the deep calm now around [him]" (393), he feels "the thrill of being alive again" because "some fashion-less form brushed [his] side — some inert, coiled fish of the sea" (393) stirs him. In Christian iconology, the fish represents Christ. I believe that the "inert, coiled fish of the sea" is Melville's superficial attempt to reconcile his charac-ter's spiritual faltering and failing. White Jacket's silence when he cannot answer the Assistant Surgeon's religious question is a denial of Christ; this passage calls to mind Peter's denial of Christ in the Christian Bible. But the interac-tion between White Jacket and the fish, if one can even call it that, nearly escapes the reader's attention, even White Jacket's; the narrator does not emphasize this scene, but still it is highly suggestive. White Jacket undergoes a symbolic death by his injury and fall into the ocean, and the fish effects a kind of rebirth. White Jacket's resurrection, as it is represented, points to *Moby-Dick*'s ending where Ishmael is saved by Queequeg's life buoy/coffin. However, Bruce L. Grenberg points out that despite the scene's rich possibilities, this religious motif only confirms the sense of ambiguity in White Jacket's life (90).

The adjectives that describe the fish muddle the symbolic strength of the scene. The fish is inert, lacking vigor and movement; this may indicate that Christ is powerless or severely limited in this world, or it may symbolize White Jacket's own spiritual limitations. Howard P. Vincent sees Melville's use of the fish as "powerful" (220). On the other hand, the fish also is coiled, which suggests the potential for power, action, and movement. The fish did brush White Jacket, which could mean the fish is slightly active, but perhaps unin-tentionally. Because the scene takes place at night and underwater and White Jacket is injured and impaired mentally, he never really sees what awakens him; it could have not happened at all. Melville is reaching for symbolic meaning here, but it is unclear what kind. That the crew ultimately rescues him suggests that Christ and man are needed together for deliverance from destruction. Along with these ambiguous elements, the overall structure of "The Last of the Jacket" chapter blurs any message the reader is meant to take. Melville may be taxing the material to make this experience fit within some religious/optimistic program. This moment is not strong enough to counter the hardships and narrowly avoided deaths White Jacket endures. While this seeming life-preserving-changing event does provide some of the momentum for the novel's final message of hopefulness, it also contributes to the unsat-isfactory tone of the ending.

Although *White-Jacket* ends on a note of hope, this conclusion is strained, illogical, artificial, unearned, and unconvincing, and flies in the face of all that has occurred. The religious optimism does not, cannot, counter the despair and offset the ever-present threat of death in the novel; rather, the ending seems as a cushion to deny the bleak conditions of navy life. John Samson notes, "The triteness of this faith and the ease with which White-Jacket, like the 'transcendental' chaplain whom he earlier lampoons, dismisses the world's evil indicate that Melville does not share his narrator's position" (162). I agree with Alan Lebowitz's interpretation; he may want to see and more importantly want to end with a cheery and light message, but his "sunny" disposition cannot cut through the dark realities that he and the rest of the crew experienced (129). Edgar A. Dryden (1968) agrees, saying White Jacket's insistence on a happy ending is at odds with itself (71). The ending cannot bear the novel's oppressive themes because it is too fragile to counterbalance them (Grenberg 91); Grenberg also adds that the ending "does not resolve life's ambiguities" (92). The ending is conspicuous, sentimental, and excessive while addressing its religious message of fortitude. It is an undeserved and unrealizable directive because White Jacket fails to enact it; it is a virtue he cannot manifest. I do not share Joyce Sparer Adler's claim that "The Ending" is "a poetic summary of what the work as a whole has had to say" (232); moreover, White Jacket does not gain any knowledge. Unlike Adler, I see the ending as a bad replica of what one should be. Christian faith does not save at the end because it did not throughout the entire novel. Yes, the warship may be hell, but White Jacket is no Dante, as Adler alludes to.

A clear example of White Jacket's lack of steadfastness in the face of opposition, hardship, and danger is when he is nearly flogged for allegedly not being at his station. He shows stubbornness and insubordination; moreover, he displays a personal affront or disgrace, an unprincipled and shameful cowardice, when addressing the captain while coping with the reality of being punished. Melville notes, "There are times when wild thoughts enter a man's heart, when he seems almost irresponsible for his act and his deed ... between him and the sea" (280). As he is about to kill the captain and himself, Colbrook, a corporal of marines, saves him by showing respect to the Captain while addressing him, an act he refuses, and bravely speaks up to authority based on truth to point out White Jacket was not derelict in his duty. White Jacket's profession of a high-minded sense of morality and divine reliance for justice is not as strong as he may want it to be. He may sound religious, but fails to express a real belief in God through his actions, just as he cannot answer the Assistant Surgeon's question. In contrast, White Jacket loses all hope and becomes reckless and very nearly violent, and does not seem all that different from the skulkers and scoundrels he condemns. He lacks any consciousness; at least Taji in *Mardi* expresses little guilt concerning his murderous act. White Jacket may be a bright, imaginative, and expressive person, but he shows no emotional and moral maturity. Forcing God's justice "to decide between [the Captain and himself]" (280) is taking justice into his own hands and thereby denying God's law. Although John, Antone, Mark, and Peter vary in their responses while being flogged, they all withstand the punishment, and even Old Ushant, the revered old tar, "only bowed over head, and stood as the Dying Gladiator" (366) when he was flogged. Christ showed dignity when flogged and crucified, which White Jacket does not even think of.

The message of the novel is conventional and expected, but it seems that Melville could not bring himself to embrace it himself. He has difficulty presenting this forced optimism:

> Believe not the hypochondriac dwellers below hatches, who will tell you, with a sneer, that our world-frigate is bound to no final harbor whatever; that our voyage will prove an endless circumnavigation of space. Not so. For how can this world-frigate prove our eventual abiding place, when, upon our first embarkation, as infants in arms, her violent rolling — in after life unperceived — makes every soul of us sea-sick? Does not this show, too, that the very air we here inhale is uncongenial, and only becomes endurable at last through gradual habituation, and that some blessed, placid haven, however remote at present, must be in store for us all?
>
> Glance fore and aft our flush decks. What a swarming crew! All told, they muster hard upon eight hundred millions of souls. Over these we have authoritative Lieutenants, a sword-belted Officer of Marines, a Chaplain, a Professor, a Purser, a Doctor, a Cook, a Master-at-Arms.
>
> Oppressed by illiberal laws, and partly oppressed by themselves, many of our people are wicked, unhappy, inefficient. We have skulkers and idlers all round, and brow-beaten waisters, who, for a pittance, do our craft's shabby work. Nevertheless, among our people we have gallant fore, main, and mizzen top-men aloft, who, well treated or ill, still trim our craft to the blast.
>
> We have a *brig* for trespassers; a bar by our main-mast, at which they are arraigned; a cat-o'-nine-tails and a gangway, to degrade them in their own eyes and in ours [398–9].

In a 6 October 1849 letter to his father-in-law, Lemuel Shaw, Melville claims that *White-Jacket* was written "not from my heart" (*Correspondence*, 138); he could not endorse a belief he could not feel. The White Jacket of this propagandistic millennial program is not the same one who was about to charge the Captain and kill both Claret and himself. It seems we should believe the hypochondriac dwellers below. Christopher Sten argues that White Jacket's reaction to his near flogging anticipates the arrival of Ahab, the character type who refuses to accept what fate has to offer (129). I do not see White Jacket as a domineering, articulate, and fearless individual as Ahab; the naval tar is insincere, unsure, and unassuming. He may protest against the injustices of the navy and world at large; however, he voices them privately, that is, as a writer. Ahab shouts at the world, and, more importantly, he is an active agent in the world. White Jacket does not fight back.

White Jacket's religion, if one can call it that, proves an inadequate antidote to his boredom. It fails him because it is mere profession. White Jacket feels no genuine joy of God. What he faces is a kind of shattering of personal values. Earlier novels tended to criticize Christianity as an institution; his critiques were not an attack on values or beliefs, but upon people who abused native people and endorsed growing imperialism in the South Pacific. In *White-Jacket* Melville gradually approaches a more personal exploration and questioning of faith. *White-Jacket* can be seen as Melville's first determined examination of religious faith as a response to boredom, but the strength and genuineness of that belief in God is murky and at the very least questionable. Kathleen E. Kier stresses that "*White-Jacket*'s deepest concerns are not fully worked out within the text of the novel" (6).

White-Jacket subtly commences a pattern that will mark some of Melville's later religiously themed literature: *Moby-Dick* (1851), "Bartleby, the Scrivener" (1853), *Clarel* (1876), and *Billy Budd* (posthumous, 1924). These works of art all have endings that close with religious hope; however, the contention over these conclusions is whether they are earned. The final chapter of *White-Jacket* forces piety in a work where religion fails to uphold its protagonist. Melville's treatment of religion in *White-Jacket* is not so much a quarrel, but, like the Biblical Jacob wrestling with God's angel, a struggle. Lawrence Thompson's *Melville's Quarrel with God* has insisted that Melville vehemently opposed a belief in God. If an atheist, why shout against God? Shelley and other nineteenth-century atheists did not verbally and passionately quarrel against God. If one does not believe, why invest so much energy toward a non-existing entity? It indicates the possibility that Melville wanted to believe, but could not find a satisfactory way of doing so.

In *Either/Or* (1843), Søren Kierkegaard observes, "Boredom is the root of all evil" (285). Boredom is not a superficial and harmless annoyance; it is a serious, dreadful, and powerful force that undermines integrity and contentment. It spawns hatred and murder; it divides, and ushers chaos. The devil loves idle hands. Man's worst arises when boredom possesses him. Melville has illustrated this unsettling and unflattering side of man in *White-Jacket*, and thus has articulated a painful and distressing insight which he had gained during his actual naval service. Compositional compromises such as public reception/success and curbing his more artistic daring caused him to soften the impact of his terrible realization that the evil that men do as a result of boredom also weakened the unity of his art.

It may be true that squeamishness and artistic immaturity still plagued him in some degree when he began drafting the first version of *Moby-Dick*. In the 1 May 1850 letter to Richard H. Dana, Jr., Melville describes some hesitancies he feels concerning the novel's composition: "It will be a strange sort of a book, tho,' I fear; blubber is blubber you know; tho' you may get oil out of it, the poetry runs as hard as sap from a frozen maple tree.... Yet I mean to give the truth of the thing, spite of this" (*Correspondence*, 162). This original draft of *Moby-Dick* is lost because Melville reenvisioned the work soon after the beginning of his famous and fateful friendship with Hawthorne; the identification with and validation from Hawthorne motivated Melville to discard it. It is only when Melville finally embraces Shakespeare and Hawthorne's powers of blackness that he is able to embrace his own dark themes. Days after the publication of *Moby-Dick*, Melville finally is able to admit to Hawthorne in a 17(?) November 1851 letter that "I have written a wicked book, and feel spotless as the lamb.... It is a strange feeling — no hopefulness is in it, no despair. Content — that is it; and irresponsibility; but without licentious inclination. I speak now of my profoundest sense of being, not of an incidental feeling" (*Correspondence*, 212). Through Ishmael, Ahab, and Moby Dick, Melville now can freely explore how deep, penetrating, and strong boredom's roots are, and how black is man's evil. He can question the validity and nature of God, and trace the deterioration and insensibility of the human soul. Melville discovered long ago that boredom undermines these entities, but it took him years to accept its grim realities.

Moby-Dick
God or the Devil

Those three great evils, boredom, vice, and poverty.
Voltaire, *Candide*

Everything good is the transmutation of something evil: every god has a devil
for a father.

Friedrich Nietzsche,
Unpublished Fragments,
Nov 1882–Feb1883

By the summer of 1850, Melville could no longer disown what had been festering in his art from the beginning. His characters immediately saw it in their island paradises, and witnessed it on their ships. There was no escaping it; evil was an inescapable component of man. When Melville as artist could not come to terms with evil, his art wavered. His need for affirmation often compromised the validity of his themes and conclusions; Melville could not bring to a close what his art unconsciously implied: the power of darkness. In writing "Hawthorne and His Mosses" (1850) Melville found liberation from the constraining, genteel, and misleading conventions of being a popular writer. No matter how much Melville longed for financial success, his greater desire to become a serious artist prevailed.

The first manuscript of *Moby-Dick* was nearly completed when he was asked to review Hawthorne's fiction. If Melville believed that "until I was twenty-five, I had no development at all. From my twenty-fifth year I date my life" (*Correspondence*, 193), it may be truer to say that the summer of 1850 was the moment that transformed Melville as novelist. Although he was praising Hawthorne's cunning in "Mosses," he simultaneously was securing his own vision as an artist handling dark themes. In the review, Melville writes, "For, in certain moods, no man can weigh this world, without throwing in something, somehow like Original Sin, to strike the uneven balance.... This black conceit pervades him, through and through" (243); he adds, "This blackness it is that furnishes the infinite obscure of his grandest conceits, the things that have made for Shakespeare his loftiest, but most circumscribed renown, as the profoundest of thinkers" (244). Through his guise as an approving Hawthorne critic, Melville allowed himself to be such a profound thinker. Melville confessed in a 1 May 1850 letter to Richard Dana, Jr., that the whale book was going to be different, but he did not yet fully know the nature or significance of this difference. By absorbing Hawthorne's influence and making himself over after the summer of 1850, Melville rewrote his *Moby-Dick* manuscript and penned his "Gospels" (*Correspondence*, 192) to reflect his new confidence in a dark literary and philosophical vision.

The acceptance of evil brought balance in Melville's art. Its presence in his art would become at times unbearable, but the struggle for resolution, hopefulness, and joy would be just as difficult to maintain. Hawthorne became a living model of the composure and discernment that Melville needed at this time to achieve his own self-possession. Eventually, the student would surpass the mentor, able to find brightness in the darkness in ways the elder could not or did not want to avow. Melville's literary demons of noontide will not let him be. They torment him with the anguish of not knowing, plaguing him with the doubt that Epicurus describes:

> The gods can either take away evil from the world and will not, or, being willing to do so cannot; or they neither can nor will, or lastly, they are both able and willing. If they have the will to remove evil and cannot, then they are not omnipotent. If they can, but will not, then they are not benevolent. If they are neither able nor willing, then they are neither omnipotent nor benevolent. Lastly, if they are both able and willing to annihilate evil, how does it exist? [as quoted in *Dictionary of Quotations*, 209].

The demon of noontide could not have expressed it more forcefully.

Bolstered by his insights into Shakespeare and Hawthorne and propelled more by his own discovery of powerful literary subjects, Melville explored in *Moby-Dick* (1851) the "lower layer" (163) of boredom. It gathers previous incomplete expressions and tepid intimations of boredom's importance in his art, and consolidates and discloses the integral nature of boredom in his characters. The novel draws together various metaphysical concerns: self-meaning, the role of good and evil, and the questionable nature of God/universe, and traces the unifying thread of boredom running through all. Boredom's power is so crushing and pervasive in *Moby-Dick* that it is as miraculous that Ishmael survives its blows as it is that he survives the *Peqoud's* stoving. Boredom unleashes the "power of blackness" in *Moby-Dick*; Melville's previous work is its trace, and his art thereafter is the shade of its darkness. I agree with Emory Elliott's summary that "All of the concerns that had been expressed in Melville's works in fragments before *Moby-Dick* come together in this work, which engages issues involving religion, ethics, morality, and metaphysics" (190). Elliot, however, does not address the role of boredom in Melville's religious and philosophical considerations. This is my task in this chapter.

Ahab

Ishmael is not alone in his shocked recognition of boredom's blackness. Even Ahab experiences bouts of boredom. At first Ahab seems too massive to fall victim to boredom; it appears as if his monomania shields him from it. But could he imagine his adversary dead? What would he do after killing Moby Dick? Could he live on? His singular concentration on the whale makes him appear to have purpose, interest, and engagement, but his principle determination is a perversion. It blocks everything else in his life: crew, wife and child, and his own well-being. He disengages himself from life itself. Ahab boasts to Starbuck that "We'll talk to-morrow, nay, to-night, when the white whale lies down there, tied by head and tail" (565); he may be able to imagine the whale in the try-works, but can he imagine the morrow without Moby Dick? He lives in the present moment, dreaming of a future with Moby Dick conquered; however, that future includes nothing else. His reality is a constant sameness, only the whale, and it occupies him both physically and spiritually. Ahab says of himself, "I'm demoniac, I am madness maddened.... The path to my fixed purpose is laid with iron rails whereon my soul is grooved to run.... Naught's an obstacle" (168). He dismisses other ships if they have no useful information about the whale; he refuses to help the *Rachel* search for her lost crew after engaging Moby Dick. Ahab does not care.

Ahab's intense singlemindedness is a variation of boredom: he takes no interest in anything but Moby Dick. The sea creature for Ahab represents in a demented pantheistic manner everything; however, if he embodies the All, then he could as well symbolize the Nothing, Ahab's spiritual void. Ahab explains, "To me, the white whale is that wall shoved near to me. Sometimes I think there's a naught beyond" (164). Staring at walls daily, Bartleby knows too what lies beyond the wall. The other side is spiritual disaster, a blankness that emerges from within, but the emptiness from behind has already begun to consume Ahab. Boredom is eating away at him. When Ahab smites his chest to indicate what a dead Moby Dick will be worth, Stubb comments, "What's that for? Methinks it rings most vast, but hollow" (163).

Because there was little for the officers in *White-Jacket* to do, they were annoyed by boredom; Ahab too endures the "ennui of having nothing to do, nowhere to go" (WJ, 176). Still in the Atlantic (and still in the vicinity of home), Ahab on deck "seemed as unnecessary there as another mast ... there was little or nothing, out of himself, to employ or excite Ahab" (125). Like the authority figures on the *United States*, the captain of the *Pequod* too is tormented by isolation and purposelessness. Melville writes, "Ahab for hours and hours would stand gazing dead to windward, while an occasional squall of sleet or snow would all but congeal his very eyelashes together" (234). His loneliness and unutilized time increase his monomania and boredom. If Moby Dick does not occupy his mind, the feelings of nothingness prey upon him. Melville notes:

> But all the witcheries of that unwaning weather did not merely lend new spells and potencies to the outward world. Inward they turned upon the soul, especially when the still mild hours of eve came on; then, memory shot her crystals as the clear ice most forms of noiseless twilights. And all these subtle agencies, more and more, they wrought on Ahab's texture [126].

The uneventfulness of the world attacks the self, and the nothingness of the self breaks out. The relative safety of position and rank does not offset the threat of boredom. It is always there, and once one's guard is weakened, danger awaits: soul damage. Ahab is spiritually infirm.

Ahab's boredom is a type that destroys every other aspect of his being except his intent to kill Moby Dick. There is no resistance against losing his spirit or humanity. Despite sounding and acting so vigorously, his life is ebbing away, his sources of life shriveling, as he becomes more focused on his quest. In his pursuit to avenge himself, he is killing himself. The joy of life is fading fast, but for Ahab this is an insignificant loss; such joy is an impediment to achieving his goal. He apparently does not sleep (127), and if he does, the sleep is not restful due to "exhausting and intolerably vivid dreams of the night, which, resuming his own intense thoughts through the day, carried them on amid a clashing of phrensies, and whirled them round and round in his blazing brain, till the very throbbing of his life-spot became insufferable anguish" (201). No rest for the wickedly bored. Just as sleep brings no comfort or peace, his pipe too "no longer soothes" (129). He says:

> Oh, my pipe! hard must it go with me if thy charm be gone! Here have I been unconsciously toiling, not pleasuring,— aye, and ignorantly smoking to windward all the while; to windward, and with such nervous whiffs, as if, like the dying whale, my final jets were the strongest and fullest of trouble. What business have I with this pipe? this thing that is meant for sereneness, to send up mild white vapors among mild white hairs, not among torn iron-grey locks like mine. I'll smoke no more [129].

Ahab acknowledges that psychological pain and joylessness have gone straight to the heart of his being. The pipe is an index of his joie de vivre, his life force promoting wholeness, and by tossing the pipe into the sea, Ahab measures the grim and hopeless nature of his existence. John Bryant calls this behavior "a rejection of geniality" (221). Like the pipe, a beautiful sunset offers no more pleasure (167), and Ahab is unmoved by the vastness and sublimity of the Pacific Ocean (483). He says, "all loveliness is anguish to me, since I can ne'er enjoy. Gifted with the high perception, I lack the low, enjoying power; damned, most subtly and most malignantly! damned in the midst of Paradise" (167). Moby Dick is a constant stinging reminder that he can no longer take delight in anything; all previous pastimes and pleasures are now useless and worthless.

With Moby Dick still alive, Ahab wonders how he can live his life. Having been crippled by the whale, Ahab prefers not to be in life for anything else but to seek revenge. Everything in life irritates him because it dulls and numbs his purpose. He has no need of anything that does not bring him closer to killing the white whale. Ahab commands the blacksmith: "Take them [razors], man, I have no need for them; for I now neither shave, sup, nor pray till — but here — to work" (489). Monkish, Ahab denies himself, and only subsists on his hatred for the whale.

This abstinence of both physical and emotional sustenance can help the individual achieve higher meaning and being; in a spiritual context, in the Christian kenotic tradition, emptying one's self physically allows for a fuller, transcendental experience. Such an experience is considered as a spiritual good; it promises a more intense contact with God. Both a physical and spiritual fast is meant to purify the devotee; thus cleansed, the individual is ready to receive God within. However, in Ahab's case, it is a perverse, unholy kenosis. His discarding of activities and objects that had brought him relative wholesome enjoyment is not a righteous or healthy action. It is destructive and evil. The noontide demon, not God, is awaiting him. Melville writes:

> A chasm seemed opening in him, from which forked flames and lightnings shot up, and accursed fiends beckoned him to leap down among them.... The tormented spirit that glared out of bodily eyes, when what seemed Ahab rushed from his room, was for the time but a vacated thing, a formless somnambulistic being, a ray of living light, to be sure, but without an object to color, and therefore a blankness in itself [202].

Formlessness, blankness, and emptiness, all the precursors of boredom, become horrifyingly real. These foretelling signs of Ahab's boredom take on dark, sinister overtones, and any equivocations concerning Ahab's feelings of emptiness are made more complicated by this representation of Ahab's animus. This passage is more than just a symbol of Ahab's demoniac impulses or an image of Ahab as possessed; it deals with deep-rooted, monstrous, and primal forces in man. Have the demons been within Ahab's empty soul all along, or has Ahab voided himself to invite evil? The chasm that "seemed opening in him" recalls the image of the Greek goddess Athena's birth; however, instead of wisdom, virtue, and purity, emerging out of the head of Zeus, the terror of Ahab's (and the universe's) emptiness is revealed.

The greatest fear that the medieval monks faced was that once having committed the sin of acedia, they would forever be lost, abandoned by God and left alone. *Acedia* was one of the original deadly sins; this trespass against God was one that drew the faithful away from God, causing them to lack joy in God's goodness and grace. *Acedia* was a wedge that separated God from man. How would they live without God's presence? Would they follow Satan, the demon of noontide who drew them away from God? Did Ahab intentionally pull himself away from God, or did God forsake him? Ann Douglas notes, "Ahab's mind may be diseased, but it is a sickness he caught from God, not man" (44). God is at once the source of the problem and the cure for acedia. The situation is chaotic, puzzling, and ambiguous. At such moments, it is difficult to decide whether one is afflicted with "good or bad" boredom (Raposa), or to ponder the possibilities of a derelict God, jilted believer, or even a defunct religion. The challenge of acedia is to decide whether there is a reason to continue to believe. This problem of abandonment, of losing one's connection to a higher, spiritual force in *Moby-Dick* becomes a significant leitmotif in Melville's art, achieving its highest point in *Clarel*.

"The Candles" chapter in *Moby-Dick* offers an index of Ahab's spirituality. It suggests a reevaluation and confirmation of his position in life, relationship to God, and sense of self. Moby Dick not only changed Ahab physically and emotionally, but also caused his fallout with the divine; for Ahab, these altercations are the same. Ahab envisions himself as a faithful worshipper, even calling himself a "Persian," perhaps alluding poetically to the depth of his devotedness. That he climbs upon the Parsee — who in name at least is a Zoroastrian, a religion that many scholars hold is the mother of the Abrahamic religions, whose followers fled Islamic persecution to India — suggests he is addressing a conflict that goes straight to the heart of faith. Ahab is not debunking religion per se; instead, as Marius Bewley maintains, "Melville is not attacking God; he is attempting to rescue the idea of the good, to push back from his darkening consciousness that instinctive reaction of the disillusioned American: hatred of creation itself" (22).

Ahab's intense interest with the transcendental suggests his spirituality was overzealous, narrow, and constraining. It had blinded him; he had lost perspective. Perhaps he even wanted a more direct, concentrated communion, taking kenotic tendencies to the extreme. Ahab says, "Oh! thou clear spirit of clear fire, whom on these seas I as Persian once did worship, till in the sacramental act so burned by thee, that to this hour I bear the scar" (507). Ahab has undergone a profound disillusionment. He is purging his dependency on this supernatural force, yet he is hesitant to break free completely. Harold Bloom's comments on Ahab's "He tasks me; he heaps me" speech also bear poignant, comparative insights for "The Candles" chapter: "To strike through the mask is to break through what the ancient Gnostics called the Kenoma, the cosmological emptiness into which we have been thrown by the Creation-Fall" (2). Ahab no longer sees God as a power of good, able to keep His promise to His fold. God is not beneficent or caring; He may be powerful, but is not an ally. God may be inept, but is a powerful bungler. By being All, He, as a result, may be nothing.

Utilizing deconstruction to highlight Nietzsche's position on God, Mark C. Taylor (1984) insists that no matter if one envisions God as the epitome of evil, by doing so, one nonetheless (and perhaps unknowingly) praises God. Similarly, Thomas Merton celebrates this gainsaying, noting, "He is so far above being that it is in some sense truer to say of Him that He 'is not' than He is" (15). God has belittled Ahab, disposed of him. God seems indifferent, unresponsive to either devotion or disregard, but He just in fact may be receptive; He may answer Ahab's passion with unadulterated, blessed fire. The flame burns, but illuminates. Ahab can see, but is blinded. Saint Paul once was a persecutor of Christians, and Saint Thomas once doubted the resurrected Christ. Ahab curses God; however, Ahab does not reject or deny God. He gains certain strength by distancing but not abandoning totally this God; he achieves a certain independence. Faith is a complex, unnerving relationship; it binds one to God, but can one ever know or feel that bond? *Acedia* always challenged the relationship between the Creator and His fold.

On the threshold of faith and denial, of embrace and recoil, and of joy and misery, Ahab exposes what he perceives to be the deficiencies of his God's intensity and relation to him; he too unfolds his own past shortcomings of his assimilation into the Godhead. He apparently stared too long, too ardently into the fire, and as Friedrich Nietzsche warns in *Beyond Good and Evil* (1886): "If thou gaze too long into an abyss, the abyss will also gaze into thee" (466). In response, God has stared back, boring right into Ahab's soul, emptying him. Michael L. Raposa has shown that this aspect of acedia, the so-called clash between "good" and "bad" boredom, must be clarified. Therefore, by identifying whether Ahab suffers from good or bad boredom will help one understand Ahab's mission. The difference between good and bad boredom is a matter of perspective. Feeling bored can inspire one to dive deeper, try harder. It is not a dead end per se; it can build character and faith. If one sees a way to alleviate this temporary boredom, and believes that it is only temporary, then this kind of boredom is indeed good. It exposes a problem not yet disastrous. One can gain benefit from the insight and improve. Therefore, one's attitude toward boredom is crucial. Ahab's contest is whether he chooses to remain devout or demonic. Ahab's kenotic rite could have been a Jonathan Edwards–like enthusiasm, of surrendering all to behold the All, or could have been the awakening to acknowledge his vulnerability and error. This great potential for either attainment or loss, contact or rift, is the edge of nihilism and affirmation.

Irving Howe's (1967) definition of the modern offers another way to place Ahab's trying situation: "[One must begin to recognize] ... the intrinsic connection between nihilism as doctrine and nihilism as experience of loss. Just as Jane Austen saw how trivial lapses in conduct can lead to moral disaster, so Dostoevsky insisted that casual concessions to boredom can drive men straight into the void" (38). Howe continues, stressing, "Fundamentally, then, nihilism comes to imply a loss of connection with the sources of life, so that both in experience and literature it is always related to, while analytically distinguishable from, the blight of boredom" (38). Ahab's experience of loss is no casual admission of failure, but the culmination of his loss of the sources of life — the joie de vivre — which, as Howe has shown, is linked to nihilism. The ultimate danger of boredom is crossing the threshold, stepping into the "realm" of the void.

Ahab can be conceived as one of Mark C. Taylor's troubled believer-atheists. In *Errings: A Postmodern A/theology* (1984), Taylor describes this group as "people who find themselves caught in the middle of such extremes. Suspended between the loss of old certainties and the discovery of new beliefs, these marginal people constantly live on the border that both joins and separates belief and unbelief. They look yet do not find, search but do not discover. This failure, however, need not necessarily end the quest" (5). Ahab's wrenching and hazardous inquisition of God can neither be successful nor end in failure. Despite his fixation on the whale, he cannot, almost does not, want to choose; and so he suffers, unable to grasp or cast away God. Ahab is caught in transition, a limbo which binds him to his obsession and scourges his soul. He cannot know that God exists, but knows that he must pursue Moby Dick as he must pursue God.

Taylor (1984) argues that deconstruction is the rhetoric that articulates/confounds this affirmation of negation and negation of affirmation. Taylor says, "Its words cannot be completely fixed, mastered, or captured in the net of

either/or. Instead, deconstructive criticism constantly errs along the / of nei-
ther/nor. Forever wavering and wandering, deconstruction is (re)inscribed
betwixt 'n' between the opposites it inverts, perverts, and subverts" (10). Ahab
is a wanderer, a vagrant who searches and sacrifices everything, emptying his
life (and crew) to touch the fin of God and to slay the divine Leviathan. In
essence, Ahab errs; however, by understanding "erring" in Taylor's theory, to
err is not necessarily a moral failing. Is Ahab wrong or sinful to drift away
from orthodoxy or belief in a traditional sense? By erring, he is discovering,
for and by himself, what he deems to be true and genuine. Public opinion
may deem his mission as erroneous; however, perhaps they have erred. Ahab
is the lost sheep; is he even lost? Will the good Shepherd look for him? Ahab
has strayed off the path. But is the trail true? Will he reach God by going the
wrong way? The disorder within form, the right within wrong, which con-
tradicts by its very nature, may in fact be the mode to reunite with God. Ahab's
body is lame, but his mind is potent. He may be demonic, but he is divinely
touched. He refuses to worship anything but the pure, true, and only God.
Ahab had defied God in his worship, like Iblis—the devil in the *Qu'ran*—
who refused God's commandment to worship Adam. Ahab defies God to worship Him absolutely and undoubtedly; by sinning and cursing, he is praising
and obeying God. To be devil-like may not at all imply disobedience, deceit,
downfall, or evil in the traditional sense; perhaps it could be piety. All things
fall apart, but the center still holds.

Yet, at the same time Ahab defines himself in relation to God. Ahab is
trying to emulate this God in order to surpass Him; his attitudes, thoughts,
and actions are colossal. Ahab's defiance suggests equality with God, a kind
of stature that can take on the divine: "I now know thee, thou clear spirit,
and I now know that thy right worship is defiance" (507). To defy is to purify
the faith. This oxymoronic language calls to mind Jesus's own baffling para-
bles and sayings; the irony of his threat to destroy the Temple only to rebuild
it in three days illustrates how destruction and cleansing are the same action.
To tear down is not necessarily an act of violence. To defy is not to blas-
pheme, and to curse is not always to sin. Ahab will not bow before Adam.
Starbuck in his piety may in fact be sinning against God; during the third
day of the chase, Starbuck cries out, "I misdoubt me that I disobey my God
in obeying him [Ahab]" (564).

Ahab does not feel any weakness or limitation. He is ready to take on
the universe. He feels invincible; nothing God can do will curb him. I agree
with Raney Stanford's argument that "other rebels elsewhere throughout European literature sound petulant and boring, as they voice their complaints
about the status of power they do not have; for Ahab's rebellion, profound

and metaphysical, is against the limits and nature of man himself. He goes further than Faust" (37). Even in seeming defeat, he can still declare a victory because God will not have the last word or act. The longer he addresses God during "The Candles" speech, the more he grows in confidence, and becomes less awed by His power; the more Ahab speaks, the lower God's stature falls. Ahab defines his very essence and identity in opposition to God; Prometheus-like, he lives despite every crushing blow against him. Ahab says:

> I own thy speechless, placeless power; said I not so? Nor was it wrung from me; nor do I now drop these links. Thou canst blind; but I can then grope. Thou canst consume; but I can then be ashes. Take the homage of these poor eyes, and shutter-hands. I would not take it. The lightning flashes through my skull; mine eye-balls ache and ache; my whole beaten brain seems as beheaded, and rolling on some stunning ground. Oh, oh! Yet blindfolded, yet will I talk to thee. Light though thou be, thou leapest out of darkness; but I am darkness leaping out of light, leaping out of thee! [507].

There is victory even in defeat; God cannot extinguish or annihilate him. He feels indestructible; his attitude is "you may injure me, but I still will be here." Ahab has the will to power. Ann Douglas emphasizes, "One could say that in *Moby-Dick*, Melville is putting the shark back into religion" (43).

Ahab has lost and cannot find the joy of God within. Possibly speculative, Elijah's anecdotal, prophetic representation of Ahab renders him as sacrilegious, but also relies on religious symbolism to depict him as such. Prior to his first fateful confrontation with the white whale, it seems as if Ahab were already in the throes of an acedia-like condition. He is a man wrestling with God, finding no peace. Offering a perspective into a different, mysterious side of Ahab, Elijah says, "But nothing about that thing that happened to him off Cape Horn, long ago, when he lay like dead for three days and nights; nothing about that deadly scrimmage with the Spaniard afore the alter in Santa?—heard nothing about that, eh? Nothing about the silver calabash he spat into?" (92). David Trotter has focused on this spitting scene; he notes, "To spit is to explode the screen (face, doubloon) onto which meanings are customarily projected. It is to inflict a part of your inside on the world's outside. Spitting is a self-exposure, a scandal, a declaration of war: to hell with the consequences" (25–6). Although Trotter deals with a rich topic, he focuses instead on the historical and post-structuralist aspects of this act. Ahab may have undergone a series of unholy kenotic acts that emptied all of his affirmative beliefs in God. Within the kenotic tradition, it is believed that God emptied himself into the form of Jesus — an emptying of divine being into a material, human being — and in turn Jesus emptied himself when he died. Ahab lying like a dead man suggests a spiritual death, the ultimate emptying out. Melville describes Cape Horn in *White-Jacket* as hellish, and so this event could have initiated a progression away from God. Ahab's apparent desecration of holy objects and places may seem to suggest malice toward Catholicism; it is too strong, however, to be just the anti–Catholic sentiment of a Yankee ex–Protestant. No, it is pure malice toward God.

Despite all of his blasphemy, Ahab still believes in God. I agree with John Bryant's assessment: "For all his rage, Ahab remains a believer, desiring contact with a sovereign father" (207). Robert Milder (1998) identifies Ahab as a Gnostic, and sees his quest for the whale not driven by revenge but a desire to become one with it (263).* I think Ahab wants both to avenge himself against the lesser God and to reunite with the authentic God. He has abandoned the flawed, limited, and knowable God, but feels a vague sense of being abandoned by the true God. Ahab is not a rebel, but a purist; he rejects one God in order to become more intimate with another. I agree with K. L. Evans who argues, "*Moby-Dick* is a take not of vengeance but of affection ... of attachment, disguised as vengeance, about the search for connection, camouflaged to resemble estrangement" (2). As William B. Dillingham argues, "Ahab is a heretic.... He is not an infidel" (159). His belief is not a pious and reverent feeling toward God. It is an acknowledgment that He exists and may have interposed, but the relationship is antagonism. Ahab does not feel small next to God and does not have any sense of orthodox obedience or submission. It is unclear whether this supernatural force is indeed God, the Christian God, because Ahab never unequivocally states whether he denies or embraces God. He also does not identify himself clearly as a Christian. There are elements of Gnosticism, Zoroastrianism, and Satanism in Ahab that complicate labeling, defining, or understanding him.

Rather than imagining Ahab strictly as subversive, skeptic, gnostic, or atheist, I understand him as a conglomerate of opposing stands toward God; he is devout, while being unfaithful. The dilemma (for critics, mainly) is which God Ahab is abandoning, and, therefore, which God Ahab is embracing. There are satanic elements in Ahab, and most critics view them as rebellious, destructive, and evil; however, I question the so-called evil nature of

*Dorothee Metlitsky Finkelstein, William B. Dillingham, and Robert Milder are among a group of critics who have studied extensively the role of Gnosticism and other unorthodox religious traditions influencing Melville's art. Finkelstein suggests strong possibilities of how Melville's readings and secondhand knowledge of various religions, including cults within Christianity, shape and complicate Melville's increasing use of religious themes in his art. Building upon Finkelstein's important work, William B. Dillingham contributes a detailed history of the available knowledge of Gnosticism during Melville's time. Dillingham points to key Gnostic concepts and shows how Ahab's egotism, intellect, and convictions are characteristics of common Gnostic behavior and beliefs.

Ahab. William Hamilton argues, "Ahab's Satanism is not devil-worship, however much his rum-filled harpoon chalices may remind us of a black mass. His Satanism is not liturgical but ethical.... Evil is there to be killed, the demons must be exorcised. This is Ahab's theological logic" (56). Hamilton adds, "Ahab's project should not be confused with atheism or rebellious unbelief. It is more like faith raised to the breaking point" (57). In the Islamic tradition, God had decried that the angels worship Man, but Satan refused, preserving, honoring the sanctity of veneration and prayer for God alone; Satan, in his defiance of God, was actually obeying God. Captain Peleg captures this seeming contradiction in his praise of Ahab when he says, "He's a grand, ungodly, god-like man" (79). Ahab embodies a spectrum of (dis)belief. Ahab's character and values cannot be partitioned; one must accept that combinations of contradictory or incongruous features are present, and are not unusual or difficult to understand.

In "The Candles" chapter, Ahab reveals an intense spiritual element. One can be spiritual without being religious. To be religious is to accept and follow dogma, and one can still believe in the Christian God and yet not be religious. Ahab could fall under this category, but it would simplify the matter. Perhaps at one time Ahab may have been deferential and ardently so. He could have wanted a deeper, more intense relationship with his God, but that God may have disappointed, forsaken, or impaired him; this ambiguity will become a major theme in Melville's later art.

Ahab's joylessness is not only a self-abnegation — a negation or emptying of self — but also an expression of his worldview. Ahab believes Moby Dick is responsible for everything that goes wrong in his life. The Whale is a wicked parody of the neo–Aristotelian belief of God as First Mover, the source of all movement, action. Having removed Ahab's leg, the Whale has set off an endless and growing circuit of pain for Ahab. This experience with the spermaceti has convinced the captain that grief is stronger, longer lasting, and more penetrating than joy. Ahab lives in a Manichean world, one that he has fashioned, even exaggerating the extent of evil's power; for him, Moby Dick is that evil source that repeats, gnaws, and taunts. Its energy of negation is so overwhelming that when his splintered false leg nearly castrates him, he discovers an insight, which helps to explain his feeling of abandonment:

> Anguish of that then present suffering was but the direct issue of a former woe; and he too plainly seemed to see, that as the most poisonous reptile of the marsh perpetuates his kind as inevitably as the sweetest songster of the grove; so, equally with every felicity, all miserable events do naturally beget their like. Yea, more than equally, thought Ahab; since

> both the ancestry and posterity of Grief go further than the ancestry and posterity of Joy. For, not to hint of this: that it is an inference from certain canonic teachings, that while some natural enjoyments here shall have no children born to them for the other world, but, on the contrary, shall be followed by the joy-childlessness of all hell's despair; whereas, some guilty mortal miseries shall still fertilely beget to themselves an eternally progressive progeny of griefs beyond the grave; not at all to hint of this, there still seems an inequality in the deeper analysis of the things [464].

The forces that oppose joy are so stifling that in his mind they oppress man for generations, even beyond death. The "Ancestry and posterity of Grief" is a direct challenge to the perennial optimism of the young American nation; it is so unsettling, dismal, and futile that nothing seems able to offset it. It is nihilism so corrosive and unrelenting that there seems no end to its despair and tragedy; it is an endless repetition of negation. Happiness has its limits, and can do only so much. For Ahab, "even the highest earthly felicities ever have a certain unsignifying pettiness lurking in them, but, at bottom, all heart-woes, a mystic significance, and, in some men, an archangelic grandeur" (464). The power of darkness is the shaping force in his conception of the universe. There is no joy or goodness that can pierce it. Even the gods grow impotent in its wake. Ahab says:

> To trail the genealogies of these high mortal miseries, carries us at last among the sourceless primogenitures of the gods; so that, in the face of all the glad, hay-making suns, and soft-cymballing, round harvest-moons, we must needs give in to this: that the gods themselves are not for ever glad. The ineffaceable sad birth-mark in the brow of man, is but the stamp of sorrow in the signers [464].

It is believed in Christianity that man is made in the image of God. But if man is perpetually and irrevocably despairing, is God too hopeless?

The power of grief to repeat itself, to promulgate becomes a curse in itself. In his attempt to avenge himself, Ahab instead has cursed himself. Believing grief to be fixed, relentless, and enduring, Ahab is scornful of the integrity of life. With all of his arrogance and blasphemy, his will to power will not offset the inevitable consequences of antecedents that have brought Ahab to this point. Pain becomes eternal, and seems to be Ahab's (man's) fate. His defiance has little to do with enduring pain; there is an element of buoyancy, the desire to be alive (joy of life) in perseverance, and so Ahab's drive to win justice (an affirmation of life) seems at odds with his convictions. Eyal Peretz notes,

> This event of wounding also intensifies Ahab's vital strength, of the *power of his life*, as if life, far from being only the physical or biological fact of existence, is an intensity and a force with the character of an open wound, which is inflamed and intensified precisely by being exposed

to external provocation. It is in this sense that the wounding whale might be said to be, surprisingly, a provocative and inspiring call for life [49–50].

The complex nature of Ahab's simultaneous impotence and energy and his unusual form of boredom, one that blocks out all irrelevant or meaningless forces and at the same time focuses solely on Moby Dick (a twist on Raposa's "good" and "bad" boredom), is both a negation and affirmation of life. Ahab is an extreme character and must be understood in extreme terms. In *Overload and Boredom: Essays on the Quality of Life in the Information Society* (1986), Orrin E. Klapp argues that an overload of information or stimuli produces its own unique form of boredom. Like Raposa, Klapp also distinguishes between "good" and "bad" boredom. Klapp's point is that one can be bored despite appearing excited, interested, or conscious. Ahab consumes everything in his path, and, if it does not satisfy his hunger to know about Moby Dick, he craves for more. His passion is like greed: no amount will ever satiate, and this constant filling suggests emptiness. His pursuit of ultimate meaning is a negation that he is not unaware of. On the surface, his disinterest in things not Moby Dick intimates discernment (Raposa); however, the nature, intent, and execution of his extreme version of boredom bears the mark of evil, in spite of his crusade to face the true Creator God.

However, "The Candles" chapter offers a qualification to this point. Ahab is a bitter man made more bitter by his severe grief and anguish, but, rather than retain it completely, Ahab releases it back to the universe; Ahab says, "Oh, thou clear spirit, of thy fire thou madest me, and like a true child of fire, I breathe it back to thee" (507). In his own way, he breaks through the hopelessness of grief, cosmos, and God. He is not a hapless victim, but a formidable foe. "The Candles" chapter echoes the swagger of the "Sunset" chapter: "They think me mad — Starbuck does; but I'm demoniac, I am madness maddened!" (168) and his abandonment of life's pleasures and of life itself testify to his fierce reluctance to give up. Ahab's disappointment and apathy over the numerous whales both he and his crew capture also demonstrates that Ahab does not accept his fate, that grief ultimately will overwhelm him. His last harpoon in hand and issuing his last anathema against Moby Dick during their decisive encounter, Ahab goes to his death fighting against impotency and grief. He wants to kill Moby Dick, the very source of his grief.

In one of the rare moments that Ahab allows himself to enjoy himself, "The Gilder" chapter, Ahab's fleeting enjoyment of the beauty and atmosphere of the ocean gives way to profound and harsh examination of man in the universe. Staring at the sea actually has touched him; his imagination and eloquence can focus on something other than his loathing for Moby Dick.

He can experience and think about life; he can be rejuvenated despite being "long parched by the dead drought of the earthy life" (492). Yet, "the ancestry and posterity of Grief go further than the ancestry and posterity of Joy" (464). While Ishmael, Starbuck, and Stubb can enjoy a pleasant moment of having nothing to do, of giving in comfortably to and enjoying their feelings of boredom, Ahab enacts his belief that joy is short-lived and weak. Although his soliloquy-like speech starts off with an allusion to balance ["calms crossed by storms, a storm for every calm" (492)], that life can be understood as having a series of both joy and grief ["the mingled, mingling threads of life are woven by warp and woof" (492)], that life is comprised of disorder and order, Ahab's vision of the world topples this dichotomy. He says:

> There is no steady unretracing progress in this life; we do not advance through fixed gradations, and at the last one pause:— through infancy's unconscious spell, boyhood's thoughtless faith, adolescence's doubt (the common doom), then scepticism, then disbelief, resting at last in manhood's pondering repose of If. But once gone through, we trace the round again; and are infants, boys, and men, and Ifs eternally. Where lies the final harbor, whence we unmoor no more? In what rapt ether sails the world, of which the weariest will never weary? Where is the foundling's father hidden? Our souls are like those orphans whose unwedded mothers die in bearing them: the secret of our paternity lies in the grave, and we must there to learn it [492].

There is only meaninglessness. Whatever cycle of time or progress there may seem to be is an illusion. Man begins and ends in chaos. During existence, man is utterly alone, not knowing himself or where he came from. In a godless universe, in a world where there are no implicit values, man is left to decipher for himself, but fails to gain certainty. He is left with "Ifs," and that realization is unbearable. Viewing the blankness of the ocean for the crew brings intoxicating enjoyment; however, for Ahab the empty panorama, no matter how transcendentally delightful, is a picture of his own spiritual desert. Striking through the mask discloses the nothingness within. This episode is Ahab's own version of Ishmael's "The Mast-head" and "The Try-Works" experiences.

If St. Elmo's fire is a sign from the Supreme Being, indicating favor, affirmation, and acknowledgement, if the corposant is a show of Ahab's acceptance and piety of the true God, then "The Candles" chapter is a highly wrought profession of Ahab's faith in a higher, more transcendent God, one that is above the Creator. The peculiarity of "The Candles" chapter lies in its shrouded and schismatic language and subject matter. Robert Milder adds, "The overt and covert levels of Ahab's hunt interweave themselves in the tangled rhetoric of 'The Candles' (Ch. 119), a chapter at once so emotionally intense and allusively opaque that Melville seems to have written it from and for himself" (261). "The Candles" chapter too is a deeply personal, cabalistic act of Ahab's religion, a vow of faith that superficially resonates unhallowed and ungracious tones, but actually offers zeal and service amounting to fidelity beyond good and evil, beyond creation and chaos. Newton Arvin characterizes this complicated duality as "the gravity and the tenderness of religious feeling, if not of religious belief" (181). Footnoting Leon Chai to emphasize his own point, Shawn Thomson stresses, "In this light, Ahab's defiance, in terms of his conception of God, is presented as "no longer merely negative but rather as the aspiration toward a yet higher form of divinity." The fire is the spark of Ahab's impulse to strike at an "impersonal personified" God (40). In *Gay Science* (1882), Friedrich Nietzsche says, "Good and evil are the prejudices of God" (218), and in an unpublished fragment dated November 1882–February 1883, he writes, "I know all evil and all good — I also know what is beyond evil and good." In "The Candles," Ahab admits he too has learned what resides in the beyond. His faith is in purity of being, not in the tainted, flawed, and decayed forms of being; he is concerned with the essence of God, not the manifestation of God. Moby Dick's crooked jaw suggests a God who is flawed in its physicality, and Ahab's holy quest to kill this lower God who has abandoned, ridiculed, and maimed him is to correct the proper understanding of God. His God has no perceivable form. William B. Dillingham believes that Ahab already discovered his (the) genuine God and therefore the source of goodness; and as a result, he wages war against the God responsible for evil and injustice (158). The God of conventional Christianity is deceitful and bloodthirsty, polluted by man's understanding of Him; this God is all too human. Ahab's version of faith in a higher Godhead at times bears some similarities with the "Death of God" movement in modern theology; however, whereas this contemporary heretical group suggests and celebrates the death of God and draws ever closer to Christ, the God who took on human form and thus understands man's plights, Ahab instead resists and defies all earthbound representations of God, and seeks the untouchable, invisible, and unknowable God. Driven by common needs, Ahab and these unorthodox theologians instead go in opposites directions. They each rebel against a tyrannical, indifferent and at times moody and belligerent God who remains above them; yet, they differ in the type of God who is more responsive, pure, and powerful. Ahab seeks a God that may seem like an extreme form of this unsatisfying God, but really this God is passionless in the sense that He is not human-like, while the other God seekers want a personable one.

Ahab also is all too human. Such a God that he believes he has discovered and placed all of his trust in would not, out of who He is, reach out to humans, even a man like Ahab. This God is beyond such contact, need, and presence; this Supreme Being would be indifferent to Ahab. If Ahab is to be perceived as a tragic hero, then his error is his notion of the divine; he has misjudged both the Creator God and Supreme Being. His drive to capture essence at the expense of sanity and certainty leads him and the others to death. I agree with William B. Dillingham's final assessment of Ahab: Ahab fails because he cannot resolve his Gnostic and atheistic tendencies (158); however, I am ambivalent toward Harold Bloom's bolder, more optimistic reading of Ahab's end, emphasizing his unwavering but faithful spirit (4). I agree with Bloom's rendering of Ahab in the sense that Ahab goes to the end fixed on his focus and faith that this version of God is flawed and must be eradicated; he remains in the mind, in art forever as God-killer, murdering the false higher being. On the other hand, Ahab for all intents and purposes is crucified on Moby Dick, made ultimately impotent by the ropes that choke him and bind him to the whale. Lear still can speak and more importantly has learned painful truths; Ahab is broken: no longer able to spit and dart his blasphemy. His final statement indeed is his dying word: "Towards thee I roll, thou, all-destroying but unconquering whale; to the last I grapple with thee; from hell's heart I stab at thee; for hate's sake I spit my last breath at thee" (571–2). Lawrence Thompson notes, "Perhaps Ahab's last words are so worded by Melville to interlock with Christ's last words" (235). Ahab perishes alone, abandoned by his Supreme Being and estranged with the Creator; part of the Godhead, Jesus too is deserted. Ahab's implied death is as tortuous as Christ's. Ahab dies on the very thing that, for him, represents limitations, weaknesses, and defects; Moby Dick represents the Creator God that cannot be killed. The sources of life remain viable; Ahab cannot dam(n) the life flow. Boredom is a powerfully ambivalent force that can protect or pollute the springs of life.

Ishmael

The sources of life are strong in Ishmael. He carefully monitors their ebb and flow, and, just as conscientiously, he bridles their fluctuations to divert boredom from overwhelming him. This attention does not always work, and his boredom often deluges him. Ishmael struggles with this psychological malady. His condition is more drastic, pressing, and severe than White Jacket's, but Quequeeg's friendship and Ishmael's decency, sobriety, and balance prevent him from the excesses of Taji and Ahab. At times, his life consists of extremes: intense enjoyment and gloomy despair, and his quest is to attain self-possession. It is a lifelong prospect; although he knows the dangers of desperate living, it is a lifestyle that proves difficult to modify. It is a tormenting and challenging call to suppress his wilder impulses and cultivate safer strategies to weaken boredom's hold. The core problem is he has not found a proven and reliable buffer against boredom. Escape, work, eloquence, and friendship are temporary remedies; what does seem to work, however, is his alertness in gauging his levels of boredom. Also, he is able to shuffle these short-lived practices in ways that overlap with one another. If self-seclusion fails, he discovers employment that soothes, and when that seizes to ward off boredom, Queequeg's devotion rescues him. Ishmael's mood is a recurrent, disabling, and potentially deadly spiritual ailment.

When the joy of life grows stale and unprofitable, Ishmael quickly wills himself to find the joy of work to reactivate his depleted soul. Ishmael is a strong man; even in the depths of boredom, he still manages to pull himself out. He says:

> Call me Ishmael. Some years ago — never mind how long precisely — having little or no money in my purse, and nothing particular to interest me on shore, I thought I would sail about a little and see the watery part of the world. It is a way I have of driving off the spleen, and regulating the circulation. When I find myself growing grim about the mouth; whenever it is a damp, drizzly November in my soul; whenever I find myself involuntarily pausing before coffin warehouses, and bringing up the rear of every funeral I meet; and especially whenever my hypos get such an upper hand of me, that it requires a strong moral principle to prevent me from deliberately stepping into the street, and methodically knocking people's hats off— then, I account it high time to get to sea as soon as I can. This is my substitute for pistol and ball [3].

The trait of pulling oneself out of boredom is common among previous Melville figures; however, Ishmael does not indulge in or enjoy his prolonged diffuse feelings of nothingness as Tommo and Taji do. He senses that the deceptions of petty criminality, narcotic-like numbness, and existential despair are not to be gulled by. The labors of the sea seem his only means to save himself; he seeks such employment, instead of neglecting and spurning work like previous figures. Unlike Melville's first heroes, Ishmael is earnest in dealing with his problems. He is determined not to succumb. His somberness is an affirmation of life; by being solemn, he saves himself from suicide and prison. There is an element of caprice and wit in Ishmael's self-humor, a kind of joking that anticipates "The Hyena" chapter. There are comical elements throughout *Moby-Dick*, especially in the opening chapter. Many critics (Bryant, Adamson, et. al.) assert that the opening sequences of Ishmael recounting his earlier gloomy self are in fact humorous, often downplaying or discrediting the dark, disturbing, and depressing tones. I accept T. Walter Herbert's (1977) characterization of Ishmael's "naïveté" (95) as the butt of these jokes, but the laughter elicited from these lines is not lighthearted. The opening chapter's misgivings about life and death have been influenced by Ishmael's "genial, desperado philosophy." "Loomings" chapter in fact looms; it ushers in the crisis between hope and despair, life and death. It is admirable that Ishmael can discover and maintain a jovial, blithe attitude, but, like the novel's ending, clings to affirmation precariously. The dark humor conceals the darkness of boredom.

In the "Call me Ishmael" opening, Ishmael reveals that he treats his metaphysical ailment himself by going to sea. He identifies the life on land as the cause of his boredom. The sea has proved to be a reliable exercise against boredom. Going to sea relieves his boredom which then eases related threats: anxiety, "hypos," suicidal thoughts, and preoccupation with death. Harrison Hayford and Hershel Parker have noted in their Norton Critical Edition of *Moby-Dick* that "hypos" is "short for 'hypochondria,' a state of depression somewhat more chronic and morbid than our 'blues'" (12).* "Hypos" is an inelegant but comparable alternate for boredom. Reinhard Kuhn notes that hypochondria is a component of ennui and can lead to suicide (20).

Living on terra firma fails Ishmael: it offers only unsatisfying employment, confinement, and mundaneness. Along with these factors, hopelessness tethers him on the brink of sanity and madness, wholeness and corruption, and life and death. Keeping on the move was more deleterious than beneficial for earlier characters; for Ishmael, his constant new jobs have clear purposes and results. Being a hand on a ship preserves selfhood. Land life (and work) drains him of energy, and he believes that the sea has a healing power; it may be his only way to survive. It is a perilous approach, but he is nowhere close to Bartleby's last chance at life.

Through his psychological epithets, Ishmael reveals that his soul sickness is brought on by the very conditions of life on land. For Ishmael, the land symbolizes finiteness, metaphysical instability, and death. Monotony is tantamount to death. The city office and country farm shackle the soul; family obligations limit independence, and demand constant attention and money to maintain it. Running to the West, in time, will also confine and slow down the individual. Ishmael has done it all on land and has been depleted by it.

---

*German E. Berrios traces the origins of "depression," and finds that "melancholia" "was re-named "depression," a term that had been popular in middle nineteenth century cardiovascular medicine to refer to a reduction in function. The word was first used analogically as "mental depression" but soon after the adjective "mental" was dropped. By 1860, it appears in medical dictionaries: "applied to the lowness of spirits of persons suffering under disease" (299).

The sea allows Ishmael to declare his selfhood. Paul Brodtkorb articulates well what the land represents for Ishmael:

> Land life tends toward the stable and the certain. Earth is the domain of the *familiar*.... In a contrary mood, however, the familiar seems aggressively boring: one is forced to turn one's gaze away from the contemplation of earth and become "fixed in ocean reveries" as a necessary respite [19].

Living at home produces boredom. The land negates the vitality and variety that the ocean restores to Ishmael. He cannot remain long on land because it is slowly killing him. Even after the loss of Ahab's *Pequod*, he returns to the sea to escape a land-bound existence. In "The Affidavit" chapter, he reveals that he returns to the water after his meeting with Moby Dick, and he apparently prefers the hazardous conditions of the ocean to the boredom of the land. Land-locked existence and the discontents of civilization are forces that drive him to sign up for three-year voyages. The perils of being a mariner seem more tolerable — even when death is a real danger every second — than the sterility of staying put.

Ishmael's account of his boredom on land is brief because his stay on land is also short. He knows that the longer he remains on terra firma, the more psychological damage he is exposed to. Despite the inhospitableness of the land for Ishmael, he returns to the port because he may want to live here and keeps trying to. He has not totally abandoned the possibility. His boredom is a deep, penetrating condition that is really independent of geography. Once docked, the old fears, terrifying memories, and sense of things to come make him act like Bulkington; he only stays so long before the November drizzle soaks him.

Not only does nautical work lighten Ishmael's intense unease, it is also profitable. In addition, it is socially sanctioned and is performed with men in such a way as to build a sense of solidarity. Physical labor on ships fortifies his being. He says, "I always go to sea as a sailor, because of the wholesome exercise and pure air of the forecastle deck" (15). The strenuous activity as a deck hand, the thrilling excitement as a rower on a whaling boat, and the invigorating sea climate all inspire Ishmael to abandon attitudes and thoughts associated with the land. Paul McCarthy also believes that it is through work that Ishmael finds little time to fall victim to soul sickness (66). Ishmael does learn to restrain his dread, and, at times, may relieve boredom and deep thoughts. Nonetheless, these activities also prove to be boring, and these duties also plunge sailors into "moody introspections." From *Typee* to *Moby-Dick*, Melville has dramatized these moments of boredom while performing ship chores, and has demonstrated that work ultimately is not a defense against boredom. Work only is a temporary solution to this devastating condition; again the medieval monks can testify to the limitations of work warding off boredom. The "great whale" (16) also is something beyond the merely utilitarian and mundane. Ishmael wants to experience nature in its fullness. He needs to feel the greatness, largeness, and openness of the world; coming close to God's sphere helps to make him feel alive. Life at sea offers deeper joy than the land.

Along with the joy of wholesome work, Ishmael strengthens his joie de vivre through storytelling. Being a storyteller affirms life; spinning yarns brings good cheer, camaraderie, and more chanteys. Song and tale do more than just pass the time away; they fill time with meaning. Even the "Town-Ho Story," a disastrous account of Moby Dick attacking a ship weakened by mutiny and envy, offers important lessons to its audience. From the boyish prankishness of Ishmael and Queequg sneaking extra chowder to *Moby-Dick* itself, Ishmael's command of narrative saves him from the darkness of boredom. He takes pleasure in the life of the mind, showcasing his inventiveness. The intensity of his intellect reflects the enthusiasm he has for life. Whereas the narrative begins by depicting Ishmael as a man of action, the plot develops into a story of how he becomes a man of the mind, a storyteller, which is much more than just a yarn spinner. He need not rely solely on risk-taking to come in contact with the sources of life.

The ocean calls out to others besides Ishmael. He points out the countless men of Manhattan who stare out to the sea suffering from claustrophobia and boredom; perhaps Bartleby is there. Ishmael believes that these men too are bored and restless with the land. He says, "These are all landsmen; of week days pent up in lath and plaster — tied to counters, nailed to benches, clinched to desks" (12). Confined to their pedestrian jobs, these men are oppressed by daily life, and their only relief is to gaze at the water. For most, it is sufficient to look at the river; however, few lucky men break from the fetters of their desks and take to the ocean. Ishmael says, "Almost every robust healthy boy with a robust healthy soul in him, at some time or other [is] crazy to go to sea" (13).

Bulkington is another example of a limited group of men who go to sea to manage their life discomfort. Ishmael notices him in a crowd of whalers at Peter Coffin's Inn, and he says that Bulkington "held somewhat aloof, and though he seemed desirous not to spoil the hilarity of his shipmates by his own sober face, yet upon the whole he refrained from making as much noise as the rest" (23). Bulkington finds the ground underfoot uncomfortable. His estrangement, uninvolvement in landbound activity, and avoidance of others suggest boredom of a deep sort. Ishmael notes that Bulkington prefers the sea, and, in fact, cannot tolerate the land and must return to sea quickly. Ishmael sees him again on the *Pequod* and he says that Bulkington has just returned from a sea voyage:

> When on that shivering winter's night, the Pequod thrust her vindictive bows into the cold malicious waves, who should I see standing at her helm but Bulkington! I looked with sympathetic awe and fearfulness upon the man, who in mid-winter just landed from a four years' dangerous voyage, could so unrestingly push off again for still another tempestuous term. The land seemed scorching to his feet. Wonderfullest things are ever the unmentionable; deep memories yield no epitaphs; this six-inch chapter is the stoneless grave of Bulkington. Let me only say that it fared with him as with the stormed-tossed ship, that miserably drives along the leeward land. The port would fain give succor; the port is pitiful; in the port is safety, comfort, hearthstone, supper, warm blankets, friends, all that's kind to our mortalities [97]

Bulkington cannot endure life on land even as long as Ishmael can. The land is immediately repellant to Bulkington whereas life on land becomes unbearable only gradually for Ishmael. For Bulkington, the land domesticates, and his moments on shore serve only as opportunities to board new ships for new voyages. Apparently, this man has no family or friends. For him, being on the shore is empty of meaning and love. The sea is the only place that Bulkington can call home or that allows a modicum of ease.

The initiation of the friendship between Ishmael and Queequeg is no doubt the most fruitful aspect of non-sea life for Ishmael. The loving nature of their relationship is an exception to the empty and painful encounters Ishmael has had with others, especially his stepmother. Ishmael deeply respects his uncle, Captain D'Wolf, but they seem to have a distant relationship. Ishmael does not show the reader moments of affection, bonding, and interaction between his family and himself. Likewise, he speaks of no land-based friends, so that his friendship with Queequeg is indeed extraordinary. Brotherly love is crucial for Ishmael's well being; his friendship with Queequeg stabilizes Ishmael's fragile spirit, and it buffers the devastating effects of Ishmael's boredom. Their friendship fills a void in his existence. After Queequeg clasps Ishmael around the waist and declares that they are "married" (53), it seems that their close association dissolves land-induced boredom; there is no further mention of "a damp, drizzly November" in Ishmael's soul.

I disagree with those critics who believe that Ishmael and Queequeg's relationship is homosexual. Although I disagree with Cesare Casarino's argument that there exists a homosexual relationship between the two, I do agree with Casarino when he says the "first encounter [between Queequeg and Ishmael] could be said to constitute the continued condition of possibility for the rest of the novel, that is, the fuel propelling the *Pequod* and all aboard in their fated peregrination" (147). The possible suggestiveness of sexuality in Ishmael's narrative about the bedroom scene and marriage seem to suggest homosexual intercourse. Laurie Robertson-Lorant challenges this claim:

> In Melville's day, same-sex friends often shared beds when visiting each other's homes, partly because houses were small, furniture scarce, and central heating unknown. Men traveling alone slept with other men at roadside inns, as Ishmael and Queequeg do in *Moby-Dick*, and young men sowing their wild oats with whores in frontier towns regularly shared sleeping quarters and often slept in the same bed [619].

Also, what Robertson-Lorant says about Melville and Hawthorne's relationship could easily hold true for the friendship between Ishmael and Queequeg. She says, "Even Melville's passionate letters to Hawthorne, so often deemed homoerotic, are bursting more with self-discovery, psychological identification, intellectual excitement, and spiritual hunger than with sexual desire" (619). Ishmael, too, in his affectionate connection with Queequeg, discovers personal growth; he develops a psychological awareness of others, and he finds a new avenue to combat boredom. Sex may be one way that friends can show appreciation for one another, but there is no clear evidence in the text to support such a claim about these two sailor mates. In "Friendship" (1841), Ralph Waldo Emerson describes the joy of friendship. Friendship is a complete giving of the self to the other; it is a communion of souls, which expands and fulfills the self, making the self a better individual. Emerson describes this transformation: "The moment we indulge our affections, the earth is metamorphosed; there is no winter and no night; all tragedies, all ennuis vanish" (202). True friendship is rare. Truth and tenderness are the two distinguishing markers that allow the self to know a true friend is had. True friendship is felt in the soul, and Ishmael and Queequeg's friendship is Emersonian. Genuine friendship helps to keep at bay boredom.

Their friendship deepens when they join the *Pequod* crew. Although Ishmael does not reveal moments of their bonding on the ship, Irving Howe (1986) believes that their "plebian brotherhood [is] murmuringly honored" through work (48, 69). If their loneliness drew them together on land, shipboard work keeps them together. Many critics point out that Melville's dropping of their onboard togetherness is a flaw of the novel; however, dramatizing their brotherhood may perhaps be unnecessary. One feels the glow of their friendship throughout. In "The Monkey-Rope" chapter, Ishmael realizes how intimately he is connected with his friend. As Joseph Adamson mentions, "The image of Siamese twins recalls the struggling brothers theme, but only to reverse its implications; instead of rivalry there is interdependency.... Ishmael adopts a self-deprecating posture" (93). Tied to his shipmate by the monkey-rope (till death do they part) while preparing a dead whale for the try-works, Ishmael gains a sober appreciation for his comrade. He says:

> For better or for worse, we two, for the time, were married; and should poor Queequeg sink to rise no more, then both usage and honor demanded, that instead of cutting the cord, it should drag me down in his wake. So, then, an elongated Siamese ligature united us. Queequeg was my own inseparable twin brother; nor could I any way get rid of the dangerous liabilities which the hempen bond entailed [270–1].

I disagree with John T. Matteson's harsh critique that Ishmael is horrified by this dependence (102). Granted, Ishmael is frightened by this situation, but admits, "this situation of [his] was the precise situation of every mortal that breathes" (271). He learns that the monkey-rope affirms their land-marriage; the two men are permanently bonded, and what affects one, affects the other. Furthermore, the rope represents their rough male marriage ring, symbolizes their union, and stands for self-sacrifice, brotherhood, and a renewed appreciation for life. The necessity for reliance on another, the appreciation of the dependency between friends, grows out of their mutual attachment. Queequeg is the living symbol of the joie de vivre that Ishmael at times lacks; he embraces life completely, regrets nothing, and decides when he will die or live. He has a warm, deep heart that holds no grudges, especially toward those who despise and abuse him. He is the paragon of virtue and brotherhood. Ishmael learns from Queequeg that life is sacred and that relationships sanctify life. Queequeg instructs his mate to see more in life and others. He teaches his comrade to respect and enjoy life; he saves Ishmael's life, bolstering his joy of life by offering up his own. Such sacrifice will only be matched by Bartleby and Billy Budd.

Although Ishmael flees the perils of the shore, he soon discovers that sea life carries its own psychological ills. Land and sea life respectively may bring out and intensify his boredom, which demonstrates that he carries his metaphysical distress with him, a condition that plagues many modern characters. Reinhard Kuhn reminds that continual movement does not permanently heal the soul of boredom (27). Ishmael knows this truth, but his many returns to seafaring suggest strongly the untenable and complicated forces motivating him. To remain still is to give in to death, a terrible realization Bartleby will discover. He needs to struggle against this gnawing, chronic, and modern condition no matter if he may lose. Boredom cannot kill, but it can lead to self-destructive acts that do kill. Going to sea is not for everyone; it is precarious, and can be unprofitable. Further heightening the danger Ishmael faces is the fact that he never served on a whaler and does not know what to expect.

Unlike the boredom that grows at home, the boredom that looms onboard is fully defined and more potent. It occurs frequently in varying degrees and is inescapable. A salvation from the monotony of the shore is that one could always escape to the sea. Confined to the whaler, there is no possibility to look elsewhere; for Ishmael, however, there is no way out. Geographical space has been exhausted, and so the only remedy left is spiritual regeneration, an inward movement. Reflection, not running away, may be his only true redemption.

Ishmael notices his boredom returning soon after the *Pequod* sails out. In "The Mast-head" chapter, he observes how high spirits at sea can become dangerously low. Isolation and the undemanding work of watch duty do little to prevent boredom. The sea is no longer a place of freedom or excitement; the ocean can cast its own spell of listlessness. Ishmael's watch duty makes for boredom. It is not physically demanding, and it is hard to keep alert; it requires a particular effort to stay awake. The tropical sun is not oppressive; its heat has a calming effect. Time begins to slow, and the afternoon sun's rays begin to have a narcotic-like influence. The mandatory two-hour watch does not feel that long; in fact, he is losing track of time. He feels at one with his surroundings, and it gives him the occasion to think heartily about the universe. For a man like Ishmael, whose wistful, dreamy tendencies often promote more meditation, this is paradise. He says:

> In the serene weather of the tropics it is exceedingly pleasant — the masthead; nay, to a dreamy meditative man it is delightful. There you stand, a hundred feet above the silent decks, striding along the deep, as if the masts were gigantic stilts, while beneath you and between your legs, as it were, swim the hugest monsters of the sea, even as ships once sailed between the boots of the famous Colossus at old Rhodes. There you stand, lost in the infinite series of the sea, with nothing ruffled, but the waves. The tranced ship indolently rolls; the drowsy trade winds blow; everything resolves you into languor. For the most part, in this tropic whaling life, a sublime uneventfulness invests you [156].

Soul diffusion is taking place. The soft, blowing winds caress, and the gentle, rolling waves rock him, softening his resistance and loosening his grip on reality. When bored, the unconscious mind flows; like the tides, and, once caught in the tide of boredom, the individual has no control of direction. Ishmael is not complaining; he is all too willing to surrender to the "sublime uneventfulness." Like many before him, Ishmael cannot repel the siren-like call; Tommo and Taji could not stand firm either.

What makes the song of boredom initially so bewitching and gratifying is the sense of privacy it produces; Ishmael feels an utter disconnection from everything around him. Like Tommo, he too enjoys the solitude, and being so far away from the pettiness, annoyance, and corruption of civilization. Perched so high, ironically he loses perspective as he gives into the feeling of expansiveness all around him. The sensation, however, is chimerical; imagining himself as Colossus, he totally ignores how close to falling he is. The escalating feelings of nothingness develop into an arrogance of invincibility. Standing a hundred feet above deck, he fails to consider if the ship were to roll; will he still feel immense? The Colossus at Rhodes did topple and shatter; will Ishmael?

Throughout "The Mast-head" passages, Ishmael simultaneously gives a direct account of his experience of boredom atop the ship, as if it is happening instantly, and offers commentary. *Moby-Dick* is filled with varying narrative perspectives and tenses that often intermingle with one another. There are two Ishmaels narrating at the same time: the one who experiences life on the ship firsthand and the other, older survivor of the *Pequod* disaster. He breaks the narrative in the midst of recalling the wonder of falling under the spell of boredom to hint at the presence of death. While understanding the seriousness of that threat, he glibly conceals how dangerous it really is to be so high. By providing elaborate detail concerning the inventor of the crow's nest, Ishmael buries in the narrative the suggestion that the masthead perch is "so sadly destitute of anything approaching to a cosy inhabitiveness, or adapted to breed a comfortable localness of feeling, such as pertains to a bed, a hammock, a hearse, a sentry box, a pulpit, a coach, or any other of those small and snug contrivances in which men temporarily isolate themselves" (156). Instead of a platform to spiritual bliss, it can become his coffin. Like Taji, once entranced, he cannot stop the metaphysical tide carrying him away; he does not even want to try. At other times, the masthead post is a place for Ishmael and Queequeg to talk, where he can throw "a lazy leg over the top-sail yard, take a preliminary view of the watery pastures and so at last mount to my ultimate destination" (158). It seems so safe, and Ishmael seems to be in control of the situation; he treats his post in the crow's nest like a boy's hideaway, a kind of tree house retreat. It may be a hundred feet to the deck, but, for him, where is the apparent danger? Is his "ultimate destination" transcendental heaven or death?

Ishmael unashamedly admits to being derelict to his post. He confesses, "With the problem of the universe revolving in me, how could I — being left completely to myself at such a thought-engendering altitude, — how could I but lightly hold my obligations to observe all whale-ships standing orders" (158). His existential crisis is profound and requires focus and strength of mind; however, is he here grappling with intellectual and spiritual matters or is he enjoying himself? Ishmael achieves significant insights after this masthead experience, not during it. Following this episode, a pattern will emerge: after each near-fatal or distressing event, he will discover valuable truths of life and death. How can he think clearly while bored? His disclosure is not honest, and is more of an excuse. It is a pretense of the intellectual. The mast-head is a precarious spot, a hastily secured barrel at best, or scraps of wood or iron at worst. This crow's nest is unstable when just spotting for whales. Standing for two hours on duty certainly tests the stoutest sailors, those who are not wide-eyed and romantic.

And Ishmael, who includes himself while condemning a stereotypical portrait of the "sunkened-eyed young Platonist" (158) and "those absent-minded young philosophers" (159), heeds not his own warning to them. He gently mocks the Transcendental type "who offers to ship with the Phaedon instead of Bowditch in his head" (158), discarding the nautical expertise found in Bowditch's mathematical and astronomical texts and embracing Plato's alleviating ones. The Pantheist disregards the experience of others and flies recklessly into oblivion; Icarus comes to mind, carelessly flying too closely to the sun. Ishmael parodies these romantics, but also recognizes the problems afflicting them: "those young Platonists have a notion that their vision is imperfect; they are short-sighted; what use, then, to strain the visual nerve? They have left their opera-glasses at home" (159). They have selective vision: they see what they want to see. They are searching for "the visible image of that deep, blue, bottomless soul, pervading mankind and nature" (159), not a pod of whales. Whaling is work, requiring sharp eyes, which makes for boredom for these visionaries.

Returning to the primacy of the actual masthead experience, Ishmael indicates clearly how insidious boredom can be to the soul, whereas White Jacket only hints at its dangers. Picking up with the passage where he spots boredom developing, he observes how boredom slowly deepens into a more serious, dreadful condition; the pantheistic glow that colors the experience begins to cast menacing shadows. He notes:

> Lulled into such an opium-like listlessness of vacant, unconscious reverie is this absent-minded youth by the blending cadence of waves with thoughts, that at last he loses his identity; takes the mystic ocean at his feet for the visible image of the deep, blue, bottomless soul, pervading mankind and nature; and every strange, half-seen, gliding, beautiful thing that eludes him; every dimly-discovered, uprising fin of some indiscernible form, seems to him the embodiment of those elusive thoughts that only people the soul by continually flitting through it. In this enchanted mood, thy spirit ebbs away to whence it came; becomes diffused through time and space; like Wickliff's sprinkled Pantheistic ashes, forming at last a part of every shore the round globe over [159].

As if under the influence of a narcotic like one of Tennyson's Lotos-Eaters, Ishmael loses all sense of time and space. Lapsing into unconsciousness, he is generating nothingness outward; he feels his life flowing out and he is losing his willpower. He is physically numbed and spiritually stupefied. The gentle action of the ocean relaxes his body and mind to a point of dangerous complacency. Herbert N. Schneidau and Homer B. Pettey point out, "Mildness and serenity in *Moby-Dick* stand for the hypocritical and delusive comforts of so-called Providence" (207); they elaborate on this point in a footnote: "The temptations of Platonic-Pantheistic thinking, in the famous chapter 35, 'The Mast-Head,' are related dangers. Falling through 'Descartian vortices' into the sea is punishment for too easy identification with the world-soul. The sea is an avenue of defiance for isolatoes, but in the end God will drown them in it" (212). Boredom only weakens this seeming insecurity in these isolatoes. These isolatoes deceive themselves by being all too trusting in those delightful, wondrous, and mystifying feelings. These experiences do not lead to contact with the All; they usher these misled individuals into oblivion — an All that is Nothingness. This feeling of oneness with the air and ocean is a death-like sleep that is so inviting and subtle that he is unaware of how infinitely enveloping it is. The ocean symbolizes his unconscious and it reveals the dark, uncontrollable, and deadly impulses underneath consciousness. The half-seen and imagined objects are so compelling, so real that they seem to him the very source of himself.

Ishmael has emptied himself, undergoing a mystical, kenotic experience. He has voided himself of all heartaches and stress; gone are all misgivings. He need not be held back by limitations. He is free; he is amorphous. He has cleared himself in order to achieve higher being or enlightenment, but that is the illusion. In his efforts to return spiritually to the fountainhead, he has effaced himself, dangerously so. By losing consciousness, he is losing his identity, and by losing his identity, he is losing his grip on life. He seemingly has prepared himself for some higher attainment of Being, possibly melding with God; however, he has become a mere shell, making himself hollow to the core. The horror is how easily he can void himself to the point of death. What had seemed so harmonious and lush is really tantamount to death. Moreover, Ishmael is stationed so high above the water that he begins to explore how close to death he is. Richard B. Sewall recognizes that "Ishmael was nevermore in greater danger than on his seemingly secure and sunny perch" (97), and Bruce L. Grenberg understands that Ishmael's delightful patheistic day dreams cannot transform the deck or the sea into something soft, safe, and pleasing; and those enchantingly romantic fantasies cannot convert the ugliness and killer instinct of life into something innocuous (112). Ishmael was never realistically closer to death on land than during his watch here. On the verge of toppling, he says:

> There is no life in thee, now, except that rocking life imparted by a gently rolling ship; by her, borrowed from the sea; by the sea, from the inscrutable tides of God. But while this sleep, this dream is on ye, move your foot or hand an inch, slip your hold at all; and your identity comes back in horror. Over Descartian vortices you hover. And perhaps, at mid-day in the fairest weather, with one half-throttled shriek you drop through that transparent air into the summer sea, no more to rise for ever. Heed it well, ye Pantheists! [159].

Ishmael nearly loses his life. Feeling the danger of falling off the mast, his awakening is a godsend at that split second. This image of a man plunging from the sky in relative calm reminds one of W. H. Auden's "Musée des Beaux Arts" (1940). Auden describes Breughel's *Icarus*, which portrays this event:

> In Breughel's Icarus, for instance: how everything turns away
> Quite leisurely from the disaster; the ploughman may
> Have heard the splash, the forsaken cry,
> But for him it was not an important failure; the sun shone
> As it had to on the white legs disappearing into the green
> Water; and the expensive delicate ship that must have seen
> Something amazing, a boy falling out of the sky,
> Had somewhere to get to and sailed calmly on [14–21].

Like the painting Auden describes, Ishmael warns us that at the brightest, safest time of the day, one can die. This encounter with death can occur anytime, and Melville does not tell us what prevents Ishmael from falling.

Producing a shiver of anxiety in the reader, he cautions us that one cannot trust in nature; nature is not benevolent. Despite the calm and innocuous appearance of the sea, it is not soothing or nurturing. Echoing Percy Bysshe Shelley's subtle warnings in "Alastor, or The Spirit of Solitude" (1816) of returning to the formlessness before the womb, Ishmael strongly advises us to be observant of the seductive nature of the void. In part, this danger was a reason why medieval monks feared the noontide demon. Appearing during the day, the noontide demon would afflict monks with boredom and drive them out of the security of the abbot and cell; if even the afternoon was now a time of danger, could there really be any sense of assurance? The devil in the light of day could lead souls to hell. Acedia, or the medieval version of boredom, was just as deadly as Ishmael's episode. Ishmael barely avoids the vertigo of boredom.

The "Descartian vortices" that Ishmael hovers over are analogous to the observation that Friedrich Nietzsche makes in *Beyond Good and Evil* (1886): "if thou gaze long into an abyss, the abyss will also gaze into thee" (466). Both Melville and Nietzsche admonish individuals against looking too deeply into evil and darkness, for the abyss or "Descartian vortices" can overwhelm us, strip us of our defenses, make us weak, and can entice us to death. They warn us not to overestimate the health and strength of the mind when we face the void. It takes strong moral powers of resistance to look without turning away. Ishmael has that strength of mind. The emptiness Ishmael sees is also an emptiness within him. The abyss is too powerful and it must be given its distance and respect.

This realization of the awesome power of the sea and its relationship with boredom shapes Ishmael's later reflections. The irony of "The Masthead" chapter is remembered in "The Gilder" chapter, but this subsequent incident demonstrates how difficult it is to keep boredom at bay. Ishmael knows that "Descartian vortices" lie hidden underneath each beautiful wave, ready to suck him in. Compounding the danger are exhaustion and dehydration. "Often, in mild, pleasant weather, for twelve, fifteen, eighteen, and twenty hours on stretch, they were engaged in the boats, steadily pulling, or sailing, or paddling after the whales, or for an interlude of sixty or seventy minutes calmly awaiting their uprising" (491). Once lowered in their boats, the crew must, if lucky, haul in a whale; but, when the whale draws them away from the ship and then goes under, they must wait, and the waiting becomes intolerably boring. Waiting for hours, which turns into over a day, truly tests the limits of how much boredom one can endure. One can talk for only so long. One must be alert, ready for the spermaceti to surface, but the mood melts into boredom:

> At such times, under an abated sun; afloat all day upon smooth, slow heaving swells; seated in his boat, light as a birch canoe; and so sociably mixing with the soft waves themselves, that like hearth-stone cats they purr against the gunwale; these are the times of dreaming quietude, when beholding the tranquil beauty and brilliancy of the ocean's skin, one forgets the tiger heart that pants beneath it; and would not willingly remember, that this velvet paw but conceals a remorseless fang [491].

No matter how comfortable, secure, and sleepy one feels in the middle of the ocean, no matter how much it lulls, the ocean at any minute can turn against you. What seems like a gentle, purring cat really is a ferocious man-eating tiger. One cannot trust one's senses, especially when affected by boredom. Boredom leaves one vulnerable to deception. Nature is not benevolent. The Siren's call, beautiful melodies sung by an alluring feminine spirit, often ended with a mariner's dying gasp. One can try to heed Ishmael's guidance, and agree that it is sound advice, but when caught under the spell, almost nothing can thwart the doomed man from ending up on the rocks.

Visions of terra firma make this particular episode of boredom in "The Gilder" chapter that much more acute. So far from home, and never stopping at an island, the men's dreams take them away from the watery waste. Ishmael imagines the blank sea as "so much flowery earth.... The long-drawn virgin vales; the mild blue hill-sides; as over these there steals the hush, the hum; you almost swear that play-wearied children lie sleeping in those solitudes, in some glad May-time, when the flowers of the woods are plucked. And all this mixes with your most mystic mood; so that fact and fancy, half-way meet, interpenetrate, and form one seamless whole" (491–2). The tiger's paw for a moment has given way to a child's hand grasping flowers; pantheistic glory can be enjoyed this time. It is a rare moment when Ishmael can abandon himself and savor his boredom.

Even Ahab falls under the allure of boredom that has transfixed the entire ship, and he too sees "grassy glades! oh, ever vernal endless landscapes in the soul" (492). In contrast to Ishmael's heavenly spiritual retreat to visionary mountains, Ahab's scene of charming nature dims over; Ahab cannot enjoy himself. His boredom leads him to gloom; his hate is so fixed, his mind narrowed in on Moby Dick, that he is forever doomed. John Bryant adds, "If Ahab speaks Ishmael's lingo, it is only for a moment, and Ahab's failed plagiary only anticipates his demise" (206). Cautious Starbuck yields to the same dreamy boredom, and ignores the tiger's paw: "Tell me not of thy teeth-tiered sharks, and their kidnapping cannibal ways" (492). Stubb's reaction is customary; he is a jolly man and that alone matters to him.

Boredom does not only assault sunken-eyed young Platonists, it besets all types; "The Gilder" chapter demonstrates this fact. As Melville pointed out in *White-Jacket*, even the high-ranking officers feel soul weary. In *Typee*, *Omoo*, and *White-Jacket*, ships lose their morale because of boredom; experiencing tedium is democratic, and it does not discriminate. In *Moby-Dick*, "the Pequod's crew could hardly resist the spell of sleep induced by such a vacant sea.... No resolution could withstand it" (282). Ishmael implies that boredom is part of human experience; there are no ostentatious displays of breeding, education, or wealth restricting individuals from ennui. Ishmael constantly witnesses and chronicles numerous times when the enchanting air and sea are too much for the entire crew to cope with; both so-called civilized and savage men go under the tranquilizing effects of boredom.

In "Stubb Kills a Whale" chapter, Ishmael is not alone when he merges with nature, relieving the monotony he feels. What started as a private affair becomes a shared experience in the masthead. Ishmael in the foremast-head and two unnamed crewmen respectively in the main and mizzen masts, all lose consciousness and lose their souls to boredom (282). The image of three men dangling atop three poles calls to mind the crucifixion scene. Death is only a slight movement away. Unlike "The Mast-head" chapter incident, a specified spur back to life is mentioned. Ishmael notes, "Suddenly bubbles seemed bursting beneath my closed eyes; like vices my hands grasped the shrouds; some invisible, gracious agency preserved me; with a shock I came back to life. And lo! close under our lee, not forty fathoms off, a gigantic Sperm Whale lay rolling in the water" (283). This occurrence is not infused with high language or thought and is not as ominous as his earlier experience, but a potential catastrophe is averted.

A growing realization throughout Ishmael's narrative is the shrouded, insidious, and nauseating presence of the nothingness of the universe everywhere; nihilism shapes Ishmael's worldview. During his first lowering to chase after the whale which takes place during the course of a squall, he becomes badly demoralized that, aside from nearly dying in the treacherous waters, the *Pequod* had given up his boat for lost (225). The dreadful feeling of abandonment which unbalances Pip later mortifies Ishmael. Man's indifference toward his fellow man emasculates him further as the universe cuts him at the same time. It is a harsh world. Queequeg's friendship is all the more indispensable, and when Ishmael is alone, the void nearly crushes him. Terrified, he begins to sense the profundity of the nothingness that resides behind the Descartian vortices; there is nothing sensual this time about the experience. His pantheistic, Platonic tendencies are stripped bare; he is witnessing both man's and the universe's hearts of darkness.

Narrowly defeated, Ishmael buoys himself with the "free and easy sort of genial, desperado philosophy" (226), which Robert Milder (1998) describes as "an Absurdist acceptance of his and humanity's position as cosmic outcasts" (257). This approach to life just buffers the shock of the world's indifference, and requires strength of mind that can allow Ishmael to laugh at himself or at least not to feel too outraged and ridiculed:

> When a man takes this whole universe for a vast practical joke, though the wit thereof be but dimly discerns, and more than suspects that the joke is at nobody's expense but his own. However, nothing dispirits, and nothing seems worth while disputing. He bolts down all events, all creeds, and beliefs, and persuasions, all hard things visible and invisible, never mind how knobby; as an ostrich of potent digestion gobbles down bullets and gun flints. And as for small difficulties and worryings, prospects of sudden disaster, peril of life and limb; all these, and death itself, seems to him only sly, good-natured hits, and jolly punches in the side bestowed by the unseen and unaccountable old joker [226].

He realizes that there is little one can do in response; in fact, he has no choice in the matter. He knows his *Ecclesiastes*: "All is vanity." In contrast, his captain feels insulted and therefore obligated to retaliate, even if it means he will die. Ahab will strike the sun. Ishmael must settle for the fact that man's lot in the end is beyond his comprehension and control. He admits all is vanity but is not dejected by this truth. Terrifying experience must be handled in a way that does not petrify; if not, life becomes overwhelmingly fearful and joyless. This way of thinking is an attempt to recapture the joy of life, no matter if it constrains it slightly. Death always is hovering, and Ishmael can die any second; it is the manner in which he will die that matters to him.

Ishmael accepts that man is a plaything of the gods (universe). Ishmael does not remain angry or disquieted for long. It is all part of the joke, the joke that is life (*Ecclesiastes*). And he is the butt of that joke. What Ishmael sees as insults to life itself, to which death makes the punch line, is the laughter of the universe. He is resolved; the indecency of the jokes makes him stronger. He might as well laugh along with the gods.

The genial, desperado philosophy gives rise to Ishmael's overall motivating principle in *Moby-Dick*. To remain intact, he must adopt this system of values. In a strange way, it claims him, making life bearable. Unnerving as they are, Ishmael's insights allow him to come to terms with nature's darker consequences. It is still life. Powerless to stop the larger forces conquering him, he has courage to look past nature's raw and merciless actions against man. His hope in life seems so inadequate and frail in the face of everything around him; and yet, Queequeg is there for him, and he can still see life's beauty. After the harshest squall, he can affirm life's possibilities, indulge in sweet nothingness, admire colorful sunsets, spin good yarns, and dream of tomorrows. Nature has darkened his views, but has not contaminated him fully; he maintains a zest for life. His age and transcendental disposition also keep him from going under; evil has not hardened him. He resists the inevitability of fate, but unlike his captain he does not defy it. There exists some good in the world, and he keeps it close to him. He says:

> Consider all this; and then turn to this green, gentle, and most docile earth; consider them both, the sea and the land; and do you not find a strange analogy to something in yourself? For as this appalling ocean surrounds the verdant land, so in the soul of man there lies one insular Tahiti, full of peace and joy, but encompassed by all the horrors of the half known life. God keep thee! Push not off from that isle, thou canst never return! [274].

Shark-infested waters, concealed shoals, mighty storms, and the ruthlessness and "universal cannibalism of the sea" (274),—all are true, but such determinism keeps man animalistic. However, Tahiti is spoiled and fallen; even Tommo's beloved Marquesas has just opened up, and the French are pounding its shore, a la Conrad's "Heart of Darkness." Paradise is an illusion; however, there always is a secluded, yet undiscovered island, and there hope abides. Taji's madness kept him looking for Yillah. Joy in some way is still possible; however, at what cost?

Spotting Descartian vortices in placid waters and locating insular Tahitis are examples of Ishmael's double consciousness. At times it appears as if hopelessness and terror inundate him, making all incidences of promise and fortune seem flat and pale. It is a Manichean world. Melville constantly tests the soundness and equilibrium of this opposition. Moments before his whale boat will slaughter a serene nursing pod, Ishmael observes:

> And thus, though surrounded by circle upon circle of consternations and affrights, did these inscrutable creatures at the centre freely and fearlessly indulge in all peaceful concernments; yea, serenely reveled in dalliance and delight. But even so, amid the tornadoes Atlantic of my being, do I myself still for ever centrally disport in mute calm; and while ponderous planets of unwaning woe revolve round me, deep down and deep inland there I still bathe in eternal mildness of joy [388–9].

The scene is so calming, it lulls Ishmael's boat mates; merging with the oneness of the mothers and their claves, the men fall under the spell of listlessness. Existential problems are forgotten for the moment; Ishmael is always ready to relieve himself of those burdens. He has found his insular Tahiti. It seems depraved to lance this pod of whales now. The shock back to life from this spell is just as horrifying as in "The Mast-head"; the sights of carnage in the distance awaken and spur them to massacre the herd. Just as there is no intact Tahiti, joy is fleeting. The misery and indifference of life is so cruel, naked, and insignificant. Is not Ahab's belief correct then that the ancestry and posterity of grief is deeper, firmer, and more endless compared with joy? It is a dilemma that Ishmael will wrestle with forever; it is the predicament of double consciousness.

The struggle to ballast the self from the onset of boredom is severely tried in "The Try-Works" chapter. This latest bout brings Ishmael to another metaphysical collapse, one that shakes him to the core. It tests the essence of all his beliefs, more so than any other experience with boredom. While on night duty as helmsman, the uninterrupted sameness of the post provokes bad visions. Amid a lurid background, Ishmael's attention lapses. He no longer sees the utilitarian effect of men working. Instead of the *Pequod*'s try-works, he sees the fires of hell, and, in lieu of his comrades, he beholds devils. The scene described recalls the ghastly horror Young Goodman Brown experiences in Nathaniel Hawthorne's eponymous tale (1835). The revered Puritan elders, including his father and grandfather, discard their respectable masks and join in an unholy Sabbath bonfire with the Devil. When his own wife, Faith, is about to enter the inner circle, Brown loses all faith, and awakens to a lifetime disillusionment. The more Ishmael looks into the fire, the longer he is mesmerized. Taken over by the scene in front of him, he grows disillusioned.

Because the job takes place after midnight, it is hard for Ishmael to remain concentrated and not to give into drowsiness. As with his masthead duties, the task of manning the helm is not physically taxing, especially at night. The inner forces that are needed when outside discipline is gone have relaxed. The devilish figures before him both unman and sedate him. Since the noontide demon terrorized him during the sun's zenith, appropriately, an eventide demon coerces him at the moon's apex. Ishmael admits, "The continual sight of the fiend shapes before me, capering half in smoke and half in fire, these at last begat kindred visions in my soul, so soon as I began to yield to that unaccountable drowsiness which ever would come over me at a midnight helm" (423). At the high points of a full day, peril always frequents him. Nietzsche's admonishment of the abyss is a difficult lesson to follow. The void is staring right back at Ishmael. The surrounding "blackness of darkness" (423) is so piercing that he barely escapes it. The flames give no spiritual light, and so, he is completely lost. This is not the Pantheistic glow he felt in the mast beforehand; there is no pleasure here.

Ishmael's complete absorption of the fiery darkness is his worst case of boredom. The emptiness he feels is blending with the darkness outside. His view of the world becomes shifting, fluid-like, and, little by little, he begins to feel his unconsciousness seeping into the outside; the terror he is witnessing reflects the inner dread he is living. The abyss is staring right at him. All safeguards have been removed, and he has a direct view of the void; he cannot rhapsodize or soften the brunt of this onslaught as before. "The Try-Works" is not a Platonic, transcendental dream; it is a nightmare, one he has been trying to suppress. The tiger's paw is about to maul him, and the horror of it is that he does not even see it approaching. What was a personal crisis grows into a larger, more monstrous condition as it now places the entire ship in jeopardy. His negligence can kill everyone. Sensing something wrong, he awakens seconds before disaster; in his trance, he somehow spun himself around, facing away from the tiller. Cesare Casarino spots veiled homosexual references in this scene. Casarino suggests that this "inversion" was a metaphor available at the time for Melville to explore Ishmael's homosexual anxiety of having his backside facing the hellish impulses of the try-works and its lustful crew (139). Casarino severely discounts the importance and graveness of this scene. Ishmael's "mere loss of bearing" is not grandiose or allegorical; it is quite real with real consequences. Casarino's dismissive tone parodies — this mocking inflection is carried throughout his analysis of "The Try-Works" — what Ishmael is experiencing. Ishmael understands what he experiences and is able to recount what he experiences; his insights into the nature of knowledge, human limitations, good and evil, and other related themes go straight to the heart of the novel. "The Try-Works" moral is not strange (138), as Casarino maintains; instead, Ishmael reveals the insidious reality of losing consciousness and moral confidence. He adds, "In an instant I faced back, just in time to prevent the vessel from flying up into the wind, and very probably capsizing her. How glad and how grateful the relief from this unnatural hallucination of the night, and the fatal contingency of being brought by the lee" (424). His genial, desperado philosophy is forgotten; its tenets are too arduous to employ, and it would be vulgar to join in the laughter of the universe.

As in "The Mast-head" chapter, his identity comes back in horror, but Ishmael issues a severer expression of the immediate peril in "The Try-Works." Melville all along has been pointing to Nietzsche's warning. The pleasing façade that covered the ferocious and heartless face of nature in "The Mast-head" has been removed in "The Try-Works." There are no benevolent and cruel sides of nature. I disagree with Julian Markels's overall reading of this chapter's key passages. Markels contends that the entire message found in "The Try-Works" is flowery, pretentious, and overwrought. He argues that Ishmael sounds like Starbuck in his timidity; in effect, he only speaks and does not act. Because, for Markels, Ishmael's words ring hollow, the eventual affirmation Ishmael discovers is cheap. As a result, Markels evaluates Ishmael's outlook as "less heroically uncompromising than Ahab's but that also provides a more dependable alternative to [Shakespeare's] Edmund and Hobbes" (109). The first paragraph in Ishmael's revelation is a statement of disillusionment. He experiences the void, enters the void, a feat which Starbuck shuns. No matter how close Starbuck may venture to understand his captain and his quest, Starbuck remains safely in his conventional attitudes and fears. Ishmael's warning about staring into the fires is not a message of submission, but a caution for strength of mind. He is informing others who pursue deep, disturbing metaphysical truths to be on guard, to be sensitive to every little tremor of the unconscious; this quake of the soul may save one's life. If Ishmael's warning were to be "Starbuckian platitudes," then the line would read, "Look not in the face of the fire," not, as Ishmael does say, "Look not too long in the face of the fire" (424). Ishmael calls for both sensitivity and sensibility: one must be aware that the flames camouflage both truth and death, and one must be able to see each, not simply to look at them. The fire can illuminate, but also burn. Starbuck has neither this kind of sensitivity nor sensibility. Ishmael has known for a long time that nature and the world are not benign, and the second paragraph of Ishmael's major insight is not an attempt to balance between Starbuckian ideals to Ahabian ones. Ahab would strike the sun if it insulted him. The Catskill eagle is not an inflated, flattering symbol, but one that can penetrate into the depths and emerge out of them intact; the bird comes as close to the leviathan. Ishmael's revelation is not a condemnation of acquiring profound and terrifying truths, but a call to be prepared for what lies beneath, for what is behind the mask.

Ishmael now sees the universe as amoral and apathetic to man; Melville is seeing naturalism on the horizon. Ishmael is forestalling the onset of despair and meaninglessness as a result of this encounter with the blackness of darkness. It puts to the test his stability and resolution. It is a sobering moment that humbles him. He has gained a deeper sense of things, admitting that even with insight, he does not, cannot comprehend everything: all is vanity. Adopting a biblical tone to punctuate man's confinement, he comes to terms with the implications of his terrifying visions. He confesses:

> Nevertheless the sun hides not Virginia's Dismal Swamp, nor Rome's accursed Campagna, nor wide Sahara, nor all the millions of miles of deserts and of griefs beneath the moon. The sun hides not ocean, which is the dark side of this earth, and which is two thirds of this earth. So, therefore, that mortal man who hath more of joy than sorrow in him, that mortal man cannot be true — not true, or undeveloped. With books the same. The truest of all men was the Man of Sorrows, and the truest of all books is Solomon's, and Ecclesiastes is the fine hammered steel of woe. "All is vanity." ALL. This willful world hath not got hold of unchristian Solomon's wisdom yet. But he who dodges hospitals and jails, and walks fast crossing grave-yards, and would rather talk of operas than hell; calls Cowper, Young, Pascal, Rousseau, poor devils all of sick men; and throughout a care-free lifetime swears by Rabelais as passing wise, and therefore jolly;— not that man is fitted to sit down on tomb-stones, and break the green damp mould with unfathomably wondrous Solomon [424].

It would seem that Ishmael is confirming Ahab's conviction that grief is the abiding energy in the cosmos; however, Ishmael is not fixed, and is able to grow and learn from his discoveries and calamities. His use of the Hebrew Bible and its outwardly dark and pessimistic accents ordains his own unsettling and gloomy outlook. It offsets the increasingly debilitating and radical nihilism growing in the narrative; it quiets Ishmael's despair and strengthens him. It does not dissolve or repudiate hopelessness and evil, but acknowledges their existence in the world, and insists man must confront them. This recognition is a sign of maturity; it forces the individual to embrace all of life, not just the pleasing and attractive side. It calls for double consciousness, for the double vision of the whale. Ishmael judges people accordingly: "This willful world hath not got hold of unchristian Solomon's wisdom yet." It is not youthful glumness. Avoiding these brutal realizations is a symptom of willful ignorance. Wisdom in *Proverbs* is a mark of distinction, of belonging to God, and it is praiseworthy because true knowledge is fear of the Lord. Melville in the following passage from "The Try-Works" quotes from *Proverbs* 21:16, altering it slightly: "the man that wandereth out of the way of understanding shall remain" (*i.e.*, even while living) "in the congregation of the dead" (424). Concordantly, a passage from *Ecclesiastes* 7:3–4 will emphasize how despite how demoralizing life may get, not facing it is far worse: "Sorrow *is* better than laughter: for by the sadness of the countenance the heart is made better. The heart of the wise *is* in the house of mourning; but in the heart of fools *is* in the house of mirth."

Ishmael's use of *Ecclesiastes* 1:2 ("all is vanity") and his powerful addition of "ALL" to it are signs of how he tempers Ahab's system of values into his own. Man's existence is vain, man's understanding is limited; however, there is a wisdom that is woe and one that is madness (*Ecclesiastes* 1:17–18). One cannot comprehend God's way; to attempt to do so is futile. A wise man is one who fears God (7:18); a wise man is one who accepts that all is vanity. Ahab attempts to know more than is humanly possible, and therefore, his mission is a massive assault on the way things are, on nature, and on God. The captain refuses consolation, and stresses the limits of morality and human existence; he rejects the Bible's profoundest maxim. He says, "I am impatient of all misery in others that is not mad" (487). Ishmael knows that "there is a wisdom that is woe; but there is a woe that is madness" (425).

There is freedom and mobility within this fundamental principle. Ishmael's genial, desperado philosophy helps to keep him in check so as both not to desecrate God's dominion and not to annihilate man's territory; the aftermath of each episode of boredom underscores this borderline. He pushes the boundaries as well, but he knows where the abyss begins. He asserts, "There is a Catskill eagle in some souls that can alike dive down into the blackest gorges, and soar out of them again and become invisible in the sunny spaces. And even if he for ever flies within the gorge, that gorge is in the mountains; so that even in his lowest swoop the mountain eagle is still higher than other birds upon the plain, even though they soar" (425). The Catskill eagle symbol is an amendment to his genial, desperado philosophy; the bird image gives him far more existential independence and dignity than before. The conceit not only is flattering, but necessary because it steadies him, giving a sense of control and purpose. The genial, desperado philosophy was developed during a time when he faced death directly, shaking him to the core; the response to terror was as terrifying and unnerving. The Catskill eagle also comes at a time when he faces immediate danger, but this current consolation truly is salutary, restorative, and humanistic. The nightmarish encounter with the void within need not remain intimidating; Ishmael is tempered, but continues to live life. As there are few individuals who possess true knowledge, there are fewer still who are Catskill eagles. They are rare because it involves toughness, wit, and cunning, all qualities that sharpen and bolster the mind and spirit to plumb the depths. It provides the courage and restraint to pull back when one dives too deeply. Being a Catskill eagle reinforces the joy of life. The image of the bird flying above the land is still a part of life on land; perhaps Ishmael has found the faith to live on terra firma.

However, based on "The Mast-head" and "The Try-Works" chapters, restraint, discipline, and work are insufficient to counter boredom. Each time Ishmael falls under the spell of boredom, Queequeg is not there to rescue him. Queequeg may have cured or at least helped Ishmael to ward off his land-based boredom, but, at sea, Ishmael alone must deal with his grave existential problem. On the other hand, Queequeg's unconditional love and spirit save Ishmael from mortal annihilation. In the "Epilogue," Queequeg's coffin/life buoy rises from the chaotic whirlpool and saves him, and he is unharmed by the sharks and sea-hawks. The ending has a more than natural, almost extraordinary, feeling as his rescue carries with it a sign of some hope in the midst of the obliteration of the *Pequod*, that love and brotherhood may save man from utter destruction. Ishmael's rebirth hints, but barely, that life can emerge from death, that joy can be sustained through tragedy. Bruce L. Grenberg also notes this shred of hope, "only in the grimmest, most ironic sense. He knows little more of the *Pequod*'s captain and his mad aspirations, little more of whales and whaling than he did" (117). Robert K. Martin remarks, "*Moby-Dick* was Melville's last hopeful fiction, and even its hope seems abandoned partway through, only to be resumed, miraculously, in the epilogue" (95). Furthermore, Grenberg forcefully observes that the remarkable quality of this miracle is the role of chance; in fact, it seems his very survival was an accident (119). Ishmael's survival may very well be an accident, but it too is part of the universe's joke. Yes, there is no reason why Ishmael alone should survive. Despite Melville's maturity as tragic artist, he could not end the novel so bleakly, so hopelessly tragic; he will save that kind of ending for *Pierre* (1852). Fedallah's replacement should not be read as Ishmael serving as substitute; they are not doubles in any sense, and there are no incongruities if a symbol of death is uprooted by one of life. If Melville goes out of his way to point out this substitution, then it is an indication of Melville's inherent need to find affirmation in the face of death, a pattern that marks his work.

The "blackness of darkness" in Melville's view of life is painful to confront uncompromisingly, and Melville's contemporary audience avoided dealing with it. *Moby-Dick* marks the emergence of his tragic vision. John Bryant believes that Ishmael's experiences approach nihilism (198). Although Bryant does not specify the elements of Melville's nihilism, I agree with Bryant that *Moby-Dick* strips illusions. Work is praised, but its limitations are shown. Work is not an ultimate defense or guaranteed safeguard against despair, boredom, and self-destruction. It is not a transcendent moral value. The authority of the captain cannot be fully trusted. Ahab is not a moral ideal; he abuses power, and his egoism destroys himself and his crew. The tragic dilemma is that the captain is the supreme law at sea even if his orders are immoral; Starbuck learns this lesson painfully. On the other hand, I disagree with Bryant because hope, friendship, and the moral principles of *Moby-Dick* can instruct those who read it. *Pierre* (1852) and *The Confidence-Man* (1857) are the epitome of nihilism in Melville's canon. Ishmael's narrow escape from the abyss prepares the reader for Bartleby, who does enter the void. Shifting his imaginative gaze from the water to terra firma, Melville's artistic treatment of the land marks a new writing phase. From the enormity and vastness of the ocean (and Ahab), Melville narrows his vision to the constricted, weighty world of Wall Street.

"Bartleby, the Scrivener"
Not Quite the Last Word

Bartleby is a man whose soul hungers. Not only is he starving himself of food — ginger nuts are the only thing he seems to eat occasionally, if at all — he gains no spiritual nourishment from the capitalist system he lives in. He apparently buys nothing, rents nothing, consumes nothing, and ultimately performs nothing; however, he does say something, and his expression of choice, indicates that he will not conform, accommodate, or obey the life-robbing enterprises of Wall Street.

Gillian Brown may be too harsh in criticizing Bartleby. Unlike Brown (149), I think there is tragedy in his death; although Brown quickly qualifies this unfavorable observation by saying that his anorexia substantiates a tragedy, Brown continues to censure Bartleby for disconnecting with life. I do not believe Bartleby avoided life or feared the openness of life; instead I believe he sought connections produced by life. I am also unconvinced by Brown's claim that he dodges, curses, and loathes all contact with life (148). I agree in part with Brown's concept of "tragedy of circulation," but for reasons not stated by Brown. Bartleby could not join in the flow of life. Part of the tragedy Brown leaves out is the recipient's, the world's responsibility in Bartleby's death. I am not completely excusing Bartleby for his suicide, but, in some respects, his messages, his "letters" to the world were returned to him. That he appeared at the Lawyer's office door answering the want ad demonstrates that Bartleby is not the agoraphobe Brown portrays him to be.

At the same time that Bartleby physically starves himself, he hungers for something more nourishing, spiritual, and profound. Soul hunger can be a manifestation of boredom. Boredom is the result of finding nothing to satisfy the self; everything becomes stale, unpalatable, and insipid. Life becomes devoid of qualities that make for spirit and character. Nausea burns, making the world repugnant; the world becomes alien to one's ideas, principles, and tastes; it gnaws, plagues, and bedevils the spirit. Jean-Paul Sartre's *La Nausee* (1938) dramatizes the intense dissatisfaction, sameness, and indifference of life that Antoine Roquentin feels. Oftentimes, Antoine feels terribly bored, which then grows into a condition he calls "nausea." Nausea is a complicated state that forces him to face the bare existence of life; stripping objects to their bare essence, he discovers that even essence is too grounded in reality, and, for him, this insight of life reduced to its purest, barest aspect is disgusting and fearsome. Taken further, nothing can ever be known, and this "meaninglessness," "nothingness" is the real essence of life. Such a realization produces nausea, or revulsion. Disgust becomes apathy, turning even against the self. There is a similarity between soul hunger and boredom; both terms describe the inner void. Nothing seems sapid to fill the emptiness. The soul grows thin, sick, plunging itself deeper into the abyss of boredom.

Maggie Helwig asserts that anorexia is not a condition triggered by a woman's desire to achieve a particular body ideal; for Helwig, starving oneself has little to do with fashion or image. Denying oneself of physical sustenance is an expression of spiritual hunger. In "Hunger," Helwig is hungry because she prefers not to approve, purchase, or validate the materialism of her society. By not consuming, she chooses not to hold on to it; she literally gives back consumerism to the system that produces it, thus spewing it. Her act is a judgment. One can hear the power and insistence of Bartleby's thrice stated message in Helwig's own judgment of the world when she says, "It is not all right. It is not all right. It is not all right" (350). The self cannot find decent, healthy, and meaningful resources to preserve and foster itself. Instead of nourishing, contributing to, and energizing the sources of life within, Helwig argues, mass culture contaminates and negates the individual's well-being. The person afflicted with anorexia chooses to abstain from food, a consumer item, because she symbolically desires something deeper, more fulfilling. What society and culture offer are unacceptable. Popular culture and its various consumer products may have an economic value; however, that worth accounts for little of spiritual value. According to Helwig, the anorexic prefers not to consume, participate, or accept what fails to feed the soul. For Helwig, consumerism devours the buyer; the consumer is ingested in the economic process.

Helwig speaks of this spiritual hunger in religious/philosophical overtones, demonstrating that it is a serious metaphysical disease. In many religious sects, fasting is practiced. Fasting is a kind of controlled anorexia: a short-term version. It is practiced to purify the spirit, to absolve oneself of sin or guilt, or to put oneself in a proper state of mind for higher spiritual contact. Fasting is an emptying out both physically and spiritually so that the devotee may be filled with God's presence/being. For Simone Weil, in fact, it is to be welcomed. It presents a chance to experience God. It creates space so that God can fill it in. In fact, one is to help create the void within (*Gravity and Grace*, 55–8). The believer is a vessel who pours herself out so as to receive God. In religious practice, fasting is considered to be favorable, sanctioned, and beneficial. Anorexia is a twisted and extreme form of fasting. As the Lawyer admits to himself: "I might give alms to his body, but his body did not pain him — it was his soul that suffered, and his soul I could not reach" (18). Helwig's conception of anorexia has nothing to do with the physical; it is spiritual, and society has difficulty, as did the Lawyer, in reaching the ailing soul. It is far easier to classify anorexia as an issue of appearance rather than to probe deeper into the condition. The Lawyer too at one time preferred to believe "that the easiest way of life is the best" (3). It is much more challenging to think of hunger metaphysically, that soul hunger is the voiding of the self; and what makes it especially lethal is that there is little in society that Melville portrays in "Bartleby" to fill the soul.

It does not seem apparent to the reader or the Lawyer himself that he has a problem spiritual in nature. The attorney does not know he indeed has the same soul sickness as Bartleby's, but in a less obvious manner; his condition also is less severe.* After all, he is a functioning and prosperous man; he is complacent and self-pleased. He does not see weakness or hypocrisy in his Christian identity; it is because of his religious faith that he takes on Bartleby, for he has, he thinks, a good heart. However, his Christianity never has been tested, and Bartleby forces his employer to become a better Christian. The old man sees in Bartleby a version of a younger self, characteristics in which he admires in himself; he likes Bartleby's incipient industry and apparent obedience, and other virtues he praises in himself. Because he feels so connected to and responsible for Bartleby, in his efforts to help Bartleby, he also tries to heal his own spiritual emptiness. Bartleby exposes the Lawyer's own emptiness, which, despite being unconscious of his spiritual fate in the beginning, is also a problem of the story. Only when the Lawyer has his insight at the end of the story that the deeper questions of what it means to be a Christian emerge and bring light to his particular form of disguised boredom. Bartleby saves the Lawyer from the lower depths of boredom, and brings him to life. "Bartleby" represents one of Melville's more optimistic explorations

---

*In the introduction to Stories of the Double (1967), Albert J. Guerard includes a brief discussion on Bartleby and the Lawyer as doubles. Guerard notes, "Yet Bartleby also functions, for the narrator, as a true double, as another self and inhabitant of the mind" (11). Mordecai Marcus, C. F. Keppler, and Robert Rogers also view these Melville characters as doubles. The doppelganger is an intricate literary-psychological concept that expresses itself in various forms. The double may be a reflection of favorable, pleasing aspects of the self, or may be a critique of the self's baser, less admirable characteristics; of course, these two approaches can be combined, revealing the interplay of opposing forces within the self.

of boredom because while Bartleby is bored to death, the Lawyer is brought to life by his connection with Bartleby.

Correcting the Lawyer's misunderstanding of his decisiveness — "You *will* not?" — Bartleby says, "I *prefer* not" (14). His resoluteness is a choice, an existential statement that punctuates his life predicament. It is not a consideration brought forward to the Lawyer so that the Lawyer can consider and grant permission. Bartleby's preference is not an inclination, one that could be dissuaded. Instead, his preference means only one thing: "No." Weinstock posits: "When he says that he 'prefers not to,' what he really *seems* to me is that he *will* not. And when he says that he is not particular, it is clear that he is very particular indeed" (33). Bartleby's "no" is taking a stand; his "no" is who he is. To say "no" is will to power. For all of his defiance and individuality, his "no" also is self-destructive. His "no" slowly negates him. His right to say "no" begins to annihilate him. If he is to be the lone voice in the wilderness, he should continue to say "no;" however, his litany of "no" consumes him as well. His adamant refusals foreshadow the "no" of Imre Kertesz's *Kaddish for an Unborn Child* (1990). And what saves his "no" from utter nihilism is the Lawyer's newfound understanding. The "no" becomes an affirmation of life; it protects one from the negating forces of Wall Street. What was for so long a crazed, indecipherable, and maddening expression becomes a rallying cry.

He will not buckle under societal pressures to work and consume according to their prescribed manner; those forces emasculate, confine, and smother the self. It is a world of endless and repetitious drudgery. The monotonous office work reflects the deterioration of the copyist's bleak existence. Bartleby's new position at the Lawyer's office is at the very heart of consumerism — Wall Street.* It is the world of money values. It is the place where everything carries a certain monetary value, as do the papers the law office handles; the trade has calculated even the worth (fee) of the copy sheets the scriveners duplicate. Everything is to run efficiently, predictably, and safely. The Lawyer — tolerating the idiosyncrasies of Turkey and Nippers and yet profiting from their ineffectiveness — makes compromises to ensure propriety, smoothness, and business. Bartleby challenges Wall Street's operations. The Lawyer undervalues the spiritual toll of business. He gently mocks the seriousness and deadliness of the desecration of life when he describes the layout of his office:

> My chambers were upstairs at No.— Wall Street. At one end they looked upon the white wall of the interior of a spacious skylight shaft, penetrating the building from top to bottom.
> This view might have been considered rather tame than otherwise,

*For an in-depth discussion on "Bartleby" and capitalism, please see David Kuebrich's "Melville's Doctrines of Assumptions: The Hidden Ideology of Capitalist Production in 'Bartleby'" (1996).

deficient in what landscape painters call "life." But, if so, the view from the other end of my chambers offered at least a contrast, if nothing more. In that direction, my windows commanded an unobstructed view of a lofty brick wall, black by age and everlasting shade, which wall required no spyglass to bring out its lurking beauties, but, for the benefit of all nearsighted spectators, was pushed up to within ten feet of my window-panes [4].

His attitude is an unsympathetic and casual dismissal; as long as money is made and reputation is maintained to ensure further business, there is nothing wrong. The office is a place to work, not to tackle the meaning of life. He feels no need to ask such questions; such inquiries entail difficulty, something the Lawyer avoids. The Lawyer tolerates slovenliness and even insubordination from his employees as long as he can profit from them. To question the (im)morality of such work is to become distracted, incompetent, and lazy. It does not matter whether the work kills the soul, as long as someone can correct Bartleby's proofs.

The work of a scrivener is sedentary, mechanical, and numbing; it is boring. Even the medieval monks wrestled with the deadening boredom that made Bible transcribing irksome; the spirit of God abandoned them, they were left sleepy, but more importantly, hollow and indifferent, and when God's presence within was no longer felt or appreciated, the gaping mouth of Hell sucked them in. A scrivener's line of work drains the joie de vivre; it is labor that does not satisfy or replenish the sources of life. Rather, it detaches one's connections to existence. It leaves Bartleby empty, creating an inner void as he stares into one in front of him: Friedrich Nietzsche warns, "And if thou gaze long into an abyss, the abyss will also gaze into thee" (466). When one sees (and works in) the void as Bartleby does, it is not difficult to see what Bartleby sees: "Do you not see the reason for yourself?" (21), Bartleby tells the Lawyer when he decides to do no more work for his employer. The Lawyer admits that the work "is a very dull, wearisome, and lethargic affair. I can readily imagine that to some sanguine temperaments it would be altogether intolerable" (20). Like the walls that entrap Bartleby, the dull and repetitive nature of a scrivener's work intensifies the feeling of going nowhere and of doing nothing. The work produces copies, not originals; there is no sense of pride or ownership in this work. There is no sense of a beginning and end; there is more of the same to be done over and over again. The staleness of such activity can plunge someone into the depths of boredom.

Bartleby's spiritual ailment is deep, and has proceeded from boredom. His case of boredom is the worst among Melville's figures. He literally is bored to death. He comes to the office in an advanced state of boredom. Hardly

anything interests him. He is visibly an unemotional man who has disconnected himself from the world, and the world too has abandoned him. He is
unable to connect with the sources of life and others. He is, to use Simone
Weil's classification, a "truly uprooted being." Weil believes that "a certain
form of food necessary to the life of the soul" ("The Needs of the Soul," 110)
is needed to counter the devastation of boredom. Weil understands boredom
to be a great threat, attacking the metaphysical roots that ground man. Some
type of fulfilling and wholesome excitement is needed to curb boredom; this
food for the soul constitutes her "need for roots," to feel connected. Without
these roots, man will suffer affliction, or *le malheur*. Affliction is a state of
being, "which means physical pain, distress of soul, and social degradation,
all at the same time, is a nail spreading throughout space and time" (81). In
"Human Personality" she writes, "Affliction is a device for pulverizing the
soul" (90). Affliction dries up the sources of life, and the resulting torment is
the soul dying; it is the soul starving to death. Bartleby is an uprooted man;
his soul is being torn.

The reader does not see how boredom infiltrated and eroded Bartleby's
will beforehand; however, the reader does see what boredom has done to his
soul. Very little is known of his past — his post at the Dead Letters Office at
Washington is an evocative indication of the bleakness of his life, and as a
result, he frustrates everyone — the lawyer, his co-workers, the attorney's
clients and colleagues, and the reader — because he is beyond understanding,
remedy, and hope. Ahab, Ishmael, and other Melville protagonists do not
hesitate telling the reader what troubles them; correspondingly, their life
predicaments, although monumental and deadly, are not as enigmatic as
Bartleby's. Bartleby is silent, and provides remote and extremely subtle indi-
cations, if at all, to what afflicts him. Speculations on Bartleby's past and present ultimately disappoint because they only hint at what might be wrong with
him. "Bartleby" is a highly disciplined, restrained story where every detail,
phrasing, and scene is vital, delicate, and tragic. There is no solution for
Bartleby's soul sickness, although everyone thinks there is. His lonely, desperate, and empty life easily is misunderstood by all, and his position in life
makes it so that he can be ridiculed and then ignored. Except for the Lawyer,
no one pities him, and, despite working as a scrivener, his class status is low.
He is one of Weil's lowly factory workers, one of the truly uprooted beings.

Bartleby upbraids the Lawyer's cheap and insincere optimism and narrow sense of things when the elderly man tries to convince Bartleby that the
Tombs, where he is confined, is not "so vile a place. Nothing reproachful
attaches to you by being here. And see, it is not so sad a place as one might
think. Look, there is the sky, and here is the grass" (31). Yes, there may be a

spot of sky and patch of grass where Bartleby stands in the prison yard, but he knows where he is; the Lawyer does not. Bartleby is in prison, hell, and the void where he continues not to participate, consume, and now not to live. In his attempt to soften Bartleby's indignity of being arrested and jailed, the Lawyer instead further debases him, reminding Bartleby that he is dying, and that nothing can be done for him. There is no life, no redemption, no freedom, and no possibility here; just because there is a view of the openness means nothing. It only is the specter of nature. And "the view from the other end" is the "surrounding walls, of amazing thickness, [which] kept off all sounds behind them. The Egyptian character of the masonry weighed upon me with its gloom" (33). The Lawyer resists the full implication of the meaning of these walls, adhering to the very end to his untroubled, straightforward, and calculated view of life: "But a soft imprisoned turf grew underfoot. The heart of the eternal pyramids, it seemed, wherein, by some strange magic, through the clefts, grass-seed, dropped by birds, had sprung" (33). Life can flourish in the harshest of places, but the Lawyer has ignored the quality of life a soul needs to flourish.

Bartleby's statement also is an indictment of the world; the world fails him. It does not satisfy him; it leaves him empty and hungry. The world starves him. His "I prefer not to" sounds his dissatisfaction and repugnance at what the world offers. Like Maggie Helwig, he will not participate; he too will not eat, partake, or consume unwholesome, artificial, and poisonous products that would kill his soul. He will not perform, condone, and assist the profit-making, life-destroying capitalist economy. He would rather die than be a part of the mechanism that dehumanizes the individual. At the expense of himself— note the irony — Bartleby is a commodity to be sold, traded, and betrayed. He becomes a byproduct to be recycled, exploited, and reviled. Should he say "yes" to this objectification? Should he "buck-up" and encourage himself to work even harder, bolstering himself with the "American dream"? With a little more money, he can find his own apartment; however, he prefers not to. By preferring not to, is Bartleby punishing the system and us? Are we conscious enough to learn from his death, and not see our own? Can we acknowledge that we too are Bartlebys? Can we imagine Bartleby's death as ours? If Melville meant for this tale to be utterly bleak, he would not have granted a new life for the Lawyer. The Nietzschean emptiness Bartleby sees in the world stares back at him; what would we recommend Bartleby do? Bartleby's own thrice repeated "no" is an indictment that all is not right, too; when he will not, he wills that "no." The system is corrupt; it degrades the soul, and Bartleby's presence says it is wrong. It also declares he is not well, that he is ill. Like Helwig's, Bartleby's efforts to save the self, to preserve his identity, simultaneously injure him. In his struggle to protect the sanctity of life, he is killing himself. Ultimately the Lawyer learns what Bartleby's supposed stubbornness and insubordination mean: all is not right. His self-sacrifice gives the Lawyer the gift of life: his own. Bartleby's life is not meaningless, and his preference is not obscene. The execution of his preference may be obscene, but it is a moral stand.

Answering the Lawyer's ad may perhaps be Bartleby's last attempt to reconnect with the world; however, the Lawyer is unfit to nurture his employee, as Bartleby is incapable of receiving his help. Bartleby is an extreme case who requires extreme measures. Indeed, how is one to help Bartleby? The Wall Street man is not a man of extremes. It appears that no matter how much can be done to assist Bartleby, it will not be enough. The old man is too safe a man to help him. Bartleby's case is beyond the attorney's range, experience, calculations, humane solutions, and versions of Christianity; his very imagination is unable to grapple with Bartleby's soul disorder. The longer Bartleby remains with the Lawyer, the longer he exists. When the old man is forced by the pressure of his colleagues to give up Bartleby, Bartleby, too, gives up. The scrivener's boss is too blind and too set in his own ways to reach Bartleby. His efforts are vain because he is not exerting himself; he does not see how perilous his copyist's life is. Firing and trying to give Bartleby money are the easy ways out. He is a superficial man who cannot deal with spiritual matters. Spiritual matters are arduous and complicated. The Lawyer sees that Bartleby is a hopeless case. Bartleby's affliction terrifies him. Simone Weil says, "Affliction ... is hideous as life in its nakedness always is, like an amputated stump, like the swarming of insects. Life without form" (GG, 73). Faced with Bartleby's nakedness, the Lawyer cannot clothe, nurse, or see him. How would Christ have fared with Bartleby?

Piety without fortitude is a weak faith; falling asleep during service, or, waiting for Jesus on Gethsemane, is not an expression of the joy of God. Acts of Christian faith without spiritual conviction undermines one's relationship with God. For the early desert Christians, such disregard or inattention toward God was sinful; it was acedia. If one, as the common expression goes, goes through the motions, one is not being sincere with one's religious beliefs, and one's uninspired actions are meaningless in the face of God.

In trying to connect with his scrivener, the Lawyer seeks Christian, spiritual profit for himself from his copyist. Concerning spiritual matters and charity, Christianity demands a genuine, unrelenting, and aggressive selflessness. A true Christian does not perform religious works for a reward. Bartleby is an unprecedented spiritual test for the lawyer, a test which is beyond him, and — it must be said — a case that may very well be beyond any human (outside) intervention. The eminently safe man is smug and pharisaical; his pity for Bartleby is motivated by his own self-interest, rather than Bartleby's interest. Melville links capitalism and charity in the Lawyer's portrait. The Lawyer's giving is governed by what he gets out of it, not the desire to emulate Christ. He may attend church service on Sunday, but the attraction of hearing "a celebrated preacher" (16) rather than a deeper conviction marks this man's religion. In the figure of the Lawyer, Melville shows how capitalism debases charity — he seeks spiritual profit from acts of charity instead of exercising his charitable acts out of Christian love, that is, selflessly. The Lawyer notes, "Yes. Here I can cheaply purchase a delicious self-approval. To befriend Bartleby; to humor him in his strange willfulness, will cost me little or nothing, while I lay up in my soul what will eventually prove a sweet morsel for my conscience" (23–4). The Lawyer feels entitled, believing heaven is naturally his just because he wants it, just because of who he is. He has done nothing to earn it (Zolgar 527). Keeping Bartleby on is not an act of goodness. It is only good for the Lawyer to employ Bartleby because he gains advantage by it. Helping Bartleby privately also provides benefits that promote a higher self-image and promote self-complacency. The lawyer cannot see that goodness is indeed good. He sees acts of kindness and good deeds as assets. He is so taken in by the reward, social standing, and comfort that charity stands for that he cannot perform charity selflessly. The dividends of goodwill are spiritual privileges that the Lawyer does not understand. Giving to the poor, nursing the injured, and acting out the Sermon of the Mount certainly can earn one entry to heaven; however, how the spirit of giving inspires, and why the giver is inspired to give, matters. On performing good deeds, John Cottingham remarks:

> If caring for your neighbour is good, then you ought to be able to *see* its goodness — see that human nature will flower and flourish through such acts of sympathy and concern, see the value of each of us treating others as they would wish to be treated themselves. So if there is a God who commands us to act this way, this must presumably be in virtue of just such features that make the action good; hence God's decrees would not in themselves generate the action's goodness, but simply confirm the goodness we can already recognise there. This not exactly to say that moral goodness is independent of God — for the theist, nothing is wholly independent of God — but it is to say that, even for the theist, there have to be *reasons* that make things good, and these reasons cannot boil down to the mere fact of their being divinely commanded [65].

The Lawyer does not have *reasons* to help Bartleby. He does not see the goodness of charity, of his acts for Bartleby; he sees only his self-image improve and possibly his social status. He is not concerned that Bartleby indeed is in trouble. He thinks by humoring Bartleby, he can gain entry into heaven; Bartleby is his pass into a safe, comfortable, and easy afterlife. His efforts are vain because he is not truly exerting himself, and his unflappable and disimpassioned form of caring is not Christianity. Christianity is not easy; in Matthew 7:13–14, Jesus says, "Enter ye in at the strait gate: for wide is the gate, and broad is the way, that leadeth to destruction, and many there be which go in thereat:/ Because strait is the gate, and narrow is the way, which leadeth unto life, and few there be that find it." Charity is to be done humbly (Matthew 6:1–4). The Lawyer says, "I am a man who, from his youth upwards, has been filled with a profound conviction that the easiest way of life is the best" (3). Choosing the easiest way of life is the wide and broad gate to destruction (hell); to be a genuine Christian, one must choose and take the hard way.

Simone Weil traces in *Gravity and Grace* (1952, posthumous) how truly arduous Christian love (charity) is. As does Melville in "Bartleby," Weil reminds the reader of the essence of Christianity: good must be done "in spite of ourselves" (92); if there are no obstacles, it is not pure. It must prove to be hard when performing good deeds; otherwise, those acts are not virtuous and pure. To be Christian at times may not be in one's self-interest; it even may be a detriment. An act of kindness is one that we do not even recognize as such. Quoting Jesus and commenting on the passage, Weil writes, "'I was enhungered and ye gave me meat.' 'When was that, Lord?' They did not know. We must not know when we do such acts" (93). Such deeds are done naturally, unconsciously; when charity is performed in this way, one then acts as a Christian. Weil challenges the would-be Christian to be in fact Christ himself. One should act directly in the sense that one just helps one's neighbor; just do it. She calls for no auxiliaries or prepositions. There is a huge divide between *for* God and *in* God and *for* God and *by* God: doing good for God versus doing good in God's name. When one performs charity in God, then it is charity. If one helps one's neighbor for God, it is not charity at all. Such gifts of oneself are not really of oneself, if one is guided, commanded, or ordered to give of oneself. Charity must be self-generated (Weil 93). The lawyer is not impelled to his neighbor by God; he goes to his neighbor not even for God. He goes to Bartleby for and by himself. He is not unrelenting or aggressive in giving help to Bartleby. The spirit of brotherhood at the work place is nonexistent.

In an earlier episode, the Lawyer recounts an earlier experience of charity when he gives Turkey, another scrivener in the office, an old coat of his. He says, "I thought Turkey would appreciate the favor and abate his rashness and obstreperousness of afternoons. But no; I verily believe that buttoning himself up in so downy and blanket-like a coat had a pernicious effect upon him — upon the same principle that too much oats are bad for horses. In fact, precisely as a rash, restive horse is said to feel his oats, so Turkey felt his coat. It made him insolent" (7). This example demonstrates the Lawyer's incapacity for real charity. He expects obedience and proper job performance; instead of charity, he is bribing his underling to work. This example is a foreshadowing of Bartleby's own version of feeling his position in the office.

Bartleby's co-workers mock him, even threatening physical violence; there is no comradeship in the lawyer's office. Far from being an arrow launched by God, the Lawyer exploits and manipulates this hostile environment in an effort to cajole Bartleby into working. Viewing himself as a victim of Bartleby's insolence and antagonism, he turns to his other scriveners for support. His tactic is to embarrass Bartleby to make him conform. His ploy is rather conventional: manipulation, guilt, peer pressure. Envisioning and labeling himself as "a man of peace" (5), the Lawyer is one only when it serves a self-purpose, if at all. He himself ponders murdering Bartleby — whether he is only half-serious is beside the point. Instead of Christian love, Bartleby elicits misunderstanding, anger, melancholy, pity, and terror.

Thus, the Lawyer's approach, posture, and outlook are barriers walling in Bartleby and himself. The Lawyer must have read his Christian Bible or heard the lesson at Trinity Church — his parish — and must have come across the passage dealing with loving one's neighbor. In Luke 10:25–37, Jesus praises a "teacher of the Law" for his answer that man must love his neighbor as himself, a commandment that Jesus instructs is vital for his mission. Nonetheless, this teacher of the Law asks, "Who is my neighbor?" and this is a question that is at the heart of "Bartleby." Is the Lawyer his brother's keeper? Is Bartleby his neighbor, and are the Lawyer's motives for aiding his neighbor as untainted, magnanimous, and self-giving as the Samaritan's? It is easier to call oneself a Christian than actually to be one, and the Lawyer clearly is not a true believer. The Lawyer becomes bitter, enraged that Bartleby is not appreciative. He wants his employee to shower him with praise; he wants Bartleby to be grateful. Such expressions of egoism are what Simone Weil discusses in *Gravity and Grace*. Weil points out, "It can also happen that the love of the benefactor is not pure. Then, in the 'I,' awakened by love but immediately wounded afresh by contempt, there surges up the bitterest of hatreds, a hatred which is legitimate" (75). The Lawyer looks beyond Bartleby, even not seeing him at all; instead, he sees an opportunity to promote his ego and to purchase his entry to heaven. Bartleby senses the old man's base motives, and of course would be angered; his refusals to cooperate are the surges of legitimate contempt toward his employer.

Perhaps what Bartleby is looking for, and the Lawyer cannot provide, is love. Is Bartleby completely a lost cause? Although the employer feels a "fraternal melancholy! For both I and Bartleby were sons of Adam" (28), he is afraid of Bartleby's plight. It is his inability to help his fellow man that shapes the tragic vision of "Bartleby" and Melville's dark view of humanity. Patricia Barber argues that "Bartleby" is a "story of failed love, a love the lawyer conceals by adopting a rhetorical tone of genial detachment" (214).* Rather than feeling love, the Lawyer grows resentful of Bartleby because he is not grateful or responsive to the attorney's gestures. Simone Weil explains that a recipient of charity feels genuine gratitude only when the kindhearted act is offered as an act of justice. It is just when it is not done because one feels sorry, regret, or impulsive. It is unjust when it is offered because one wants reciprocation or advantage. It stems from something nobler (*Gravity and Grace*, 118). It comes from excellence, from self-excellence.

Along with his anticipated heavenly incentives, the Lawyer expects to receive gratitude from Bartleby, but his sense of entitlement makes his interest in Bartleby corrupted and blatantly self-serving. Any expectation of acknowledgement for helping others is not philanthropy; it is not an act of loving man, but of loving oneself. Recognition of good acts becomes a business transaction, a receipt of service, and an advertisement. Again, the Lawyer may have forgotten his Bible teaching: "Therefore when thou doest *thine* alms, do not sound a trumpet before thee, as the hypocrites do in the synagogues and in the streets, that they may have glory of men. Verily I say unto you, They have their reward / But when thou doest alms, let not thy left hand know what thy right hand doeth: / That thine alms may be in secret" (Matthew 6: 2–4). The Lawyer is not modest. He feels as if Bartleby has given him insufficient attention and appreciation; in his eyes, Bartleby has no propriety and good taste in conducting himself. The copyist has failed to thank him. Simone Weil explains that what one perceives as rudeness, ingratitude, and betrayal when one hears no thanks is really a small sampling of the daily insults, frustrations, and belittlements the "ungrateful" one endures. For Weil, this brief and supposed indignity felt by the selfish individual is an introduction to the poor soul's affliction. And for Weil, this experience is the beginning step not only to genuine gratitude, but also genuine charity and Christianity (*Gravity and Grace*, 74). For a moment, the Lawyer sees who Bartleby is, but that experience is too much to bear for him. What the Wall Street man is getting in return is what Bartleby is enduring daily: the effects

---

*Patricia Barber does not fully explore this rich topic of love in "Bartleby." Instead she proposes the idea of viewing Bartleby as a woman. Gillian Brown also likens Bartleby to a woman.

of the void of boredom; he is experiencing on a small scale what it feels to be Bartleby. Along with sharing in the affliction of Bartleby, the old man is receiving justice for his unprincipled and selfish behavior. Profiting from Bartleby's pain, exploiting the class/power difference, and abusing Christian tenets, the Lawyer, wrapped in his own comfortable cocoon, believes he is affronted by Bartleby's thanklessness. He wants his underling to be a submissive and ingratiating employee; how could Bartleby not be grateful toward his boss? How dare he slight, disrespect "a rather elderly man"? Ingratitude for insincerity and selfishness is justice.

If the Lawyer's gestures were unblemished by his own self-serving program, perhaps then Bartleby might have responded to his tokens; however, as Bartleby discovers the extent of the Lawyer's selfishness, he realizes that the Lawyer cannot help or save him. And if indeed this stint were Bartleby's last chance to reconnect with life, it has failed. The Lawyer confesses:

> as the forlornness of Bartleby grew and grew to my imagination, did that same melancholy merge into fear, that pity into repulsion. So true it is, and so terrible too, that up to a certain point the thought or sight of misery enlists our best affections; but, in certain special cases, beyond that point it does not. They err who would assert that invariably this is owing to the inherent selfishness of the human heart. It rather proceeds from a certain hopelessness of remedying excessive and organic ill. To a sensitive being, pity is not seldom pain. And when at last it is perceived that such pity cannot lead to effectual succor, common sense bids the soul be rid of it. What I saw that morning persuaded me that the scrivener was the victim of innate and incurable disorder. I might gives alms to his body, but his body did not pain him — it was his soul that suffered, and his soul I could not reach [18].

Bartleby horrifies the Lawyer. The attorney has seen Bartleby in all of his defenselessness and nakedness. The Lawyer stumbles upon Bartleby half-dressed in the office. And so, the attorney quite literally has seen Bartleby naked, but, more importantly, metaphysically. Emmanuel Levinas describes this moment in *Totality and Infinity* (1961); he writes, "The face has turned to me — and this is its very nudity" (75). In *Is It Righteous To Be?* (2001), Levinas defines "face": "like a being's exposure unto death; the without-defense, the nudity and the misery of the other" (48); he adds, "This nudity which is a call to me — an appeal but also an imperative — I name *face*" (115). The old man has seen Bartleby's nudity, his abject existence. In all of his misery, Bartleby is standing before the Lawyer completely revealed. Whereas Levinas insists that when one encounters the other's face, nudity, there automatically emerges an "obligation" (133), a "an appeal or an imperative given to your responsibility: to encounter a face is straightaway to hear a demand and an order" (48) and "At no moment can you leave the other to his own destiny" (99), the Lawyer cannot undertake such a demanding ethical command to embrace Bartleby unconditionally. Could the Lawyer's failings here demonstrate the impracticality, the impossibility of Levinas' ethics?* In *Otherwise than Being, or Beyond Essence* (1974), Levinas urges that "The neighbor concerns me before all assumption, all commitment consented to or refused. I am bound to him, him who is, however, the first on the scene, not signaled, unparalleled; I am bound to him before any liaison contracted" (87). The extent of this obligation is hyper-selflessness. Levinas stresses, "To give, to-be-for-another, despite oneself, but in interrupting the for-oneself, is to take the bread out of one's own mouth, to nourish the hunger of another with one's own fasting" (56). The problem with Levinas' ethical demand is that it is unreasonable, which Levinas himself admits in *Is It Righteous To Be?* Bartleby's face, his nudity terrifies the Lawyer into resignation. Everything the attorney believed in and patterned his life on, Bartleby's nudity has debunked. The old man wants to help the young gentleman, but his face is too intimidating, too real, too nihilistic.

To help Bartleby requires more than the Lawyer has to give. The Lawyer's insight is an admission of failure; he has realized that he cannot do anything. In *Waiting for God* (1951, posthumous), Simone Weil observes, "The capacity to give one's attention to a sufferer is a very rare and difficult thing; it is almost a miracle; it *is* a miracle. Nearly all those who think they have this capacity do not possess it. Warmth of heart, impulsiveness, pity are not enough" (64). Bartleby demands a miracle, and the Lawyer cannot perform one. He comes to realize it is difficult to be truly virtuous: "But this mood was not invariable with me. The passiveness of Bartleby sometimes irritated

---

In a series of interviews published in Is It Righteous To Be? *Levinas tries to convince skeptical interviewers how to embrace and feel responsible for the other. "But it is a crazy demand" (54), says Francois Poirie after hearing Levinas' justification for his extreme form of selflessness. In many of the interviews a pattern develops, one that suggests a didactical insistence on this responsibility and hyper-selflessness. In order to dissuade and win over his interviewers, Levinas quotes often a Dosto-evsky passage from* Brothers Karamazov*: "We are all guilty for everything and toward everyone and I more than all the others." However, as many of the suspicious interviewers express, Levinas's system of ethics seems to be an impractical, naive, and unrealistic demand in an age after Auschwitz. This misgiving about Levinas is often overlooked. Murder still exists, despite Levinas's insistence that the face is an undeniable call to holiness, sacrifice, and selflessness. Levinas holds firm that his approach is sound, but buckles when he must deal with the Barbie trial in France. In "On the Use-fulness of Insomnia" Levinas uncharacteristically shows a limitation in his "limitless" philosophy; he cannot embrace the face of, accept responsibility for, or see the holiness, sacredness of Barbie, a French Nazi collaborator. In response to the question: "Does this man remain 'other' for you?" Levinas responds, "If someone in his soul and his conscience can pardon him, let him do it. I cannot" (236). This answer reveals a glaring central inconsistency in Levinas's philosophy, one that has gone virtu-ally ignored, and it suggests an irreconcilable feature in his work.*

me" (13). It is a terrible disillusionment: the Lawyer's cherished complacency has begun to slip. His Christianity is sparse, his way is insufficient, and his action is defective; it is a realization that he is a failure, too. The Lawyer is a reluctant Christian. He is a Christian in name rather than heart, and his heart lacks the warmth, impulsiveness, and pity which Weil admits are not enough.*

Moreover, the Lawyer does not attend church after discovering Bartleby living in his office. The church, which deals with spiritual matters cannot soothe or aid the Lawyer. Discovering Bartleby's secret life has unnerved him, but joining fellow Christians in worship should help him. It does not. His motive for going is not a deep spiritual one and his faith is shallow. The purpose of faith is not for self-aggrandizement or self-improvement (i.e. to improve one's self-interest). Genuine Christianity is selflessness and self-sacrifice. It is to love one's neighbor as thyself. It means one single action is not enough; it always calls for more. One must involve all of one's self, or else it is not Christianity. And it is this revelation that also horrifies the Lawyer.

Yet, the Lawyer identifies with Bartleby, and that is why he cannot fire or remove himself from Bartleby. The Lawyer's life is as joyless, hopeless, and terrifying as Bartleby's. The copyist's loneliness and isolation resemble his own. He too suffers from soul sickness; his spirit also hungers. Bartleby is a part of himself he has ignored, and Bartleby is forcing his employee to confront his own suppressed despair by compelling the safe man to wrestle with the meaning of his (Bartleby's) existence. The void he senses in Bartleby is in the Lawyer as well. The elderly man acknowledges this recognition with his scrivener: "The bond of a common humanity now drew me irresistibly to gloom. A Fraternal melancholy! For both I and Bartleby were sons of Adam" (17). Love thy neighbor as thyself. He can help neither Bartleby nor himself, and his anxiety, frustration, and inability to understand his underling highlights his own self-misconception, or rather his fear to grasp his own existential crisis. Once the Lawyer penetrates his own surface (smugness, vanity, prosperity, composure, indolence), by degrees, he grasps Bartleby (and him-

*Levinas's imperative to the other bears a striking resemblance to Christian tenets. If one questions his approach and emphasis, then a similar misgiving must be raised toward Christianity. What both Levinas and Weil insist is that behaving ethically or giving oneself to the other goes against reason. In Otherwise than Being, Levinas says, "To reduce the good to being, to its calculations and its history, is to nullify goodness" (18). It is an honorable, virtuous quest, but even Levinas cannot look upon the nudity of Barbie. Perhaps a more achievable and modest goal would be to try to reach the ideal; however, that is not enough, and that is the dilemma: trying and doing are not the same. The challenge is what kind of a Christian the Lawyer wants to be, and how it will affect his relationship with or responsibility for Bartleby. Perhaps the Lawyer is approaching Bartleby the wrong way; instead of reasoning with Bartleby-and the Lawyer admits that Bartleby is unreasonable-trying to understand Bartleby, he must be unreasonable himself. In fact, to be a true Christian is to defy reason.

self). Before he attains his revelation at the end of the story, the Lawyer attempts to take Bartleby home with him in order to save Bartleby from the authorities, a move that is unusual, radical, and unexpected. It may well be the Lawyer's first ever offer of real charity, and at the same time may be an act of desperation, which is understandable; this extreme offering may be the thing needed to penetrate both the Lawyer and Bartleby. Bartleby prefers not to and is arrested (30).

Can one impose an obligation to feel (the Lawyer), and just as important, can one dictate a commitment to accept (Bartleby)? If one finally discovers a Christian sympathy and now acts on it, what is one to do if thy neighbor refuses it? Can one force thy neighbor to accept one's philanthropy? How is one to help thy neighbor if thy neighbor refuses that help, but continues to look to one for sustenance? This problem has vexed many critics, turning their critiques toward Bartleby, who is, in their eyes, entirely at fault. If there is love, there is no need for politeness or accountability; tenderness is given because it is good. Goodness because it is good. Cottingham says, "If caring for your neighbor is good, then you ought to be able to *see* its goodness — see that human nature will flower and flourish through such acts of sympathy and concern" (65). I think the Lawyer is insisting on legal tender, not, as Weinstock argues (36), tenderness; there can be no bottom line in ethics. Weinstock's proposal is exactly the problem: the Lawyer's economic language, values, and outlook corrupt any spiritual "exchange" that could have taken place (Weinstock 36). There is no exchange or transaction of one tender for another; one cannot purchase genuine tenderness with legal tender. The Lawyer discovers this impossibility when he tries to buy Bartleby with twenty dollars. To coerce Bartleby into accounting himself is to annul his life and death crisis; it is to declare a victory for Wall Street. Forcing Bartleby to account, to be accountable is to negate the spiritual "demands" he seeks. The Lawyer knows this, eventually. When Bartleby refuses to do any work, he tells his employer, "Do you not see the reason for yourself?" (21). The elderly man looks at the dead brick wall Bartleby is staring at, but fails to see or to feel what it is that is starving the copyist. To make Bartleby accountable is to confine him further in those walls. Furthermore, the words of Jesus, "Render therefore unto Caesar the *things* which be Caesar's, and unto God the *things* which be God's" (Luke 20:25), complicate the Lawyer's (and Bartleby's) problem. Instead, the Lawyer wants to join both Caesar and God in his dealings with Bartleby, and tries to force his worker to adopt the same viewpoint. It cannot work, and their interactions prove it cannot.

Unfortunately, many critics believe these opposing outlooks can be married. Is one, then, to give up hope, and still remain a Christian? Is a Christian to stop being one if the world thwarts his identity, or because it is hard? I do not accept Harold Schechter's thesis that "Bartleby, the Scrivener" is a statement of the irreconcilability between the ethics of the divine and world (366); Schechter imposes upon "Bartleby" the ideology of Plotinus Plinlimmon from Melville's *Pierre* (1852) that argues that Christian ethics or chronometrical (heavenly) ways naturally fail because they run counter to normal human psychology or horological (earthly) means. Plotinus Plinlimmon is not an admirable figure in *Pierre*; traditionally, critics have viewed Plinlimmon as a parody of Ralph Waldo Emerson, and so this fictional character is not an appropriate model to compare with the Lawyer. A confirmation of our indifference and cynicism is not what Melville was attempting to articulate in this story. "Bartleby, the Scrivener" is not *Pierre* or *The Confidence-Man*. The short story has bleakness, but it is saved by the ethics the Lawyer (re)discovers at the end. Like the miraculous and glorious ending of *Moby-Dick*— one that is delicate and almost unbelievable — the ending of "Bartleby, the Scrivener" too is astonishing. Because Christian virtue is difficult to enact does not mean one should not attempt it. I agree with Dan McCall that the story compels one to ask of oneself, "What [do] you do with Bartleby?" (113). I would add to McCall's point that the tale also obliges one to ask of oneself how is one to live an ethical life, and, if one is Christian, how is one to live a Christian life, free of acedia.

The longer Bartleby remains with the Lawyer, the nature of the old man's behavior changes, specifically his concessions. His relinquishments no longer are the compromises of a man unwilling to confront problems, but the gestures of an individual who is more humane, philanthropic, and sensitive. From downplaying the oppressive quality of his office surroundings to tolerating his employees' eccentricities, from bridling his anger to permitting, apologizing, for his scrivener's "passive resistance" (13), and from pitying and fearing Bartleby to loving him, the Lawyer learns to avoid a fate similar to Bartleby's. Bartleby stirs him to life; he saves the old man from dying a hopeless and terrifying death. Initially, his accommodations were acts of charity, which means they were self-serving; however, when Bartleby dies, it is then that he can see beyond himself: "Ah, Bartleby! Ah, humanity!" (34). He now feels his own heart of darkness within as he learns to understand Bartleby's. When he visits Bartleby on the day he dies, the Lawyer admits for the first time the profoundness of the walls. He says, "The surrounding walls, of amazing thickness, kept off all sounds behind them. The Egyptian character of the masonry weighed upon me with its gloom" (33). He acknowledges that Bartleby is not alone; in fact, everyone is a Bartleby. There are countless other Bartlebys in the world, and there are millions of people who suffer from soul sickness. Bartleby is not a bizarre, outrageous, or freakish isolato; he is one of us, and the Lawyer is, too. The Lawyer teaches us how to bring Bartleby, even if we fail, into our lives, how to tear down our prejudices, complacencies, and limitations to learn how to live and, in particular, how to live with others. The Lawyer's final statement is a declaration of his birth of consciousness. Graham Nicol Forst finds the ending of the story as the Lawyer's conversion as a confirmation of the spiritually deep effects of Bartleby on the Lawyer's life (269). Forst adds that the short epilogue is a reminder for the Lawyer to discover who he is now and the kind of life he wishes to have now (268). The Lawyer has learned and becomes emotional as a result of comprehending finally the meaning of Bartleby's life and death. The Lawyer's conclusion is an introduction to life, his life. Therefore, I disagree with Rosemarie Garland-Thomson's reading of the Lawyer's final statement, "Ah Bartleby! Ah humanity!":

> Such resignation rather ironically replicates the fatalism of the residual religious model of suffering that surfaces in the interstices of the liberal subject's relentless effort to improve, redeem, and govern the world — a position that the aging lawyer occupies with the greatest ambivalence. Perhaps the fetal position of resignation and surrender that the dead Bartleby resorts to at the Tombs suggests the narrator's projection onto Bartleby of his own forced concession, his impotence before the problem of redeeming unfitness [799].

The Lawyer's final cry is not an admission of failure, voicing his unpreparedness and aversion because he could not save Bartleby, and thereby not save the world. The Lawyer's final utterance is not a cry of absolute hopelessness, not a lament of failed action, and not a scream of maddening frustration; his last spoken words are an embrace of Bartleby, even if he is dead. The last lines are not "thick Victorianism" (118), which Kingsley Widmer maintains "must be read with some irony" (119) in order to avoid "a maudlin hypothetical picture of Bartleby as Dead Letter clerk" (119). The unnamed protagonist has gained strength, vision, and sensibility through Bartleby. The words are emotional because he has attained an emotional life; the heart of his message is optimistic, but has been earned. It is not cheap, moralistic, or forced. That he finally utters these words at the end suggests that it took the Lawyer some time to understand Bartleby; his revelation is not immediate, although his disillusionment with his own life had been occurring slowly throughout the story. His retelling of the Dead Letter rumor is not simple gossip. I agree with Bruce L. Grenberg's analysis on the report because the hearsay has substance because the Lawyer finds meaning in it (176). He can imagine what it may have been like to work in the Dead Letters Office. Bartleby's death is tragic, but "Bartleby" also is hopeful, life-affirming, in the sense that the Lawyer will not have to endure a fate similar to Bartleby's. Bartleby has died so that the Lawyer may not have to die the same disheartening death. I accept the critical tradition of viewing Bartleby as a Christ figure, particularly sent to save the old man. There is life even in death, and the Lawyer no longer is living a living death. For the first time, he is living. Therefore, the ending is not a failure, as Charles G. Hoffman has maintained, whose view has influenced generations of critics.

"Bartleby" is tragic because there is nothing that can save Bartleby; it is man's inability to help his fellow man that shapes this dark view of humanity. It is only when Bartleby dies that the attorney gains a tragic sense of life. The lawyer's final utterance represents his developing tragic vision. Developing his insights into Bartleby's existence and learning of a rumor about Bartleby's past job at the Dead Letter Office at Washington, he says:

> Dead letters! does it not sound like dead men? Conceive a man by nature and misfortune prone to a pallid hopelessness, can any business seem more fitted to heighten it than that of continually handling these dead letters, and assorting them for the flames? For by the cartload they are annually burned. Sometimes from out of the folded paper the pale clerk takes a ring — the finger it was meant for, perhaps, molders in the grave; a bank note sent in swiftest charity — he whom it would relieve nor eats nor hungers any more; pardon for those who died despairing; hope for those who died unhoping; good tidings for those who died stifled by unrelieved calamities. On errands of life, these letters speed to death [34].

For the first time, the Lawyer understands that work can deaden an individual, especially dull, depressing work. He no longer is smug and dismissive about "Life." I agree with Graham Nicol Forst who says, "he now clearly brims with it, having learned about suffering and despair, about human hope and hunger; having clearly heard the cries for compassion and brotherhood" (268). Bartleby's example has taught him to respect life; he is able to imagine — to become aware of and vicariously experience the feelings, thoughts, and experience of another as if his own (yes, indeed, his very own) — Bartleby's pain, despair, hunger. I disagree with Gillian Brown's reading of the Lawyer's new understanding of Bartleby. Brown sees no change of heart, or gaining a heart, but a reconfirmation of the power of consumerism and sentimentalism (149). Like most critics who view Bartleby unsympathetically, Brown believes that an economic or commonsense approach is needed to correct Bartleby's "unreasonableness." Harold Schechter finds Bartleby's behavior toward the Lawyer as disdainful (361). Such a reading softens and glosses over the Lawyer's own behavior, which offers a way to "sympathize with the lawyer" (Schechter

364). To feel; the Lawyer has been shocked into recognition. To touch; he has connected himself to others. To see; he has opened his eyes. His senses have awakened. Bruce L. Grenberg is one of the rare critics to praise the Lawyer and acknowledge his conversion. And for Grenberg, when the Lawyer touches the dead Bartleby, it is that contact that ushers in understanding. With one touch of the dead Bartleby, he now understands who Bartleby was (175). There are stirrings of life in the Lawyer. Unfortunately, it is a connection that could not have been made while Bartleby was alive. Richard J. Zlogar is unconvincing in his reading of this passage. Zlogar is too literal when he disapproves of the Lawyer's supposed hesitation or more precisely his unconscious, perhaps unintended touch. His reading of "Something prompted me to touch him" elicits harsh disapproval:

> The narrator's laying on of hands, which on the surface indicates acceptance of the unclean, is actually far removed from Christ's pronouncedly active response to the leper: "And Jesus, moved with compassion, put forth *his* hand, and touched him, and saith unto him, I will; be thou clean" [528].

The "something [that] prompted" the Lawyer to touch the dead Bartleby is love emerging; he is no longer afraid. The loving gesture is natural, unconscious, and freely given. There is no calculation, no deliberation.

Todd F. Davis, however, does not see a dramatic, life-changing experience which turns the Lawyer into a selfless and empathetic individual. Davis argues, "I am not, however, as confident that the narrator has learned all that Forst claims. Rather, he seems, through the act of writing, to be restating the problem of the human condition, and, as the narrator of *Pierre* explains, perhaps the illustrations of this problem are the only possible human solutions." Davis's assessment is harsh, unsympathetic, and bleak. The postscript is more than just a rumor about Bartleby's Dead Letter Office days; the Lawyer is revealing himself in a way he has not done before. He no longer is petrified by Bartleby's bleak existence; his heart has been roused. This last addition to the story is utterly selfless; he does not mention himself at all in the passage. He is able to imagine Bartleby's life without bringing himself into it. He sees Bartleby as a human, not a bizarre, possibly insane scrivener. He sees how dark forces in the world can smother life. Bartleby is not a pathetic man, subject of ridicule and revulsion. He was a man who needed help. The Lawyer's disillusionment is not an uprooting of values, but an invigoration, fortification, inspiration of values. Perhaps a reason why he never reveals his name to the reader is that he has learned to be self-renouncing, that is selfless; he is not self-flaunting anymore.

The Lawyer's change is more than an illustration, and certainly Bartleby is more too; they are human. Charity becomes fundamentally imperative; it now is a rescue from the void. To help the other is to unite with him, to reconnect him with the sources of life, and to feed the soul. Altruism restores spiritual peace and renews hope; life is possible. The world is indifferent to the plights of the individual, and the Lawyer painfully gains consciousness of this fact. There is hope and aid, but fate interrupts the delivery, and the messages of love end up in the flames. Was there hope for Bartleby? Did he die unhoping, stifled by unrelieved calamities? Would the Lawyer now be able to help him? Yes, I believe he would have had a better chance reaching Bartleby.

These failures of human connection emphasize the death impulse found in boredom. Bartleby's death is the first and only one in Melville's oeuvre linked to boredom. The inevitability of death is the outcome, end-point, and the logical extension of boredom. All attempts to deal with boredom in "Bartleby" fail. Without any viable and consistent forces to counter the devastating pull toward lethargy, inactivity, and death, elements of nihilism characterize Melville's grim outlook on how boredom affects life. "Bartleby" underscores the dangers of failure to communicate, connect, extend oneself, and forge bonds with others. Set on terra firma, this short story offers no escape or relief from soul sickness. Melville's nautical-themed work always presented the open sea or island hideaway to ease boredom. Nature or the outdoors no longer provides a temporary respite from boredom. Bartleby's death extinguishes hope in work and human relations, and presents these two means to counter boredom as ineffective and unreliable. Religion, if pure, might offer some help, but the Lawyer demonstrates how difficult it is to attain it. Melville has become uncompromising in his presentation of darker themes. Boredom limits action, expansion, and life, and this force molds Melville's tragic vision. Bartleby was incapacitated with his soul-deep despair, and Melville saw that there was no solution. Accepting that there was no solution, Melville matured as a tragic thinker. Melville offers no social reform, or systematic humanization of business methods; nonetheless, the Lawyer has been "born," so the story holds out a faint hope, and his loving gesture of sharing this tale about Bartleby provides, as Edgar A. Dryden (2004) acutely describes, "a decent burial and final resting place" (26).

Bartleby's death is a frightening realization that boredom is a dreadful, soul-killing disease. Tedious, repetitive, and life-draining work contributes to the deterioration of the soul. Possibly along with other unspecified episodes, Bartleby's Dead Letters Office position may have begun to deaden his spirit. The dead letters symbolize that there is no communication between others. Work does not invigorate, protect, or save; rather, it has deleterious effects. Also, the spirit of brotherhood at the work place is undermined. There presumably was no comradeship in the Dead Letters Office and there is none in the Lawyer's office. All of these failures or misunderstandings emphasize the death impulse found in boredom. Bartleby's death, however, is not quite the last word on the subject of boredom; Melville will resurrect this theme, and explore further the religious dimensions of boredom in *Clarel.*

Clarel

The Noontide Demon Can
Quote Scripture, Too

It might seem logical that Melville's treatment of boredom should die with Bartleby; however, Melville returns again and again to characters who are plagued and endangered by the "noontide demon" of boredom. In *Clarel* (1876), the culmination of Melville's life-long meditation on this devil, he explicitly links boredom and religion. In doing so, Melville draws upon a long tradition in Christianity. For historic medieval desert monks, boredom, then understood as acedia, was one of the deadly sins, an evil corrupting one's soul and relationship with God. Portrayed as the work of the devil, acedia was often described by the desert monks, making prayer and devotion to Gods feeling tedious and meaningless; to feel acedia is to doubt God's existence. The remarkable similarity between the language Melville uses to describe boredom and the medieval religious formulations of acedia reveals a much deeper philosophical kinship. By turning explicitly to the language and landscape of religion in *Clarel*, Melville is able to articulate most clearly and emphatically the threat of boredom, its alliance with evil, and its crucial position at the heart of his dark vision. Melville's epic poem offers faith as an alternative to the despair and boredom that haunt man in a Manichean universe; however, whether that faith in God ever is achieved or sustained is uncertain. The dilemmas of belief, often precipitated by boredom for Melville's characters, are harder to deal with in *Clarel*, and the convenient narrative solutions to boredom, which Melville employed in earlier works, are not available here.

The Syrian monk episode of *Clarel* illustrates with particular clarity the precise nature of the relationship between boredom and the crisis of religious faith. Stan Goldman argues, "No passage in *Clarel* can better convey the bitter sense of the tremendous distance between God's hiddenness and the human desire for divine presence than the prayer of the Syrian monk" (19). When Clarel and his fellow pilgrims encounter the Syrian monk in the desert, which is the traditional battleground of the noontide demon, the monk is afflicted with a severe case of acedia. Melville's holy man is desperate to prove his faith, but his acedia is far stronger than he imagines it to be. Although he claims a victory over his noontide demon, he is not a faithful believer; he does not feel the joy of God within. Careful examination of the unrelenting and corrosive action of boredom on the Syrian's soul sheds new light on the entire Melville oeuvre. What was an implicit and sustained preoccupation with boredom in early works is brought to full imaginative realization only in *Clarel.*

The demon of noontide also persecutes Clarel. Clarel is an American divinity student, and so it is easy to view him as a monk in the Holy Land, one of the desert anchorites who combated with the noontide demon:

> The demon of ἀχηδια, also called "noontide demon," is the most oppressive of all demons. He attacks the monk about the fourth hour and besieges his soul until the eighth hour. First he makes the sun appear sluggish and immobile, as if the day had fifty hours. Then he causes the monk continually to look at the sun to see how far it still is from the ninth hour, and to look around, here and there, whether any of his brethren is near. Moreover, the demon sends him hatred against the place, against life itself, and against the work of his hands, and makes him think he has lost the love among his brethren and that there is none to comfort him. If during those days anybody annoyed the monk, the demon would add this to increase the monk's hatred. He stirs the monk also to long for different places in which he can find easily what is necessary for his life and can carry on a much less toilsome and more expedient profession. It is not on account of the locality, the demon suggests, that one pleases God. He can be worshipped everywhere. To these thoughts the demon adds the memory of the monk's family and of his former way of life. He presents the length of his lifetime, holding before the monk's eyes all the hardships of his acetic life. Thus the demon employs all his wiles so that the monk may leave his cell and flee from the race-course [Evagrius, as quoted by Wenzel, 5].

This evil force troubled, haunted, and tempted those monastic brothers, and it too tests Clarel's fortitude and faith in God. Clarel's strength as a devout Christian is questionable; does he truly believe? He never confidently or unambiguously answers this crucial question. Perhaps his pilgrimage to Jerusalem was meant to awaken him spiritually and rejuvenate his faith by enabling him to find God within. Instead, it has inspired more despair and more doubt. Exasperated over his disappointing reaction to the City of God, Clarel says, "Like the ice-bastions round the Pole, / Thy blank, blank towers, Jerusalem" (1.1.60–1). The sacred land leaves him spiritually blank. He knows prior to setting off to the holy site of the three great religions that "Salem to be no Samarcand" (1.1.64), but is still demoralized by the sterility and lifelessness of the city; Salem and its surrounding environs are covered in dust, which becomes a key symbol. The aridity of the desert and dust represent the spiritual dryness found in *Clarel,* and perhaps of religion itself.

Clarel's Jerusalem in effect can be compared to Bartleby's New York City, the city of staleness, isolation, and death. If Clarel cannot regain, or rather discover, his piety by retracing the steps of Christ, the founder of Clarel's religion, in the same city, what can he do? In fact, the key question of this epic poem asked by many characters in it is "Without religion, what then?" How is Melville's figure to live in a world where science has undermined belief in God?

As the demon of noontide made prayer and devotion to God feel tedious and meaningless for medieval monks, Clarel too cannot pray or keep his thoughts on God. He broods in his room, questioning, "Theology, art thou so blind" (1.1.22), and cries, "Can faith remove / Her faith" (1.1.18–9). In despair he tries to pray, "Dropping thereat upon the knee, / His lips he parted; but the word / Against the utterance demurred / And failed him" (1.1.121–4). Similar to White Jacket who could not answer the Assistant Surgeon's question "Full of theological hypos" (*WJ*, 329), Clarel too is quiet during important religious moments; these two literary characters pass as Christian, but cannot firmly voice their faiths. The words fail Clarel because they are not rooted in his heart; he does not feel those words of God in his soul. They are not there. It is very likely that the noontide demon afflicted Clarel before, long before this trip to Jerusalem; prayer most likely was a daily exercise which became routine, uninteresting, and tedious.

The significant fear the early Church Fathers had concerning the noontide demon was that the monk plagued with this devil would abandon his faith and works of God. This serious threat to Christianity — the noontide demon — became in an earlier version of the list of primary sins one of the deadly sins, acedia, which for some scholars morphed into its final form, the sin of sloth. The devil made prayer, Bible scribing, and other devotional works boring. Was God boring, too? Patience, fortitude, and work were the prescribed cures for the drowsiness and temptations the monks had to endure. Although there were other brothers at the monastery, some cenobites took vows of silence and were hermits. They were often isolated and alone, despite being "brothers" and occasionally living together; the demon would lure them outside, to the city and talk. Expanding the distance between God and His monks, the devil ironically brought monks closer to his secular community. The desert was where religious men tested their endurance and faith. Even Christ went to the desert and faced his demon of noontide, and in Raposa's opinion, the Apostles experienced boredom while waiting for Jesus when he prayed for "help" on the night of his betrayal.

Bartleby and Clarel are Melville's literary monkish types: Bartleby the scribe whose last weeks and death are filled with religious meaning and Clarel the initiate who tries to forestall a spiritual death. Whereas Clarel seeks unsuccessfully a mentor who will solve his doubts, Bartleby tries to look to the Lawyer for guidance and support. These two young literary characters are "afflicted by that noiseless calm" (1.2.141) of boredom. Clarel desperately tries to counter it by employing previously successful Melvillean strategies against boredom: intellectual camaraderie, and work. As in all the works studied here, *Clarel* (1876) explores the efficacy of these defenses against boredom. The tactics become ambiguous in *Clarel* because Clarel is too dependent on others to ease his spiritual disquiet. As in *Redburn* (1849) and *White-Jacket* (1850), friendships are morally questionable in *Clarel*.

Jerusalem is filled with many like Clarel. The city dwellers and visitors no longer are moved by God's love or feel that joy of God. The demon of noontide has done his work. He has made believers lose interest, devotion, and passion. Christian holy places are just stone ruins or dusty, time-worn areas. Spirituality has become meaningless. Commenting on the sacred spots that Clarel and other travelers are visiting, the narrator observes, "little here moves hearts of some; / Rather repugnance grave, or scorn / Or cynicism, to mark the dome / Beset in court or yard forlorn" (1.3.119–22). The hallowed locations do not inspire. The Spirit of God is not there, and the people there do not see, feel, or hear God. To come to such a realization so early on a pilgrimage arouses despair. To be vexed "by Europe's grieving doubt / Which asks *And can the Father be?*" (1.3.135–6) in the City of God produces hopelessness. If one can only see within the walls of Jerusalem "where no life harbors, peers or calls —/ Wild solitudes like shoals in seas / Unsailed; or list at still sundown.... / Under such scenes abysses be" (1.16.25–33), then how is one to believe? If one sees an abyss in the Holy Land, does that confirm the absence or death of God? And if one perceives an abyss, is there one within? Friedrich Nietzsche warns the reader about staring into the abyss in *Beyond Good and Evil* (1886): "If thou gaze long into an abyss, the abyss will also gaze into thee" (466). In *Clarel*, Melville confronts the wasteland.

Glaucon, a wealthy, soon-to-be married pilgrim who briefly attends Clarel's wandering party, also speaks of the boredom and hopelessness in the desert on the way to Mar Saba. He notes, "This same dull land so holy / Which breeds but blues and melancholy" (2.3.63–4). Once a region to find God, to test one's faith, and to fortify one's devotion, the desert has lost its biblical and spiritual power for the pilgrims depicted in *Clarel*. It does not rejuvenate; it now stifles. The desert reflects the spiritual aridness within. Glaucon acknowledges that the desert is "so holy," which could mean that the area may still retain its sacredness, but it may suggest that man has lost his connection to the divine there. God could exist, but man cannot sense Him there. Consciousness always has been crucial in Melville's art as an index of how well characters survive in their worlds. Like Clarel, Glaucon sees an abyss which is mirrored by the one within; or rather, his own deep sadness and boredom are projected outward.

The desert traditionally is the site of spiritual contests, and in *Clarel* the desert also is a battleground between faith in God and indifference, disbelief, or boredom. Moses and Jesus underwent trials of faith in the desert, and many desert monks reenacted the desert sojourns of these holy figures to gauge their convictions. The arid and barren features of this land materialize the psychological and spiritual attributes of boredom. To test one's devotion under extreme conditions, in an area endlessly the same and with no support, is to stage a contest between boredom and faith.

Many early Christian writers addressed the dangers of boredom (*acedia*) and suggested safeguards against it. Theodora, a well respected woman ascetic, from whom males monks accepted advice, instructs how to combat *accidie*. This example belies the common notion that women and other groups traditionally only suffered so-called occasional and insignificant boredom; women also experienced severe and dangerous boredom, a so-called "male" problem. She says:

> It is good to live in peace, for the wise man practises perpetual prayer. It is truly a great thing for a virgin or a monk to live in peace, especially for the younger ones. However, you should realize that as soon as you intend to live in peace, at once evil comes and weighs down your soul through *accidie*, faintheartedness, and evil thoughts. It also attacks your body through sickness, debility, weakening of the knees, and all the members. It dissipates the strength of soul and body, so that one believes one is ill and no longer able to pray. But if we are vigilant, all these temptations fall away [quoted in *The Sayings of the Desert Fathers*, 71].

Anthony the Great, a reclusive Egyptian monk who begrudgingly founded an order, was afflicted by *accidie* in the desert, and Saint Athanasius wrote about the ordeal Anthony the Great experienced:

> When the holy Abba Anthony lived in the desert he was beset by *accidie*, and attacked by many sinful thoughts. He said to God, "Lord, I want to be saved but these thoughts do not leave me alone; what shall I do in my affliction? How can I be saved?" A short while afterwards, when he got up to go out, Anthony saw a man like himself sitting at his work, getting up from his work to pray, then sitting down and plaiting a rope, then getting up again to pray. It was an angel of the Lord sent to correct and reassure him. He heard the angel saying to him, "Do this and you

will be saved." At these words, Anthony was filled with joy and courage. He did this, and he was saved [quoted in *The Sayings of the Desert Fathers*, 1].

Heraclides, a relatively unknown desert monk, describes his tutelage of a troubled man who was attacked by the devil filling him with *accidie*. Heraclides stresses that one must have fortitude to resist the demon of noontide. After that troubled man gives in to the devil and *accidie*, he seeks out the monk. Heraclides tells him, "'You suffered that [*accidie*] because you did not keep to my instructions.' Then, according to his capacity, he taught him the discipline of the solitary life, and in a short time he became a good monk" (62). Although the usual pattern for monks, which in itself proved to be boring, was to be alone, a community or at least a teacher-student relationship is needed for the novice monk to learn how to contend with the devil's *accidie*. Only the psychologically and spiritually robust, tenacious, and firm could live alone, and oppose the demon of noontide. The less strong needed guidance, a father figure.

Clarel is irresolute and in need of a chaperon, too. While in Jerusalem and before embarking on his pilgrimage, he seeks a mentor to solve his personal and religious dilemmas. By finding a trusted counselor, he believes that he will undergo a divine experience to ease his spiritual ails. He is admitting his helplessness; he is deeply aware that his soul is endangered, and he needs assistance. He cannot do it alone. Clarel says:

> I too, I too; could *I* but meet
> Some stranger of a lore replete,
> Who, marking how my looks betray
> The dumb thoughts clogging here my feet,
> Would question me, expound and prove,
> And make my heart to burn with love [1.8.46–51].

This desperate need for a mentor, a father figure and friend, shapes the entire epic poem. Clarel believes that this person exists and hopes he will stir him out of his doubt and boredom. He wants comradeship to restore his faith. Nehemiah initially fulfills this role for Clarel, but fails the divinity student; on the other hand, Clarel places too much faith in Nehemiah and becomes disillusioned and disappointed with his ultimately unrealistic, simple, and naïve attitudes. Nehemiah is what Clarel at one point wants to be: strong in faith and untouched by uncertainty. Since Nehemiah dies because of a sleepwalking accident, a highly strange death, perhaps Melville is suggesting a certain blindness to reality. He is too innocent, pure, and virtuous to be a viable standard. Unlike Dante's Virgil, Nehemiah does not lead Clarel to God; he is more like Prince Myshkin of Dostoevsky's *The Idiot* (1868), a holy fool who is oblivious to the evil of the world, and instead of bringing hope and good-ness, causes much harm.

The desert demon of boredom brings to mind Satan who tempted Jesus in the desert. Melville apparently thinks so in 2.18, "The Syrian Monk" sec-tion of Part 2, "The Wilderness." Part 2 takes places in the desert regions of the Holy Land, and Clarel and some of his fellow pilgrims meet an unnamed Syrian monk who "for forty days, / Not yet elapsed, he dwelt in ways / Of yonder Quarantanian hight, / A true recluse, an anchorite / .... [And] 'Twas sin, he said, that drove him out / Into the desert — sin of doubt" (2.18.30–8). This hermit must have been plagued continually by the "demon of noontide" or *accidie*. The devil likely made the monk's cell oppressive. It can be imag-ined easily that the devil nagged him, interfered with his service to God, dis-torted his vision, and fatigued his strength, all of which brought tedium, ushering doubt. Interpreting Aquinas's understanding of *accidie*, Michael L. Raposa says *accidie* is the converse of the love and ecstasy of God. It drains the goodness and joy found in a religious experience. And for these reasons, medieval theologians considered this problem as a serious cardinal breach of spiritual wholeness. Moreover, for these specialists in the study of faith *acci-die* demanded serious attention (13). I would emphasize that *accidie*, joyless-ness in/of God, is a sin, a grave and even most dangerous and serious sin against God. To be joyless is depression, and to feel *accidie* is in essence to not believe in God or at the very least to doubt His role in human affairs. Life without God in medieval times clearly would be cause for depression and fear. What would happen to the soul after death? Hell? Melville's Syrian monk is melancholy, depressed in our current understanding, and his soul is endangered.

Outwardly, the Syrian monk appears pious and determined, and initially is unwilling to address Clarel's group of pilgrims. This reluctance to speak with them is admirable; he is not engaging the world and is behaving as a hermit should. The narrator emphasizes his holiness: "Pure did he show as mountain-leaf / By brook, or coral washed in reef"(2.18.13–4) and "unworldly was the face, / He looked a later Baptist John" (17–8). The monk looks the part, but like Clarel, he lacks the steadfastness of a true believer.

Both the Syrian and American are plagued by the "sin of doubt." These men are on separate quests to find personal meaning and rediscover God's grace; not only have they lost their connections to God, they have lost them-selves. Their religious uncertainties have quaked their foundations of self. There is no spiritual consolation for their world-weariness, and so how would they find significance in a world where God may not exist or in which He may not participate? Matthew Arnold also voices Victorian uncertainty in "Dover Beach" (1867); he writes:

> The Sea of Faith
> Was once, too, at the full, and round earth's shore
> Lay like the folds of a bright girdle furled.
> But now I only hear
> Its melancholy, long, withdrawing roar,
> Retreating, to the breath
> Of the night wind, down the vast edges drear
> And naked shingles of the world [21–8].

The personal loneliness each man feels is quite possibly an effect of their spiritual abandonment of God and/or God's abandonment of them. Who really has forsaken whom? The "sin of doubt" gnaws him, and his youth and inexperience augment an already overwhelming life emergency. He is not wise of this world and heaven; he is naïve concerning these two worlds.

Wishing to redeem and purge himself of the "sin of doubt," the Syrian monk enters the desert and finds "that a wrecked chapel marks the site / Where tempter and the tempted stood / Of old" (66–8). The hermit wants to test himself and defeat his demon of noontide on the same spot where Jesus confronted his and won; hoping to follow in the footsteps of his savior, the monk, however, fails. His *accidie* is too entrenched. Desire is insufficient to keep the noontide demon at bay, and the anchorite's strength of will to carry out his wish to regain faith also is weak. The Desert Fathers counseled tyros that self-restraint, forbearance, and mortification were needed to repel the full force of *accidie*. But Melville's desert monk shows no such virtues. He notes:

> I sat me down to brood
> Within that ruin; and — my heart
> Unwaveringly to set apart
> In meditation upon Him
> Who here endured the evil whim
> Of Satan — steadfast, steadfast down
> Mine eyes fixed on a flinty stone
> Which lay there at my feet. But thought
> Would wander [68–76].

As time goes by, that steadfastness erodes. Sitting in that "wrecked chapel" — a sign of decay, neglect, disuse, and instability that represents a loss of faith — the Syrian grows complacent, a condition which afflicts many Melvillean characters and leads them to deeper boredom. The masthead in Melville's sea novels similarly is a breeding ground for complacency, boredom, and near-death experiences. He tries to concentrate — picking up a stone and squeezing it — to become more intent on his purpose there, but his mind is somewhere else. The monk does not say what those other thoughts are.

The historical Egyptian monk Anthony the Great notes that during a bout of *accidie*, an angel visited and inspired him by demonstrating devotional works to ward off this deadly condition. By the same token, Melville's Syrian monk has a vision from God. After squeezing a rock until his hand bleeds, he first sees "the Saviour there — the Imp and He: / Fair showed the Fiend — foul enemy; / But, ah, the Other pale and dim: / I saw but as the shade of Him" (79–82). Returning to the spot where he was victorious over the devil, Christ is fighting for this lost sheep, and is providing more than just moral support for his charge; he is reengaging his battle with evil. Despite his work on earth and resurrection, evil is powerful. Christ's appearance suggests God's existence or at least indicates that the monk still believes in Him. However, Christ's image is fading, which intimates that the monk's faith is waning, and the Devil's form is intensifying. It is a Manichean world; good cannot overcome evil in this world. This noontide demon is incredibly strong, and the monk's *accidie* is so deep-rooted that there seems little anyone can do, even Christ. The monk's self-inflicted wound recalls Christ's crucifixion wounds, but the monk's is a superficial injury, an indication of the shallowness of his faith, unlike the wounds of Christ, who died for his belief. The monk may want to get closer to God by imitating Christ, but cannot. His unconscious senses it, and if this holy/unholy vision is only a figment of the imagination, the monk's deep inner self is telling him he is a doubter.

The Syrian monk fails his first serious test; his *accidie* is stronger than he is and continues to be so. The vision of the devil disappears, but returns and is relentlessly yet deceivingly cordial to the monk. The monk is possessed by the devil (2.18.87), and the demon speaks through the religious figure. Essentially, what the devil thinks, the monk says, and so if the devil through the monk speaks unchristian, skeptical things, the monk may in fact be speaking what he truly feels. Because the devil enters the monk and takes some control away from the man, this possession can be seen as the monk's unconscious talking: no restraint to police what he wants to say or do. Psychoanalytically this episode perhaps is the first time he speaks freely; with no religious or authority figure to damn him as sinner, heretic, or disbeliever, he is testing religion itself. He has told Clarel and his group that he committed the "sin of doubt," but he has not come to terms with what that means until now when he relates his spiritual possession. Before the devil entered him, the monk's "sin of doubt" was an abstraction, something he never understood. More importantly, though, his wrestling with the devil at the end does not bring him closer to understanding his uncertainty or winning back his faith.

The devil is not imposing alien ideas or manipulating key beliefs to cause bewilderment and helplessness for the Syrian monk; rather, the hermit already is spiritually astray. He himself has questioned and doubted God. The devil simply is completing the process of the monk's uncertainty. Christian teaching instructs that the faithful should imitate Christ; however, the devil challenges the monk to live up to this ethical demand. The man is naïve to think he can just stand where Christ faced off the devil and succeed, too; he must demonstrate the same resolve, courage, and endurance Christ had shown. The devil tempts the monk in the same manner he enticed Christ: "'Why Strife? / Dost hunger for the bread of life…. / True faith could turn that stone to bread, / That stone thou hold'st'" (2.8.89–93). Jesus, faced with a similar question, answered, "Scripture says, 'Man cannot live on bread alone; he lives on every word that God utters'" (Matthew 4.4). Melville's Syrian monk must have forgotten Christ's reply: "Mute then was my face / I lifted to the starry space; / But the great heaven it burned so bright, / It cowed me, and back fell my sight" (2.18.93–6). In *White-Jacket* (1850) White Jacket felt the stars gave him some protection while he was up in the masthead; when he no longer saw the constellations, he drifted into boredom and near death. In *Clarel* the Syrian monk finds no such comfort or inspiration with "the starry space" he sees. The heavenly stars are meant to provide direction, but the hermit is silent and does not know what to do. He is intimidated. He lacks faith, and one recalls again White Jacket's silence when faced with the Assistant Surgeon's question, "Are you pious?" He is unable to declare his religious faith. Vocal declaration is the gauge of Melville's characters' faith. The devil is right when he says to the monk, "Thou lackest faith" (2.18.91).

Taking advantage of the monk's silence, the devil presses further the hermit's insecurities. The devil only is playing upon the doubter's fears; it really is too easy. It seems not much of a temptation. This situation calls to mind Nathaniel Hawthorne's "Young Goodman Brown" (1835) where Brown and the Devil meet and discuss the inherent evil of mankind. The insights the Devil speaks of are "so [apt] that his argument seemed rather to spring up in the bosom of his auditor than to be suggested by himself" (62); Hawthorne's fiend is verbalizing what the young Puritan already is thinking. The dark view of humanity the devil supposedly reveals to Brown has been there in Brown's mind long before their nighttime meeting. The vision truly is his, not the devil's; the devil has simply materialized Brown's pessimistic outlook. Hawthorne's Brown and Melville's Syrian monk do not fight their devils.

Finding no relief in God and undergoing a sudden overpowering terror, the Syrian monk tries to respond to the devil, but sounds unconvincing and unsure of his own replies. Taking advantage of the hermit's fear and disquiet, the devil gauges his doubt; the devil questions his belief in the existence of God: "'Is yon the Father's home? / And thou His child cast out to night? / 'Tis bravely lighted, yonder dome'" (2.18.97–9). Satan has characterized the anchorite as a kind of forsaken son; again the devil uses the monk's own self-image that he is Christ-like to attack his inherent doubt. On the cross, Jesus cries out, "My God, my God, why hast thou forsaken me?" (Mark 15:33).

Has the monk forsaken God, or has God abandoned him during this crisis of faith? Is he the one lost sheep that the shepherd Christ is searching for, or is he running away? The monk seems to profess some kind of assurance of God's being: "Part speak'st thou true: yea, He is there" (2.18.100). The monk implies that he is not a castaway, and perhaps that is what he meant by "Part speak'st thou true"; however, his reply is ambiguous. It is not a strong or confident "yea," and the relatively few words he speaks, compared to the devil, also intimate an unconscious skepticism. Since these words are his first rejoinder, they show none of the certainty of Christ's own first quick, incisive answer to the devil.

More importantly, the devil can hear in the monk's remark his lack of confidence: "Yea, yea, and He is everywhere" (2.18.101). The devil mimics the monk's "yea," and by repeating it twice, the devil is voicing the anchorite's lack of conviction; the monk's "yea" is wavering, shaky, and fragile. The devil's "yea, yea" sounds the indifference of the man, as if to say, "I don't believe you" or "you don't mean that." By extension, the phrase "and He is everywhere" also repeats the monk's uncertainty. "He is everywhere" at first may appear as an affirmation of God's omnipresence, but the devil seems to be pointing out God's scattered, airy, and potentially nonexistent presence. The devil's expression also suggests a casual dismissal of what the monk has said; it can be easily imagined that the devil nonchalantly waves his hand down when he speaks this line.

As this temptation scene continues, the conversation between the devil and Syrian monk becomes difficult to follow; one no longer is sure who is speaking. Melville's use of dashes to indicate when each character speaks becomes confusing at times because whoever is talking sounds as if he were a believer in good or God. The effect is to bewilder the reader, to make us as confounded as the monk. The result is unsettling. How can one ever argue or overcome the devil, the Father of All Lies? Since the hermit is possessed, the devil in effect is speaking. Or is he? As the Syrian monk becomes entangled in the devil's logic, it shows how dangerous a crisis of faith is. This crossroad between certainty and doubt completely disorients the hermit, and this state of confusion regarding his identity in general is a type of nihilism. There are no fixed or confirmed values which the monk believes in. The Syrian sees the emptiness within, and reflects his despair outward.

The next series of exchanges is clear because the devil completely overwhelms the hermit's insecure response of "Faith bideth" (111). His reply, however, just flies in the face of what has been happening in the scene. He has no abiding faith; his words gesture toward something he wishes he had. His faith does not remain, and does not carry him through. He is vulnerable. The devil deconstructs the monk's wishful idea of "Faith bideth," and shows that faith has no future, that it does not last. The demon says:

> Noon, and wait for day?
> The sand's half run! Eternal, He:
> But aye with a futurity
> Which not exceeds his past. Agree,
> Full time has lapsed. What ages hoar,
> What period fix, when faith no more,
> If unfulfilled, shall fool? [111–7].

Not only does the devil cast doubt concerning faith but also God's ontology. He turns God into a physical reality, one that ages, and will die. Comparing God to the sand in an hourglass, there is not much time left; the expired time exceeds that which is remaining. The devil sounds logical: "time has lapsed." The devil is questioning the Syrian's grip on reality; if nothing lasts forever, neither do faith and God. Dumbfounded, terrified, defenseless, and impotent, the monk steadfastly is mute.

After some time the monk replies, "And death?" (120), but his answer, if one can call it that, demonstrates his pathetic state. Is the hermit looking for a way out through death, or do his words suggest that death will ultimately test whether there is a Christian afterlife? After all, Christians believe that Christ conquered death and ensured eternal life for the faithful through the Resurrection. The hermit seems to be grasping at straws, rather than confidently voicing tenets of faith. And since many of the hermit's replies to the devil are questions, they strongly hint to his overall uncertainty. Why would he be asking the devil questions about faith in God?

The devil attacks the anchorite's feeble response and exposes his insubstantial, misleading, and illusory belief in the promised afterlife. The devil thinks the human is not serious, that he is failing to confront his doubt directly. Every time the man scrambles to think of some response, it is just not good or strong enough to neutralize the devil's threat. The evil spirit says: "Why beat the bush in thee? / It is the cunningest mystery: / Alive thou know'st not death; and, dead, / Death thou'lt not know" (120–3). One can never know either way; it is an unsolvable mystery. Only faith can answer this enigma. One really must depend on faith, and the question is having faith. One cannot ever confirm faith. However, the monk at last thinks he has the upper hand, and will trump the devil: "The grave will test; / But He, He *is*, though Doubt attend; / Peace will He give ere come the end" (123–5). He may have doubts, but believes he will discover the truth when he dies. More importantly, "He *is*" is an affirmation that is unearned, illogical, and counterfeit; it is false because spoken by a man who has little faith. He has not felt at peace with himself or the grace of God. He has not said anything to corroborate this statement. It would be a powerful response, only if he meant it.

The monk's statement falls flat because the devil severely and decisively unravels him; the evil spirit has revealed the hermit's deep rooted lack of faith. I disagree with Vincent Kenny and Stan Goldman's insistence that the Syrian is secure in his faith. Simply because the monk has a "need for faith" does not mean he has faith, nor does the monk attain respect, as Goldman maintains (89), from the pilgrims. Satan's rebuke is a mocking exposé which leaves the religious figure bare. The demon says, "Ha, *thou* at peace? Nay, peace were best" (126). The fiend is much more honest and focused than the man; the human is trying to fool the arch deceiver and thinks he can succeed. It is as if the devil is saying, "How could you say that?" In what I interpret as an unconvincing aside, the monk cries out, "Could the unselfish yearner rest! / At peace to be, here, here on earth, / Where peace, heart-peace, how few may claim, / And each pure nature pines in dearth" (127–30). The devil's response is precise: "Fie, fie, thy soul might well take shame" (131), and the doubter knows it, too: "There sunk my heart — he spake so true / In that" (132–3). Indeed he did.

Feeling helplessness and dread over the enormity of his "sin of doubt," the monk calls out to God to intervene and save him. This cry of desperation is a final plea for clarity; he wants to know now whether God is there. It is a prayer for acknowledgement of the man's Creator. It brings to mind again the crucified Christ, moments before he dies and demands to know why God has left him alone. The monk feels he has been forsaken; he sees God as being elusive, remote, and apathetic. The hermit's state is ambivalent in the sense that he has become isolated as well. Adding to the equivocal nature of his situation is that Christ's image did appear to him at the start of his temptation scene with the devil, but vanished as the devil's image strengthened; the pale spirit of Christ suggests a hesitancy to embrace him, an indecision to believe that he truly exists and is capable of defeating evil. The faintness of Christ is an index of the monk's faith. When he recounts his experience, he says, "O God (I prayed), come through / The cloud; hard task

Thou settest man / To know Thee; take me back again / To nothing, or make clear my view!" (133–6). William Potter believes that the monk's cry reflects "the desire for annihilation, the fearsome burden consciousness presents to many in the poem" (116). Potter's use of "annihilation" calls to mind Hawthorne's 20 November 1856 entry in *The English Notebooks* where he transcribes his and Melville's last meeting in Liverpool, England. Hawthorne writes, "Melville, as he always does, began to reason of Providence and futurity, and of everything that lies beyond human ken, and informed me that he had 'pretty much made up his mind to be annihilated;' but still he does not seem to rest in that anticipation; and, I think, will never rest until he gets hold of a definite belief" (651). Potter does not notice this highly suggestive coincidence, which would render the reading of these lines more poignant. Since some critics understand Melville's grim admission as suicidal, perhaps too the Syrian is on the verge of taking his own life. In "Timoleon" (1888) Melville dramatizes this feeling of abandonment and need of man for God to make some sign:

> Yes, *are* ye, gods? Then ye, 'tis ye
> Should show what touch of tie ye may,
> Since ye, too, if not wrung are wronged
> By grievous misconceptions of your sway.
> But deign, some little sign be given —
> Low thunder in your tranquil skies;
> Me reassure, nor let me be
> Like a lone dog that for a master cries [165–172].

Unlike Timoleon, the Syrian monk had his "little sign"; however, it seems barely sufficient. What would satisfy him? Asking for lucidity or annihilation, the monk has chosen the void; dissatisfied with what he has seen or not moved strongly enough by the sign, he chooses nothingness. The dread he feels is the chaos before birth, before the creation of the universe. God seems to be present, but the monk fails to acknowledge Him; each wavers.

Unconsciously finding solidarity with the devil, the anchorite has been speaking the devil's words as if they were his own. Melville's narrative technique thus allows for subversions and uncertainty to be spoken; to have a demon deconstruct the monk's faith, or at least question the soundness of that conviction, makes tangible what the monk is afraid to say himself. The devil is an acceptable, convenient, and unambiguous figure of dissent, rebellion, and chaos. He is the unconscious manifestation of the monk's own internal discord. For the monk, it is certainly easier to have the demon dispute the existence of God because of who he is. The devil's identity is based upon being against God, and the monk's supposedly is founded on his closeness to God.

It inspires less guilt to be horrified at the devil for speaking blasphemy than to admit honestly that the monk too feels this way.

Apparently, the devil has been entering and leaving the monk's troubled soul during their conversation. It seems that the evil force takes possession of the religious figure's spirit when he wants to inspire further doubt in the monk, and leaves him to allow horror and pain to settle in; it is a form of spiritual terrorism. If the monk finds any comfort, either false or true, the devil sees through it, and says, "Content thee: in conclusion caught / Thou'lt find how thought's extremes agree,—/ The forethought clinched by after-thought, / The firstling by finality" (140–3). The dash in this comment is unlike the others throughout this section; it does not indicate a shift in speakers. The demon is speaking here with no interruption. I cannot agree with William Potter's claim that in these lines the monk is on the verge of relief. I also fail to sense the faint voice Potter hears in the desert which tempers the monk's heart (116). Whatever triumph the monk believes he has over the devil, the diabolic spirit reminds him how unearned his assurance is; in this situation, the devil ironically is calling for honesty.

By forcing his sense of confidence in God and himself, the hermit also is showing how shallow his faith is; the devil is saying the monk's position is made of two extremes, and in essence they are the same thing. In his efforts to show his faith, he instead has demonstrated the lack of it. Because the devil managed to undermine and twist everything the monk has said, it is as if he said one thing but meant another. "Thou'lt find how thought's extremes agree." This insight devastates the religious man, and then the devil disappears forever. The monk cries out, "His will be done" (145) as a way to seek forgiveness and affirm God's existence. Adding to this effort to portray himself as devout, he drops the stone he has been holding since the start of his temptation; his bloody palms suggest the passion of Christ, the intense physical and spiritual torment he endured. Again, he wishes to emulate Christ, but he falls short of his savior.

Just like the devil that saw through the hermit's charade of faith, Rolfe, one of the pilgrims with Clarel, is skeptical of the genuineness of this faith. Rolfe says, "Surely, not all we've heard: / Peace — solace — was in end conferred?" (150–1). Rolfe's observation attests to the monk's wanting faith; hearing Rolfe's mistrust in his story, the monk despairs and leaves the group. William Potter finds the monk's experience as representative of the poem's overall theme of spiritual crisis (116). And Vincent Kenny finds no peace of mind or spirit gained through a mystical bind with God in this section of *Clarel* (137). Rolfe adds, "And this but ecstasy of fast? / Construe then Jonah in despair" (157–8). Perhaps Rolfe is too kind to call the hermit "Jonah";

Jonah reconciled with God, unlike the Syrian. All throughout this scene, Clarel has been silent. The monk's story evidently hit home; the monk's story is his own. The monk's silence is loud. I do not accept Stan Goldman's assertion that God's silence is affirming. Defending his claim by closely reading Scripture, not lines from *Clarel*, Goldman maintains that God really is not silent; one can hear Him, not with anatomical ears, but with spiritual ones (104). The juxtaposition of the biblical with the literary does not work well in this case; Melville's poetry defies such a reading.

Another important figure in *Clarel* caught between the wish to believe and tendency toward disbelief, Celio wrestles with his own demon of noontide. Celio is one of the many unsure and troubled men in Jerusalem who lack the joy of God in their lives. Although it seems that a kind of brotherhood — of fellow doubters — exists in the Holy City, Celio is an outcast; he suffers from a bodily malformation, and is considered by many critics to be one of the four monomaniacs in *Clarel*. Celio's deformity dramatizes and symbolizes his tortured soul. He may be crippled, but Celio is formidable, and reminds one of another monomaniac, Ahab, in his tenacity to seek God despite a corrosive and agonizing doubt. Celio repudiates God in the sense that God has not answered or eased his uncertainty. Vincent Kenny interprets Celio's death as a rejoinder to God's exit from the world; if God has abandoned the world, Celio too, in response to that departure, withdraws from the world (73). Celio, however, is neither atheist nor agnostic: he does not deny the existence of the Deity, and he does not say that the Godhead is either certain or impossible. William Potter argues that in spite of Celio's Christian crisis of faith, he ventures to find peace and hope in Christian terms. No matter how much he tries to run away from orthodoxy, he cannot keep away from it (80). Yes, Celio is skeptical but he is also deeply spiritual. Spirituality does not always connote religiosity. To be spiritual is to be concerned with higher questions of existence. Celio is interested in matters pertaining to metaphysical being. He struggles to be spiritual, but moreover to be religious; whether he allows and accepts God's presence in his life, even Celio cannot answer this dilemma.

Celio's intensity and acumen characterize him as a man who could be reverent toward God. He is single-minded concerning issues of faith. His drive to know is a declaration that he is neither atheist nor agnostic. In spite of that, Celio cannot be called a firm believer. I cannot agree with Stan Goldman's suggestion that Celio's outcries reflect a deep faith. Goldman finds divine affirmation and glorification in Celio's "crying to God" (23). His crying to God does not bring forth tears of joy. In fact, they may be tears of joylessness. Celio's grief is of despair, the acute realization that God, if He exists, is indifferent. He has no settled convictions of faith. He is plagued by disappointment, frustration, and uncertainty. He may very well be willing to believe, and his desperation testifies to his need for faith, but he falls short of devotion. He may curse God, and torture himself, but he cannot totally abandon God; his acts and thoughts involve God, and no matter how much he shouts at God, God still is a part of Celio's life. God structures his life, even if Celio blames Him for his misfortunes. If one overlooks Celio's illusory impiety, he in fact glows with divine light. Potter does not see Celio's character as contradictory; in contrast, he considers Celio as a "theological poet" in line within the Giambattista Vicoian tradition (123–4).

Not only haunted by his own demon of noontide, Celio is in the company of demoniacs. Initially, Celio appears possessed, and the suggestiveness of his spiritual state is heightened by Clarel's comment: "And did Christ come? in such a scene / Encounter the poor Gadarene / Long centuries ago?" (1.11.35–7). The Gadarene Demoniac is a possessed man whom Jesus exorcised, an act which is considered a miracle for Christians. This Christian biblical account of a demoniac saved demonstrates that despite being possessed by a legion of devils, the Gadarene still shows piety toward Christ. Clarel's observation, which is minor and said in passing, nonetheless is powerfully allusive. Christ did come, and was welcomed by the Gadarene; however, Celio keeps Christ at a distance, even taunting him. Celio's noontide demon seems to be a far stronger opponent than the Gadarene's. Or has Celio turned away from God and become Satan-like? Possibly anticipating the Syrian Monk passage, Melville could be intimating that both man and God have forsaken each other. Tracing some of the footsteps of Christ during the Passion, Celio visits the Arch of Ecce Homo and recounts Jesus's words on the cross, which seem more appropriate for Celio: "*My God, my God, forsakest me?*" (1.13.47). An outcast of society, Celio feels more like an outcast of heaven. Again, he is not an atheist; he may be blasphemous, but still views the world in the context of God.

The demon of noontide infected medieval monks with the utter lack of joy in anything associated with God. Celio too finds no elation in God. As if seeking an intervention by God to right his situation, Celio "glared at heaven / Then lapsed in sullenness again" (1.13.32–3); instead of peace, he finds torment, and in lieu of fulfilled expectation, he receives silent rejection when he turns his gaze toward the skies. The injustice of his life — his deformity — feeds the inequity he thinks God's absence in his life is inflicting. His cry of "*My God, my God, forsakest me?*" is a plea that goes unanswered, but more importantly demonstrates his sense of violation; God has sinned against him. And Celio behaves as an enraged yet impotent god; he wants to punish God, but how? Infuriated, vengeful, yet not entirely hopeless, he still looks to God. Again, he is not an atheist; why glare at heaven if one does not believe in the existence of God? Although he does not deny God, he finds no peace, harmony, or joy. It seems God is Celio's adversary, and this attitude once more recalls Ahab. Celio views his troubled relationship with God in sadomasochistic terms: "Upbraider! we upbraid again; / *Thee* we upbraid" (1.13.48–9). Each abuses the other. Pain, not joy, marks their interactions; God is not a source of joy but of discontent and agony. Certainly Celio's deformity has twisted the concept of God to match his own torment. Life may be joyless for Celio, but it is framed by God. It is God's irresoluteness in Celio's life that oppresses him. He is giving God chances to prove Himself, but these opportunities go unutilized.

So why does Celio continue to believe in, or at least not to deny, God's existence? This problem is precisely the issue in *Clarel*. Rolfe, an admirable figure in the poem, attempts to answer this question: "But though 'twere made / Demonstrable that God is not — / What then? it would not change this lot" (1.31.191–3). Rolfe is pointing to the modern dilemma — life without certainty. Who or what can replace God? Rolfe accepts science and sees that it is eclipsing religion, but it does not comfort. Crises of faith always have vexed men of all ages, including the era of Christ's presence on earth. Rolfe notes, "And indeed / His age was much like ours: doubt ran, / Faith flagged" (1.32.236–8). Doubt in God is not an uniquely nineteenth-century problem; divine skepticism is part of man's history. If God is denied, negated, erased, what is next? It may not prove Rolfe's own affirmation of faith, but he is aware of the awesome power the idea of God exerts in man's life. Science may answer questions of the physical and material, but becomes mute to issues of the spiritual and immaterial. Science does not necessarily deal with morality. Science makes day-to-day living easier; however, can science, as Elizabeth Kubler-Ross has stressed, improve the process of dying with dignity?

Apparently a friend of Celio, Rolfe eulogizes over his grave: "to moderns death is drear, / So drear: we die, we make no sign, / We acquiesce in any cheer — / No rite we seek, no rite decline. / Is't nonchalance of languid sense, / Or the last, last indifference?" (1.41.53–58). God's absence in man's life makes for a harsh, grim existence, but at the time of death, man faces the grave alone. Making the sign of the cross might bring some solace, having a priest administer the final rite could offer some consolation, or performing something of the religious ought to offset the terrifying nothingness which faces him, yet the faithless modern man dies without God and, in a sense, without anything. Even Celio has a gravestone that reads, "I know THAT MY

REDEEMER LIVETH" (1.41.48). In spite of all of his uncertainties, Celio did not completely exclude God from his life. Those sympathetic monks who cared for him briefly likely may have inscribed an emphatic and unmistakable vow of belief, but Celio did die with God, even if on questionable terms. Celio's death was agonizing like his life.

Modern man's indifference toward God is unlike Celio's joylessness of God. The secular person is too casual, withdrawn, and lukewarm to matters beyond the physical world. Absent from the nonreligious individual is any emotional reactions to higher, larger forces or concerns. Does he even have any connection to life itself? His sin is remaining unmoved. He may call his lack of response nonchalant, and he may feel complacent, but is he aware, does he even care to be, of the danger that awaits? A solitary death. His indifference toward God is far worse than Celio's blasphemy. Despite finding no transport, Celio cannot be said to have no passionate reaction to God, or to wish to be a non-believer; his indignation proves he is not tepid and certainly not secular. Uncertainty does not make one faithless; even Thomas the Apostle had his questions. Celio's demon of noontide may make him, at times, joyless, but he is not indifferent toward God.

Both the indifferent modern man and Celio suffer boredom in its broadest sense, but the boredom of the secular man is far more insidious. The impious person feels uninterested, discontent, and spiritless. What I mean by "spiritless" is lacking enthusiasm or energy, but the term also pertains to the nature of the spirit. The rapid advancements in technology and radical demythologization of science replace faith and inspire a kind of brazenness which Ungar, another worthy man in the poem, points out:

> The impieties of "Progress" speak.
> What say *these*, in effect, to God?
> "How profits it? And who art Thou
> That we should serve Thee? Of Thy way
> No knowledge we desire; *new* ways
> We have found out, and better. Go—
> Depart from us; we do erase
> Thy sinecure: behold, the sun
> Stands still no more in Ajalon:
> Depart from us!"—And if He do?
> (And that He may, the Scripture says)
> Is aught betwixt ye and the hells?
> For He, nor in irreverent view,
> 'Tis He distills that savor true
> Which keeps good essences from taint;
> Where He is not, corruption dwells,
> And man and chaos are without restraint [4.21.28–44].

Bored with age-old and outmoded values and practices, modern man, as Niet-zsche has documented, is killing God. Tempted by fresh, modernistic, and exciting promises of Progress, man abandons God. Vincent Kenny describes Ungar's vision as that of a man who "is on his own willfully and perversely, cutting God out of his life in a substitution of modern world's humanism" (195). There is no need for God. He has found a new (in)dependence in/of Science. Science breaks down boundaries at the expense of God. The non-believing person has brokered a Faustian compact and is unaware of the fine print. Knowing the cost of such a bargain, Ungar observes, "Now the world cannot save the world; / And Christ renounces it" (4.20.34–5). Dominating the entire poem is the theme of abandonment or forsaking, and it shapes Ungar's thoughts as well. Science ushers in the supposedly mutual abandon-ment of God and man, and this desertion is a kind of murder. William Pot-ter suggests that Ungar's anger is over "the social reform of the modern liberal state [that] is all head and no heart and treats the needy and impoverished in a patronizing way" (133). The individual is left on his own, and science is seen as killing the world. Science cheapens the dignity of man with its "haste" (4.21.105) but more importantly with its introduction of the commonplace. In Ungar's viewpoint, religion preserved the importance and uniqueness of the individual; a person was sacred. The world may have thought it was lib-erating itself from God, but instead imprisoned itself through science; its jailor is mediocrity. Ungar states:

> Myriads playing pygmy parts —
> Debased into equality:
> In glut of all material arts
> A civic barbarism may be:
> Man disennobled — brutalized
> By popular science — Atheized
> Into a smatterer —[4.21. 127–33].

The "*New* way / We have found out, and better" is boring. It is boring because the new way is uneventful, unpromising, and unexceptional. Everyone and everything is the same. Science lumps everyone together; identity is erased. This kind of egalitarianism is uncritical and superficial; it seems like the most ideal form of humanism — of total inclusiveness — but smacks of conformity, mediocrity, and, worse, inferiority.

It must be said that Ungar is part Native American. As a minority, as the Other, Ungar is deeply concerned with the moral effects of so-called Progress. Hilton Obenzinger says his "'Indian heart' appears to collapse or at least con-fuse the distinctions between colonizer and colonized, for he embodies both poles of the settler/native dialectic" (145). Rather than continual improvement, as is expected from Progress, the world becomes more vulgar, brutish, and obtuse. C. Vann Woodward describes aptly Melville's rendering of Ungar's diatribe as "the blackest commentary on the future of his country ever written by an American in the nineteenth century" (116). The world becomes dull, filled with bores. Uniformity does not inform who an individual is; shared qualities make a community, but subjectivity makes an individual. To speak without fluency, to think without exactness, and to live without passion are nightmares. Excellence is never achieved, consciousness is never attained, and selfhood is never established. This base existence is tragic in the sense that it is "new confirmation of the fall / Of Adam" (4.21.124–5). It is tragic because it initiates the "Dead level of rank commonplace" (4.22.136). Boredom is tantamount to death and since modern man has repudiated Christ, God will not save him. Man will die and face dread alone. Ungar warns a pilgrim in Clarel's group, "Woe / To us; without God, 'tis woe" (4.20.132–3).

Preserving religion's status in a segment of a middling, yet nominally observant society, Derwent is an Anglican priest whose chirpy and unearned optimism whitewashes all misgivings. He discounts, even scorns any heresies that disrupt his favorable view of man and religion. He interprets uncertainty as youthful and fashionable glumness. Asking too many questions is courting disaster, reading controversial or critical books is inviting despair, and befriending dark and intellectual men is guaranteeing faithlessness. In Derwent's understanding, all of these behaviors cause Clarel to have no comfort in religion. Feeling a paternal and professional obligation toward a fellow cleric, Derwent instructs Clarel, "Be not extreme. Midway is best" (3.21.278); in essence, he is telling the younger man to be like him: avoid thorny issues and embrace tradition. In this case, religion safeguards the status quo, cuts down everyone to size, instills uniformity, and makes for boredom. Skepticism upsets the social and moral balance and challenges established types, like Derwent. Viewing Clarel's astute friends (Rolfe, Vine, Ungar, and others) as immoral influences for being deep thinkers, Derwent warns him:

> Alas, too deep you dive.
> But hear me yet for little space:
> This shaft you sink shall strike no bloom:
> The surface, ah, heaven keeps *that* green;
> Green, sunny: nature's active scene,
> For man appointed, man's true home [3.21. 306–11].

Derwent's advice goes against what Melville himself believes. In a 3 March 1849 letter to Evert A. Duyckinck, Melville writes, "I love all men who *dive*. Any fish can swim near the surface, but it takes a great whale to go down stairs five miles or more; & if he don't attain the bottom, why, all the lead in Galena can't fashion the plummet that will" (121). Derwent is a fish. For Derwent, deep diving yields unnecessary and damaging effects, a kind of spiritual "bends," best to be avoided. Walter Bezanson describes him implicitly like Ralph Waldo Emerson, in the same way Melville parodied him in the Duyckinck 1849 letter: "For Derwent there is no crisis simply because he refused to see any; a rainbow-catcher from way back, he does not propose to have his digestion or his professional equilibrium upset" ("Historical Note," 573–4). Although Derwent represents a quality that goes against Melville's personal credo, Derwent does remain with Clarel to the end of the pilgrimage—one of only four among the original nine pilgrims—and "was loth, / How loth to leave him" (4.32.9–10) during Clarel's time of mourning for his deceased fiancée, Ruth. Many commentators who criticize Derwent for his easy, untroubled affirmation do credit him for his loyalty toward Clarel, as I do.

Even if individuals are not religious, the illusion of Progress contaminates their lives. Science demystifies but it also sterilizes. The human body becomes an anatomical specimen. A mountain transforms into a geological projection. In *Life on the Mississippi* (1883), Mark Twain expresses his horror and outrage concerning the effects his nautical education had on his love for the river; Twain writes:

> Now when I had mastered the language of this water and had come to know every trifling feature that bordered the great river as familiarly as I knew the letters of the alphabet, I had made a valuable acquisition. But I had lost something, too. I had lost something which could never be restored to me while I lived. All the grace, the beauty, the poetry had gone out of the majestic river.... The romance and the beauty were all gone from the river. All the value any feature of it had for me now was the amount of usefulness it could furnish toward compassing the safe piloting of a steamboat [54–5].

Similarly in *Clarel*, Derwent relates the destructive result when science dominates our understanding of the human condition:

> Tell Romeo that Juliet's eyes
> Are chemical; e'en analyze
> The iris; show 'tis albumen—
> Gluten—fish-jelly mere. What then? [4.18.98–101].

Echoing Rolfe's insightful realization that if God's existence finally is proven to be false "What then?" (1.31.193), Derwent too asks what is the alternative. Why replace faith in God if it means that beauty, love, humanity, and qualities that ennoble man and woman are to be dissected, scrutinized, and disparaged? Once more Mark Twain tragically notes what is lost when science presides over aesthetics:

> To say that De Soto, the first white man who ever saw the Mississippi River, saw it in 1542, is a remark which states a fact without interpreting it: it is something like giving the dimensions of a sunset by astronomical measurements, and cataloging the colors by their scientific names — as a result, you get the bald fact of the sunset, but you don't see the sunset [3].

Does the scientific knowledge of the biochemical composition in Juliet's eyes help to mesmerize Romeo? Is love nothing more than the interaction of pheromones? Does medical information interpret love poetry? Can love be more than just a genetic exchange? Science dissolves the essence of man. Is man more than only the sum of his body parts? Ask Romeo.

This drab, utterly scientific approach to life functions as one dramatic highpoint in Part 2: *The Wilderness* section. During an argument in which he defends Catholicism against the pilgrims, the Dominican says, "Science but deals / With Nature; Nature is not God; / Never she answers our appeals, / Or, if she do, but mocks the clod" (2.25.144–7). Stan Goldman interprets the Dominican's defense as "a veil of human limitations [that] lies over all knowledge of nature in Clarel.... The Dominican monk insists upon the human need for God" (27), and argues that "science is as futile in the pursuit of knowledge of God as nature is, for science deals only with second causes — nature" (28). Science is not the dominant, sole answer; it is, after all, made of many theories. It does not necessarily deal with morality. It can be said that science is amoral. The "*new* ways" do not promise answers to all questions. Questions can and are thrown back into our faces, emphasizing our earthly limitations. Those who embrace the "*new* ways" are too sure that they will find what they are looking for.

If the Dominican's opinions are meant to uplift religion and man, the next segment in this sequence featuring Margoth lessens the Catholic's supposed respect for life. Margoth is a Jewish atheist geologist. Parodying the Catholic's prediction that if Catholicism fails, all religions will die, Margoth responds:

> The broker take your trumpery pix,
> Paten and chalice! Turn ye — lo,
> Here's bread, here's wine. In Mexico
> Earthquakes lay flat your crucifix:
> All, all's geology [2.26.9–13].

Although he sounds like the skeptic in *Ecclesiastes*, echoing "All, all is vanity," Margoth accepts none of the Bible's inherent faith in God. But how will geology answer our appeals? William Potter points out that Margoth's program:

> will ultimately fail, the poem implies because it cannot penetrate to the very source of belief, the mysterious human psyche. A major religious idea expressed in *Clarel*—a very Protestant one — is that destroying the mystery of sacred sites and relics ... will not destroy true religious belief itself because the locus of that belief is in the imagination and the tempered heart [117].

Granted, the poem remains ambiguous as to what kind of appeal the Dominican is thinking of, but I assume it is metaphysical and pious. Unlike Margoth, fellow scientist Charles Darwin himself wrestled with atheism and belief. In *The Autobiography* (1887), Darwin confesses:

> [It] follows from the extreme difficulty or rather impossibility of conceiving this immense and wonderful universe, including man with his capacity of looking far backwards and far into futurity, as the result of blind chance or necessity. When thus reflecting I feel compelled to look to a First Cause having an intelligent mind in some degree analogous to that of man; and I deserve to be called a Theist.
>
> This conclusion was strong in my mind about the time, as far as I can remember, when I wrote the *Origin of Species*; and it is since that time that it has very gradually with many fluctuations become weaker. But then arises the doubt — can the mind of man, which has, as I fully believe, been developed from a mind as low as that possessed by the lowest animal, be trusted when it draws such grand conclusions....
>
> I cannot pretend to throw the least light on such abstruse problems. The mystery of the beginning of all things is insoluble by us; and I for one must be content to remain an Agnostic [92–4].

Often misleadingly portrayed as responsible for the erosion of faith in society, Darwin himself has misgivings, deep moral and spiritual doubts, concerning the integrity of his own evolutionary work. Scientific data supports Margoth, but Darwin seems to imply that no matter how many discoveries, proofs, or arguments weakening biblical authority, he cannot accept them fully. Having once prepared for the clergy, Darwin struggles between his life as man of science and man of devotion. He is caught between two worlds, equally convincing but failing to draw him. Darwin is an example of the strain of uncertainty running in major Melville figures who, like Darwin, cannot commit to either side. They find the choice to be unattainable, hopeless, and self-defeating; the decision is an unfair one because neither alternative is satisfying. They must settle for limbo: they will face a lifetime of waiting, struggling, and looking for some sign of God, while at the same time they feel abandoned and despondent.

The tendency in Melville's art to conclude on a hopeful and promising note in accordance with morality and faith in God continues in *Clarel*. The problem with these endings is whether their generally favorable constructions of God's role in the universe are plausible; do the actions portrayed in Melville's art support and warrant such a belief? Given Melville's evolving Manichean worldview, is Melville forcing conclusions that fly in the face of what the art presents? Such dilemmas exist in *White-Jacket*, and the parallels between that text and *Clarel* are immediate. Like its predecessor, *Clarel* too contends with the margins of religion's role in society. It wrestles with the idea and need for belief in spite of the overwhelming forces countering faith in God. The major protagonists in the respective works cannot affirm their faith, although they pass as nominal Christians. Are they or are they not believers? Neither one nor the other comes close to a profession of faith, and their bouts with boredom worsen their hesitancy and silence. Both White Jacket and Clarel want to believe, but each character responds differently to their doubts. White Jacket forces himself to have intense and extreme experiences, and is willing to self-aggrandize his wishes to appear as an observant Christian. This faux self-presentation contributes to the unsatisfactory and flawed ending. As in *Clarel*, ambiguity of the text and self complicates one's reading of the conclusion.

The "Epilogue" in *Clarel* verges close to the millenarian "Ending" in *White-Jacket*, but with key and subtle variations. The poem's ending is much more elaborate, problematic, and ambivalent. Although the "Epilogue" ends on a note of Christian "victory," the piece is saturated with skepticism. On the other hand, its message of promise is not earned based on the circumstances of the epic poem, and therefore I disagree with Stan Goldman's thesis that the "Epilogue" is an "epilogue of hope" (52). His fiancée dead, his pilgrimage friends leaving him, and his religious doubts unresolved, the concluding affirmation that "death but routs life into victory" (34) sounds hollow, even paradoxical. Clarel's wife-to-be, Ruth, is Jewish and did not convert to Christianity, and so "The cheer, so human, might not call / The maiden up; *Christ is risen:* / But Ruth, may Ruth so burst the prison?" (4.33.64–66). Clarel does not believe so, and when the narrator posits in the "Epilogue" that "Even death may prove unreal at the last" (4.35.25), has he Ruth in mind? Will Ruth be an exception, or will she be forgotten? Given the rather short and impersonal courtship and the long separation the couple endured, how solid is the relationship? Similarly, male friendships are morally questionable. The promise of genuine comradeship exists in *Clarel*, but no one seems willing to forge a lasting union. Clarel begins and ends his stay in the Holy Land alone and skeptical. He arrived there to find answers to his questions about existence and religion, but he ends up with more confusion. I agree with Alfred Kazin's assessment of *Clarel*:

> What I carry away most from *Clarel*, for all the wonderful travel atmosphere, is that even among so many appeals to "love" and "faith," there is no "communion true" and no fulfillment for those "seeking" it here. Those who already had faith may always have it. The past holiness of the land does nothing for those who bring nothing but their uncertainty. There is no magic in relics. Melville by the end affirms nothing but the Cross as the pain we must carry [105].

The future, which the "Epilogue" attempts to predict, looks bleak.

Yet, the oxymoronic message of the last line of the "Epilogue" could mean that "victory" is indeed a triumph and therefore a qualified but earned endorsement of hope. The mysterious and unfathomable nature of religion always will elude and frustrate; religion is an amalgamation of contradictions. "[T]hat death but routs life into victory" is the Resurrection. *Clarel* takes place during Holy Week and ends on Easter. Countering his repeated failures to connect spiritually with Jerusalem, to pray successfully to God, and to answer soundly his doubts, Clarel's determination to continue, to find faith in God, suggests that his gnawing doubts ultimately do not get the best of him. He is strong. He is more honest than the Syrian Monk and Derwent, and sees Rolfe as a model for a believer who somehow abides despite the discoveries of science. *Clarel* is far more complex, deliberate, and measured in its explorations of selfhood, boredom, and religion than *White-Jacket*. If *Clarel* ends on a Christian sense of hopefulness, no matter how equivocal it may be, it is tempered by Clarel's defeats, making its hope more palatable than that found in *White-Jacket*.

A double vision is needed to understand the "Epilogue." This short section consists of contrasts which do not necessarily negate one another. The last stanzas of the poem admit that neither science nor religion contain all the answers; Darwin's own uneasy concession to agnosticism comes to mind. The narrator seems to say that these diametrically opposed forces need each other, even if proponents of these extremes try to undermine the other. In a sense, skepticism can strengthen belief by compelling it to deal with difficult questions and vice versa; Pascal and Montaigne are considered to be Christian skeptics who tackle challenges to faith while embracing those very same questions about piety. Melville writes, "If Luther's day expand to Darwin's year, / Shall that exclude the hope — forclose the fear? (4.35.1–2). If the theory of evolution explains that human history is much longer than the Bible insists or that the earth itself is much older than theologians want to believe, does science ease the anxiety of existence? Can it answer questions beyond the earthly realm? Can science explain the meaning of life? Will technological advances really make one happy? Religion attempts to deal with these dilemmas that science tends to ignore. Belief persists in opposition to the onslaught of science: "But Faith ... / With blood warm oozing from her wounded trust, / Inscribes even on her shards of broken urns / The sign o' the cross — *the spirit above the dust!*" (4.35.8–11). Fragmented, faith transcends the physical and simultaneously leaves its mark on those urns. Even "if there be no God" (17), science does not soothe the plight of man. Science improves physical life, but fails to comfort the soul: "Wherefore ripen us to pain?" (4.35.20). Melville writes, "The harps of heaven and dreary gongs of hell; / Science the feud can only aggravate— / No umpire she betwixt the chimes and knell: / The running battle of the star and clod / Shall run forever" (13–17). One cannot mix the physical with the metaphysical; science is an inappropriate means for dealing with matters of God. Science may explain the origins of life, but shrinks from moral and ontological matters. It cannot decide what is good or evil. Science limits the view of the world while its scientists think religion occludes the vision.

Faith always is called into question; one is never confident or firm. Charles Olson describes *Clarel* as a "rosary of doubt" (99). Even Saint Thomas the Apostle doubted the risen Christ; in fact, all the Apostles questioned whether Jesus indeed would resurrect. Clarel's hesitancy and inability to arrive at some pleasing and tangible form of faith is an echo of the very problem of Christianity: how can one believe if one does not witness the resurrected Christ? The desire to believe is not piety, nor is mere appearance of the follower sufficient; one must feel God, experience a Jonathan Edwards–like great awakening. Among Melville's figures, only the Lawyer experiences the birth of genuine Christianity and Clarel lacks his enthusiasm. Perhaps age plays a factor — old age tends to inspire more interest in religion — but Clarel too has intense experiences, which fail to produce an enduring credo. *Clarel* is an annex to "Bartleby, the Scrivener" suggesting how tenuous, fragile, and provisional faith is.

This drive to attain faith and the consequent denial of a comforting and valid faith is reminiscent of Mark C. Taylor's work on erring and a/theology. The poem's conclusion can be understood as a statement of affirmation in the sense that Clarel is a wanderer who errs and continues to err. Rolfe is a more confident erring believer, but the poem rests on Clarel; even Rolfe's mentoring cannot inspire Clarel. Clarel is a problem, as is the poem; the question is whether to interpret failure as defeat or as an assertion of belief. Taylor's concept of wandering does not imply being lost, having no longer purpose, confidence, and faith visible; rather, being unable to find the way suggests there may not be a way. Getting lost, off the familiar, accepted, orthodox path has been a strategy for many to find their way back; being found or having found one's way has many religious sources and implications, and perhaps Clarel will find his way. In the meantime, he finds himself among Taylor's so-called marginal people who "constantly live on the border that both joins and separates belief and unbelief. They look yet do not find, search but do not discover. This failure, however, need not necessarily end the quest" (5). Clarel remains a nomad; he has no home, no one, and no God, but roams, strays, and drifts. Using Taylor's terminology (1984), Clarel becomes a man deep in "Nomad Thought" (13). As Taylor maintains, being a heretic is not to be fixed in his ways; it allows one to be "always in transition." It may seem haphazard and profane; however, this itinerant state of existence rescues Clarel from the profound depths of the abyss.

For Clarel, leading a roamer's life is not hopelessly in vain; the poem leaves an ambiguous possibility that hope is there, if only it can be found. Such potential can inspire excitement, movement, and a turn to God. It is philosophically and perhaps artistically pleasing. One can question, search, and attempt to answer for as long as one is able and strong enough. There is no need to settle or accept; one can remain on the quest indefinitely. It is a respectable position to maintain. One is seen as neither agnostic nor atheist; one is not necessarily a believer or doubter. It is even healthy to be occasionally skeptical of one's uncertainties. It is a young man's pursuit for those who have time to tackle duplicities, ambiguities, and even nihilism. However, for Melville, at age fifty-seven, is it as satisfying personally? John T. Shawcross argues that the temptation to hear Clarel's or even Melville's voice in the narrator of *Clarel* is irresistible; however, one must stand firm and not replace one for the other. It is not a harmonious blend, one is not a substation for the other. However, even Shawcross cannot abide by his own cautionary discourse: "The distance between the Clarel of Canto 34 and the narrative voice of Canto 35 is the difference between the Melville of the past and the Melville who has learned the efficacy of Conscience" (86). The problem Shawcross points to about critics fulfilling their image of Melville with the material in *Clarel* is also readily apparent in the splintered critical voice on the "final" meaning of *Billy Budd*. Critics desire a certain kind of Melville giving his last and definitive statement on good and evil, the individual, and the world. Twenty years earlier, Nathaniel Hawthorne recorded in his diary that Melville told him he had "'pretty much made up his mind to be annihilated'; but still he does not seem to rest in that anticipation" (651). In his last encounter with his friend, Melville still imagined himself— that is, according to Hawthorne— as a roamer: "It is strange how he persists — and has persisted ever since I knew him, and probably long before — in wandering to-and-fro over these deserts, as dismal and monotonous as the sand hills amid which we were sitting" (651). At fifty-two, Hawthorne does not share Melville's intensity or concern to pursue those unsolvable metaphysical crises, while at thirty-seven, Melville still had strength to chase after existential problems.

Does he retain that strength at fifty-seven? James Duban (1991) proposes that the "Epilogue" contains a "final utterance of hope" which must be understood by a Hawaiian expression for hope, *manaolana*. Duban suggests, "It is *manaolana*, or the *swimming thought*— faith floating and keeping its head aloft above water, when all the waves and billows are going over" (476). Duban's vision of Clarel/Melville in the ocean with his head above water symbolizing enduring faith, or faith abiding, is philosophically pleasing; however, it has the potential to end badly as it did for Pip. Ishmael is a rare case of the Melville protagonist maintaining faith despite the worst, and Clarel does not share his conviction, intensity, or confidence. It is far more difficult to account for Melville. Hilton Obenzinger is intrigued by Duban's proposition of "Hawaiian" hope, but as Obenzinger points out:

> As compassionate as is the appeal in the "Epilogue," the sudden appearance at the end of the poem of the "swimming thought" provides only the barest of life preservers. Ishmael at least can rely on the very materiality of Queequeg's coffin to keep him afloat, but Clarel is asked to grasp only the insubstantial "mind" of *manaolana* to keep himself above the stones of Judea. After the death of Ruth, after Clarel's curse upon the Jews, and after 149 cantos of anguish, *manaolana* seems small consolation, a flourish of stoic counterpoint at the very coda of textual instability" [78].

Has the death in 1867 of Malcolm, Melville's first-born son, emasculated or, to use Melville's own language, unmanned him? Has his own "swimming thought" saved him, or has he sunk to the bottom? Does Melville want to believe in the "Epilogue" of *Clarel*? Vincent Kenny (1986) says: "All of *Clarel* comes down to this dilemma: a wish to believe and an inability to find the way" (402). Does Melville want to find the way, or is he comfortable with his "rosary of doubt"? If Ruth is denied Clarel, perhaps God too is held back. Melville continues being the artist — while Hawthorne could not — he still continues to search, which is a kind of affirmation. The "Epilogue" does not restore or protect faith; it poses a challenge to maintain faith. Stan Goldman says, "The Epilogue of *Clarel* is a combination of the turn to and away from God, a combination of love and protest, a faith tinged with obstinacy: protest theism" (163). To abandon faith after such an emotionally draining journey (both physical and inward) is difficult to accept. Its ambiguity allows for a "stirring peroration" and profound melancholy and incompleteness; moreover, it seems Melville's indecisiveness — "He can neither believe, nor be comfortable in his unbelief" — will not allow for finality. Melville cannot come to terms with faith or incredulity, and the "Epilogue" offers both ways: belief and unbelief. As quoted by John T. Shawcross, Stephen C. Ausband and Susan Y. Lail note:

> [The "Epilogue"] offers the only kind of answer Melville could come to. Melville had wrestled with his own despair — over the inscrutable evil of the world, over human frailty, over the death of a son — and he had come to understand that the beauty of life cannot entirely be destroyed even in the despairing nineteenth century. Something remains, the heart. The beauty of human life is perennial, like the early-budding crocus. Belief in that beauty redeems us [71].

Both faith and skepticism are veiled, neither approach clarity or dominance; however, Melville confirms once again what he already knows: ambiguity reigns. There was no strong pressure on Melville to please the reading public and/or critics with *Clarel*; it was a small publication, financed largely by his uncle, and poetry of this magnitude never does well. As a result, Melville could take more liberties and risks, and feel less inhibited to reveal his desire to believe, and his inability to find a way that does not compromise his core values. *Billy Budd*, written in relative obscurity, will not have the pressure of contemporary audiences or reviewers, and its search for faith/doubt will be just as difficult to attain.

Billy Budd
Ode to Joy

One tends to search for finality, comprehensive meaning at the culmination of an artist's career, especially in a masterpiece like *Billy Budd*. The desire to find resolution and an acceptable or pleasing conclusion to a lifelong exploration of a theme sometimes can distract, mislead, or disappoint the critic, thus undermining the integrity of the art. A critic's need to achieve a conclusion truncates Melville's art, and abridges any kind of victory or defeat found there. Forcing a more pleasing finale to an artist's career reveals more about the reader's need for closure, order, and gratification. To reduce Melville's lifelong intensely emotional artistry to a single work or last struggle is to muffle Ahab, to ridicule Bartleby, or to dismiss Clarel. Melville himself struggled to achieve a satisfactory resolution. Nancy Ruttenberg argues that *Billy Budd*:

> categorically rejects precisely the type of either/or reading to which it has historically given rise in the still vital "acceptance" and "resistance" schools of *Billy Budd* criticism; instead it upholds an alternative to the various sacrificial solutions to the novel's paradoxes.... The novel offers Melville's retrospective and metaphorical account of his own professional failure, his inability or refusal even to dissemble the "innocence" that might have quieted critical fears of his lack of "veracity".... It is not that Melville denies innocence a place in human experience; rather, he refuses to sentimentalize it, acknowledging instead the destructive potentiality [87–8].

For an artist like Melville whose creative powers did not wane and whose artistry always displayed an ardent conscientiousness, old age and impending death can give the impression that the end is near and artistic consciousness is at its fullest, thus giving an artistic last will and testament seems imperative and logical; however, there is no apparent completion of the theme of boredom in *Billy Budd*. As was seen in "Bartleby, the Scrivener" and *Clarel*, Melville manages to find new, surprising, and mystical ways to examine the crisis of boredom. Melville's artistic representation of boredom has undergone a profound, involved, and subtle transformation in meaning and function. *Billy Budd* (posthumous, 1924), Melville's last work and indeed a masterpiece, does offer a hope not found in "Bartleby, the Scrivener" or *Clarel*. Although Billy must die given his nature, the circumstances of war, and the unprovoked enmity he inspires in Claggart, he is an ideal, an inspiring image, and an American hero. He lives on in the imagination, in the future, as Bartleby cannot. In this work, Melville offers a vision, a possibility of hope which transcends the overwhelming bleakness of "Bartleby, the Scrivener" and *Clarel*.

Over the course of his career as artist, the theme of boredom started as an indistinct and unconscious state of mind, and became a problem that encompasses multivalent issues and emergencies. Through his use of metaphysics and a heightening sense of questions concerning the meaning of life, Melville discovered that boredom is inescapable and perilous. Boredom is so entrenched and pervasive in man's existence, and so capable of darkening the very fabric of life darkened by its grayness and mustiness, that only a radical overturn of one's core values will forestall the descent into the void; the Lawyer from "Bartleby, the Scrivener" demonstrates this revolution of the spirit.

The problem for Melville's seafarers was how to escape the confinement of boredom; bound to their vessels, the only way out — aside from jumping ship — was to turn inward and ponder the significance of their lives. Of course, Melville's more intellectual and mature protagonists were better able to journey within, curbing their wilder, more reckless impulses toward action. Such responsibility and restraint are incredibly difficult even for Ishmael; Rolfe is a landlocked former mariner, and whatever strategies saved him from oblivion remain enticingly uncertain. The marriage at sea between the intellect and action is too ambiguous to earn unanimous praise. Granted, Tommo/Typee, White Jacket, Ishmael, and Rolfe, in varying degrees, survive their voyages, and all but Rolfe narrate first-hand their experiences of life at sea; however, not all are faithful to the life of the mind. The irritability, frustration, and numbness caused by boredom are so repugnant that the Melville oceanic hero is prepared in mind and by disposition to risk everything to deflect boredom's pull.

Melville's romanticism — his artistic tendency for his characters to evade full responsibility for their actions, thus gravitating toward willful naiveté, an utter and contemptible failure to use normal, healthy, and sensible rationality and perception — is a deep-rooted characteristic, and to resist its enchantment over him, Melville must, in effect, kill Billy Budd, the epitome of romanticism in his art — to free himself from it. Melville's romantic impulses are strong and determined, but his more pessimistic strains have become equally powerful, if not more so. The darker his material becomes, the less certain his faith in actions becomes; as his literary depiction of the journey inward eventually grows in permanence, stature, and command, his conception of boredom is shaped by his tragic vision. Melville's tragic vision — his artistic realization that his characters can no longer evade self-responsibility, indulge in reckless behavior, and persevere with an abiding faith in action alone, in which his darker, less forgiving and philosophical tendencies dominate — enables him to bear the emotional and creative costs not only to plumb the depths of boredom but also to impugn his most cherished literary assumptions and figures.

Billy Budd is the representation of Melville's esteemed literary values. Billy is an attempt to recapture the innocence, the idealized sense of self during those early experiences in the Pacific islands; however, as Tommo/Typee can only hint at, the narrator of *Billy Budd* emphasizes with tragic force the vulnerability of innocence. Melville's tragic vision has tempered his romantic one. It is painful, but he knows Billy must die; it hurts because Billy's execution is a kind of judgment on Melville's earlier self. Innocence is akin to recklessness. Anticipating Joseph Conrad's own artistic conflicts with a similar character type, Melville is setting the (final) staging between the exuberance of activity and sobriety of the mind. When consciousness comes, the glow of purity, guilelessness, and juvenescence dims, disappearing because innocence cannot last. Darkening this conflicting is war; it looms over individual dilemmas and all three men: Vere, Claggart, and Billy. The best that can be done is done, but Vere perishes. Claggart is a given as Satan is a given in Melville's literary world; it is there: a defect according to nature. Billy lives on in memory, but is guilty.

The crisis of boredom has become ever more perilous, and Melville's dramatization of it has remained just as complicated, unexpected, and subtle. Boredom no longer is an immediate dissatisfaction with the present; Melville's religious and existential motifs now are crucial factors in understanding the dynamics of boredom's deterioration of the self. The religious elements in *Billy Budd* reflect the influence and stature of the archetype of the Handsome Sailor; this sailor-hero is not only a working man's male ideal, he also, in Melville's depiction of him, combines almost divine qualities with the secular. In Melville's hands, the Handsome Sailor Billy Budd takes on profound social, moral, and religious significance; the blending of the secular and religious serves to bring together many diverse yet related existential concerns that broaden the theme of boredom in Melville's art. Melville's own personal religious doubts are a reflection of this complicated fusion of apparent opposites.

The problem of boredom in *Billy Budd* can be understood as a version of a secularized form of *acedia*. Acedia was one of the original deadly sins, and also was a forerunner of modern boredom. The medieval battle for the soul of the monk waged by the demon of noontide is in essence the war between good and evil (Budd versus Claggart). In Melville's more mature work, there seems to be a fragile balance between good and evil; however, in *Billy Budd*, Melville seems to suggest that his literary world is more Manichaean. To be more specific, Melville's dramatization of the clash between Budd and Claggart conveys a mutually negating collision; both the seaman and petty officer are destroyed. The tacit moral assumption shaping this work of art is also the tragic import of the novella: extreme good cannot coexist with radical evil. Good cannot overcome evil and endure without suffering severe blows; therefore, good is limited. Evil operates unrestrictedly, deforming or discoloring good, until it is undone by its own defects (according to nature) and even by the enviable virtues of Billy. The moral failings brought out by boredom take on ever more subtlety in *Billy Budd*.

Moreover, the inherent joy of life in Billy and the apparent joylessness in Claggart illustrate this particular secularized form of acedia functioning in the story. Billy's existence is free from this taint of joylessness; he is the Handsome Sailor. Claggart's cheerless and polluted existence is a reflection of the poisoned sources of life; he forever is doomed, the tragic consequence damning him and Billy to death. Without Vere's intervention and the crewmen's exaltation of Billy, the darkness of the joylessness that infects Claggart would be the underlying message of the novella; however, because of the last few chapters emphasizing Billy's goodness and stature, Melville intimates that goodness may prevail, that the joy de vivre can live on in memory. At the end, boredom's darkness is not utterly black. One does not see the abyss staring right back. If one perseveres, one can see the sparkles of hope.

Billy Budd

Billy Budd is shielded from boredom by his un–self-conscious joie de vivre. He approaches life simply and naturally. He is the human being in full glory without awareness of it; like a creature of nature, he is fully alive. The joy of life is not simply just to subsist, survive, it is to have life. It is not to be slowed down, hampered, or intimidated by life's destructive, ugly forces. It is to be. He is open to life's richness and beauty. This embrace of life is at the heart of Billy's heroic demeanor. The foretopman receives whatever comes into his life pleasantly and agreeably. Melville writes: "As to his enforced enlistment, that he seemed to take pretty much as he was wont to take any vicissitude of weather. Like the animals, though no philosopher, he was, without knowing it, practically a fatalist" (49). Ultimately his life is not in his own hands; he does not have choice, but is not fazed. His joie de vivre offsets any perceivable sting. Easy come, easy go. For Billy, life is full of surprises, which he enjoys. There is nothing harmful or potentially disastrous that he can see in his future. Billy forever is energetically optimistic, but dangerously so. He is in line with Tommo and other earlier Melville characters who lead reckless lives, lacking full consciousness. Whereas Tommo escapes death, Billy will not.

Consciousness or the lack of it shapes Melville's treatment of the joie de vivre. Would a thinking and speaking Billy still be the Handsome Sailor; would he still manage to live with the joy of life? The admirer of the Handsome Sailor may philosophize on Billy's existence, but to do so is already complicating and burdening his life. He just lives with it; he need not know it to enjoy it. He is unassuming and unreflective. A speaking and thinking Billy no longer would be who and what he is or how he lives his life. Billy is handsome, not only physically; he has moral beauty, which is a significant attribute everyone loves about him. And it is this moral beauty which matters more than his mere appearance. Those who respect him are drawn to his good nature, and he brings out the better half in his fellow sailors. The shipmaster of the *Rights-of-Man* describes Billy as "a Catholic priest striking peace in an Irish shindy. Not that he preached to them or said or did anything in particular; but a virtue went out of him, sugaring the sour ones" (47). Captain Graveling also adds that the crew "all love him" (47). Billy emanates a love that inspires fraternity and esteem. It is a love that is a joy to be around. By its very nature, the joy of life delights others. It is contagious, uplifting, and radiates affirmation. It promotes health, well-being. Billy even makes a bud out of Red Whiskers, the bully of the merchant ship. Although he must use force to make peace with the heckler, he nonetheless is called the "peacemaker" (47).

Billy enjoys his life, and loves fulfilling his duty, reveling with his friends off-duty, and delighting in the advantages of being the Handsome Sailor. Commanding almost universal respect and love, he leads a carefree existence out at sea. This is not to say that Budd is indolent, neglectful, or shiftless; on the contrary, he is rated as an able seaman, the highest of three classes for crewmen; as Melville points out, the Handsome Sailor was "invariably a proficient in his perilous calling, he was also more or less a mighty boxer or wrestler. It was strength and beauty" (44). I agree with Harrison Hayford and Merton M. Sealts when they say in their "Notes & Commentary" to their edition of *Billy Budd, Sailor*: "Critics of the novel have tended to overlook Billy's manly strength and skill while emphasizing such attributes as his beauty and his childlike simplicity — perhaps taking too literally his nickname 'Baby' (Leaf 112). His 'important variations' from the typical Handsome Sailor (Leaf 10) were certainly not shortcomings in professional aptitude and proficiency" (139). Billy's strength and beauty are manifestations of the joie de vivre; he is the embodiment of health, contentedness, and valor. Even Captain Vere "had thought of recommending him to the executive officer for promotion" (95). Relaxed in attitude, but always aware of his obligations, Billy is Melville's idealized hero. The countless biblical and mythological allusions bolster his qualities, and add another dimension to his joie de vivre. So few have the joy of life that Billy seems otherworldly.

Billy's beauty is a type that cannot be described adequately, but it has a palpable impact on the viewer. Billy's "significant personal beauty" (77) ignites Claggart's natural depravity, but it is not sexual in nature. Melville writes that Claggart's envy and antipathy "partakes nothing of the sordid or sensual" (76). Claggart and Budd's relationship lacks any explicit dimension of the sexual, but I agree that there is a vague, formless undercurrent of the homo-erotic. Eve Kosofsky Sedgwick argues that Claggart is homosexual (92), and that his depravity is perverted because of his "homosexuality" (96). Kosof-sky Sedgwick claims that *Billy Budd* is a dangerous book to come with questions about the essential nature of men's desires for men, since those desires could go either way (94). In spite of this premise, such impulses do not over-whelm Claggart. He is supremely self-controlled, calculating, and secretive. He is a man of intellect, and the sexual element is raised to a high aesthetic level, like the connoisseur appreciating the painting of a nude. The narrator reports that Captain Vere "had congratulated Lieutenant Ratcliffe upon his good fortune in lighting on such a fine specimen of the *genus homo*, who in the nude might have posed for a statue of young Adam before the Fall" (94). Vere has no sexual desire (conscious or unconscious) for Billy; his appreciation and love for the foretopman is asexual, even fatherly. Vere admires Billy's physicality like the fan appreciating the athlete. As Melville writes, "Claggart's was no vulgar form of the passion" (77).

While a source for good, Billy's strong life force and his nautical stature do limit him. Our admiration goes so far. Fundamental flaws such as his stunted consciousness (not a thinker or speaker and his naiveté) and uncon-trollable violence (the beating he gave Red Whiskers and death blow to Clag-gart) darken and mold his otherwise outstanding characteristics. When one thinks of Billy in his better light, there is an understandable propensity to overlook and disregard his defects and crimes; like the members of the drum-head court, one chooses to concentrate on his good cheer, looks, and inno-cence. The court officers try desperately to save Billy; they are willing to neglect their duty, and, in essence, commit treason. Nonetheless, trying to save Billy is trying to save themselves, ourselves, to prevent evil from winning, to preserve the joie de vivre. The law must be upheld, and no dangerous precedent must develop to complicate and worsen the atmosphere of mutiny already brewing.

Not only does he voice the court's aversion to execute Billy, he speaks ours as well. Vere too expresses compassion for Billy. He would like to save Billy just as much as the members of the drumhead court. He even admits that it is natural to feel this way. But what is unnatural for Vere, a military officer, is to be overruled by emotion. An officer's duty is his allegiance to his King; Vere and his staff are bound by their oath to preserve the King's order. As are the epaulets of his subordinates wear, Vere's buttons are daily and real reminders that he and his men are not free and natural men. They belong to the King. They chose to be officers. They sought their own commissions. Once accepting their positions in the Royal Navy, they no longer are ordinary subjects or free men. They must obey — that's an order. In an age after the Nuremberg Trials, such views are perceived suspiciously. Many readers who despise Vere renounce him for his cold, inhuman rhetoric and adherence to obedience and conformity. But these critics ignore Vere's moral crisis dealing with Billy's case. As commanding officer, he must maintain order, and set the example for his men to follow. His duty is not to please his men; his task and purpose is to lead them in battle. Vere never says that his adherence to duty (and law) is easy.

If Vere were truly tyrannical and stony hearted, then why would he carefully and slowly explain to his staff why it must be so and later to Billy? As the highest-ranking officer, his word is law, but he does not abuse this position. He wants his men to understand. He is not obligated by duty to do so, and yet he feels he must; he is compelled by morality to do so. He is a teacher, and the lessons seem profound and complex because they go against their nature and ours. They are not to concern themselves with innocence in abstract, metaphysical terms; they are not God on Judgment Day. Nor are they judges in civilian courts. They are who they are — according to their natures — and they must behave as they are — according to their natures. His commitment to instruct these men suggests a higher and nobler motive, and it also implies that in a way he is not just bound by the King. He seems to have found a way to accept the dictates of his position with his conscience; however, I am not saying that he approves or endorses it privately.

This court-martial has nothing to do with justice or morality, and to say this is not a condemnation of Vere. It is a time of war, and, during war, discipline must be kept at all costs. Vere sympathizes in a fatherly way with

Budd's fate; however, as Vere says, "Though as their fellow creatures some of us may appreciate their position, yet as navy officers what reck we of it? Still less recks the enemy" (112). This case is before the Nuremberg Trials; to modern eyes and ears, Vere's defense of the system may be considered damnable. However, it is a time of massive nineteenth-century revolutions, which threaten the stability of England, and the *Bellipotent* is not the *Rights-of-Man*. The law must be carried out, even for Billy, the same Billy who was pampered onboard the *Rights-of-Man*.

Billy's sense of personal responsibility is undimmed. He is unconscious of his own limitations and existence; in fact, he is oblivious to such questions. What need would prompt him to even ask? What would he ask and how? What would he say? How would he understand? Would what he found darken his sunny disposition? Would he still be the Handsome Sailor? No, and his joie de vivre would suffer. Whatever thinking he does is limited to shipboard activity. Based upon what he knows, his range of experience is narrow, and his will is weak; he rarely, if ever, exercises it. Because his faculties are unsubstantial, he has little volition. He lacks deliberateness in creating and managing events. Experience is created for him; he is passive. His attitude is happy-go-lucky. Free of worry and effort, he is bound or hemmed in by fate. He does not even complain.

The naïve, romantic, and adolescent streak common in a young man, a would-be "adventurer" who recognizes the rather pedestrian, uneventful tone of his own life, which composes at the same time his innocence, is the real danger facing Billy. Old Dansker calls Billy "Baby" (70), an apt way of understanding him; Billy is like an infant: powerless, helpless, and immature. Such faults undermine Billy's sense of personal responsibility. The pampering, like a spoiled child, he received on the *Rights-of-Man* (47) only stresses his quality of unpreparedness. This spirit of the perennial young man who cannot mature is also found, for example, in Shakespeare's *Romeo and Juliet*: they cannot grow old and cannot maintain the intensity of their love. Furthermore, Conrad's *Lord Jim* (1900) and *Nostromo* (1904) portray male characters that remain, in essence, adolescent.

The joy of life cannot shield Billy from human wickedness and does not save him during his trial. Although his demeanor is sweet and gentle for the most part, strong, adversarial stimuli unleash his powerful and deadly nature. His stutter is symbolic of his insufficiency dealing with intellectual matters, and is representative of the fundamental American resort to violence. Although found on a doorstep in Bristol, England, there is no evidence to suggest Billy is British by birth. Given his inclination to violence and inability to vocalize, his "defects" suggest American characteristics. His stammering is a kind of violence. It intensifies his violent, unconscious behavior. The less he is able to control himself or speak, the less he belongs on the ship or in this world. As Claggart abuses him, he becomes less and less the Handsome Sailor. The joy of life leaves Billy, and he becomes less than ordinary; he loses his ennobling qualities. He no longer is the "peacemaker." With the devilish accusation leveled against him, so shamed, humiliated in front of the man he loves (Vere), Billy cannot deal with Claggart's profound violation. He is overwhelmed by the sheer evil of Claggart's accusation which is indicative of his inexperience.

Violence is Billy's only recourse. He sees nothing morally wrong with using his fist. Ironically, it is how he makes peace with Red Whiskers on the merchant ship. Violence is his way of dealing with confusion, conflict, and uncertainty; no matter how virtuous Billy may be, his potential for violence, and hence criminality, is real. One must not forget, ignore, or downplay that Billy indeed attacked an officer. In the grip of uncontrollable passion, Billy becomes blank and numb, and is unaware of his deadly blow against Claggart.

Billy is morally outraged by Claggart's treachery and his anger triggers a bout of stuttering. As he tries to explain, it only worsens his speech patterns, frustrates him, and makes him angrier. The stuttering is his only expression of his moral outrage, and is an extension of his inexperience in life; his only answer to an accusation, insult, or confrontation is the fist. The angrier he gets, the more he feels defiled, and he feels less and less in control; his disbelief, in essence a kind of disillusionment — as if to say, "How could the master-at-arms say that of me, the Handsome Sailor?" — is characteristic of his unpreparedness. His stammer is crucially symbolic of his immaturity. This faltering of words normally occurs in young children, as speech is developing and as consciousness is maturing; Billy unfortunately is a "Baby."

When he tries to speak or think, only violence (vocal and physical) unfolds; for Billy to articulate or reflect is an act of violence. Aggression is far easier than to find the words. Violence is natural for Billy; his striking fist is an automatic response to confusion. He does not think when he uses force. How would Billy learn to avoid succumbing to violence when other alternatives (e.g., speaking out) are unavailable? And when those substitutes are impossible, what could he do? When he does try to talk, it only shows how unrealistic that possibility is. His speech is violent as is his action. Billy can control neither one. When Vere attempts to calm Billy so that he can find the words, using "words so fatherly in tone" (99), Billy was touched, and it "prompted yet more violent efforts at utterance — efforts soon ending for the time in confirming the paralysis, and bringing to his face an expression which was as a crucifixion" (99). For Billy to think is to be put on display, to be cruelly humiliated because he cannot do it. His flaws are exposed in front of his beloved Captain. The longer he struggles, the more he looks like an unhandsome fool.

Becoming uncomfortable with himself during his court-martial, Billy wrestles with the guilt of not reporting his incident with a suspicious afterguardsman. Questioned about his possible knowledge of mutiny, Billy's "reply lingered" (106), meaning he stammered. Even when his life is at stake, the ugliness of being a rat deters him from answering truthfully. The stuttering is an expression of guilt, of being caught, and of moral self-judgment. He knows he has done wrong. He fails to realize that he already is condemned to death — striking and killing an officer. He does not understand he already is in trouble. His real fear is being punished for withholding his knowledge of potential mutiny when he first came across it, not for Claggart's death. He is protecting another criminal, one potentially fomenting real discontent and rebellion; he is unknowingly to himself or the court incriminating himself.

The officers of the drum court take for granted Billy's speech impediment. As he was unable to answer Claggart's insidious suggestion, they seem to accept Billy's present difficulty as being just as understandable. They do not believe themselves that Billy could be involved; after all, he is the simple Handsome Sailor. So, in a sense, Claggart was right in describing Billy as he does to Vere: "You have but noted his fair cheek. A mantrap may be under the ruddy-tipped daisies" (94). Billy's clash of values — obeying his captain versus protecting his fellow bluejacket — indicates how unsuited and unprepared he is to deal with evil. Like a child who lies to his parent to avoid disfavor, Billy lies about his knowledge of mutiny.

Billy feels no moral anguish over killing the master-at-arms. Stammering, he tells the court officers that he is "sorry that he [Claggart] is dead. I did not mean to kill him. Could I have used my tongue I would not have struck him. But he foully lied to my face and in presence of my captain, and I had to say something, and I could only say it with a blow" (106). Guilt involves a sense of punishment over real or imagined wrongdoing. Billy feels no guilt about killing Claggart; yes, he feels regret that he is responsible, but experiences no moral torment. His sense of violation, of embarrassment, and of dishonor annuls his sense of culpability. In his mind, Claggart is the one who committed a crime, not he. He feels personally disgusted that the man who considered him to be a categorically decent man could make such a charge; in essence, Billy cannot accept that Claggart could be malicious. He takes for granted that as the Handsome Sailor, everyone will love him and treat him well; even Red Whiskers melted and embraced him. Claggart is different, and a part of Billy's mistake is to think that the master-at-arms is like everyone else. Billy considered Claggart's "manner rather queer at times. That was all" (88). As Claggart reveals his other, more sinister side to Billy, Billy sees it as an offense, injustice, and that the master-at-arms somehow is guilty; Claggart is lying. Billy has fulfilled his duty and obeyed his superiors: "I have eaten the King's bread and I am true to the King" (106).

But is Billy completely honest? Has he been true to the King? Billy refuses out of principle ("it would savor overmuch of the dirty work of a telltale" [85]) to report his knowledge of potential mutiny brewing onboard. As Melville writes, "It was his duty as a loyal bluejacket to report in the proper quarter" (85). He is guilty by implication; by not informing what transpired between he and the mysterious afterguardsman who tried to entice him with two guineas to join a supposed conspiratorial coup, he is guilty of mutiny. Claggart's indictment of Billy participating in a plot is accurate. A Handsome Sailor would not rat and therefore betray his fellow sailor, even if it is an afterguardsman. His heroic role involves honor, which seems far stronger than allegiance to the crown; his loyalty is closer to his crewmate than the royal seat. Unknowingly he is undone by his own sailor ethics. His silence or rather not saying anything about this intrigue is akin to his difficulty speaking during his confrontation with Claggart. By not speaking, he does not understand he is in jeopardy, and by not telling, he is doomed. Being challenged as never before, Billy barely scolds the stranger for his insult, stammering a warning to leave him; he is unprepared to deal with such evil intentions. Ironically, the Forecastleman, a fellow foretopman as Billy, chides him: "And is that all you did about it, Foretopman?" (83) for letting the stranger off easy. Even Old Dankster often repeats his warning that Claggart is "*down* on you" (85).

Claggart

Claggart's despair as expressed by his "envy and antipathy" (77) is a kind of secular acedia, a profound joylessness of life itself. Billy's sources of life/joy are Claggart's sources of hopelessness/misery. Claggart hates Billy not only because he was young and hale and an ideal mariner, but also because "the spirit lodged within Billy" (78); this is not the spirit in a religious sense, but rather the spirit of ease with which Billy's lives his life, an existence in which he does not struggle, doubt, or protest. Every aspect of his life is a joy; everything comes to him naturally. Describing Claggart's reaction to Billy, Melville writes:

> If askance he eyed the good looks, cheery health, and frank enjoyment of young life in Billy Budd, it was because these went along with a nature

that, as Claggart magnetically felt, had in it simplicity never willed malice or experienced the reactionary bite of that serpent. To him, the spirit lodged within Billy, and looking out from his welkin eyes as from windows, that ineffability it was which made the dimple in his dyed cheek, suppled his joints, and dancing in his yellow curls made him pre-eminently the Handsome Sailor [78].

Billy's freedom is marked by a total lack of reserve and unpleasantness, and a sincerity distinguished by an absence of artificiality and deceit. He is what he is; there is no façade. The thrill of life pulses throughout his body. In contrast, Claggart's excitement for life has been dulled. Billy and Claggart are opposites. The "man of sorrows" (88) "saw the charm of it [Billy's joie de vivre], the courageous free-and-easy temper of it, and fain would have shared it, but he despaired of it" (78). There is still a part in Claggart that would join with Billy, and take pleasure in life. In spite of that potential to share life joys, it is not enough. Claggart's darker, more sinister disposition is so entrenched in his nature that he is powerless to resist. There is an urge to be like Billy: "to be nothing more than innocent" (78), but an opposing passion to destroy him overrides it. To be like Billy would mean to master his nature; to live like Billy would require Claggart to counterbalance his utter discontent with life. How would a man like Claggart change his nature? Would he allow himself to change? Melville's conservative outlook foresees no such chance, and it is this disposition toward the impossibility for change that shapes his tragic vision. There is no remedy, no chance for either Budd or Claggart. They are what they are. Claggart is aware of this, and it is this awareness that wounds him, keeping him miserable. Claggart is resigned to his joylessness.

The more Billy acts like himself and the more he radiates his joie de vivre, the more Claggart gives in to his joylessness. By being near Billy, Claggart becomes enraged, knowing he cannot be otherwise than himself. By watching the Handsome Sailor enjoy himself and life, Claggart plunges deeper into his abyss. Billy's smiles elicit "incipient feverish tears" (88) in Claggart; Billy's good cheer saddens him. He himself smiles to Billy, but it is an expression of profound grief. "To be nothing more than innocent" (78) tortures Claggart; it is a kind of self-punishment that pits Billy against himself as well as Claggart against himself. And he uses Billy as an instrument of affliction to tear himself apart. Every gesture and laugh cuts him; every time Billy is in the center of attention, he feels slighted, wronged. Of course, Billy is doing no such thing, but in Claggart's mind, it does not matter. He views Billy as his source of despair.

Unlike Billy, Claggart knows the difference between good and evil, and chooses evil. Thomas Hove takes a slightly different view on Claggart, saying, "his "elemental evil" is simply a more powerful kind of energy than his relatively low degree of natural virtue.... What makes him tragic is not some inner conflict between a lesser spiritual good and a more powerful bodily evil. Instead, his tragedy lies in a distribution of energies that threatens his physical and psychological well-being, and in his unfortunate placement within a situation that brings forth these harmful energies." There is an element of willpower involved so that "it is protectively secretive, which is much as to say it is self-contained" (76). It is more insidious, treacherous because "it folds itself in the mantle of respectability" (75); Claggart disguises his immorality in a mask of virtue or seeming cooperation. He hides his true nature, which is depraved: "Natural Depravity: a depravity according to nature" (75). This condition is existential in the sense that Claggart recognizes his malicious nature and acts upon it, chooses to be what he is by nature. One could in these circumstances suppress one's impulses (willpower) and try to act in a conventional, decent way; Claggart prefers not to. He can "direct a cool judgment sagacious and sound" (76). I tend to agree with Thomas Hove's claim that Claggart lacks self-control in any traditional sense. The master-at-arms is in control of his mind.

Claggart's hints of nobility are already in decay. Claggart is not physically infirm or lacking in energy. He is a man doomed to unhappiness. Claggart is a man deprived — his life force dimmed, the joy of life forever out of his reach, even as he recognizes and appreciates it in Billy. Claggart is spiritually sick, but he could live out his allotted years. Budd's virtues, exemplified in his optimistic nature, youthful invigoration, and spiritual innocence, are Billy's sources of life which Claggart lacks. Claggart identifies some past and lost beauty in himself that he sees in Billy that painfully reminds him of the larger, richer human being (lofty, noble, courageous, loved) that he might have been or become. Such a daily reminder must be destroyed. This sign of envy also appears in Shakespeare's *Othello*, when Iago says of Cassio, "[He] hath a daily beauty in his life / That makes me ugly" (V.i.19–20). Tracing this insight, Hayford and Sealts have noted that similar expressions of envious aggression appear in earlier Melville works: Jackson from *Redburn* and Radney from *Moby-Dick* ("The Town-Ho's Story").

He is constantly stung by the richness and beauty of Billy. He is driven like Milton's Satan to make Billy fall as Adam and Eve; he is driven like Shakespeare's Iago to see Billy humiliated, defeated. He must be victorious; he must put down Billy.

In *Paradise Lost*, Milton crafts scenes of Satan admiring Eve's beauty even though he knows he must destroy her that remind one of Claggart looking on Billy admiringly and enviously. Claggart's traits imply a sort of beauty that has lost its wholesomeness and vitality. Having once been handsome himself—physically and morally—but now living in a state of decline and unfitness, Claggart is like Satan who cannot regain that glowing beauty that once was. Physical unattractiveness manifests itself metaphysically. It is the same technique used in characterizing Billy, only in reverse. Moral comment is implied in Claggart; Melville writes:

> His brow was of the sort phrenologically associated with more than average intellect; silken jet curls partly clustering over it, making a foil to the pallor below, a pallor tinged with a faint shade of amber akin to the hue of time-tinted marbles of old. This complexion, singularly contrasting with the red or deeply bronzed visages of the sailors, and in part the result of his official seclusion from the sunlight, though it was not exactly displeasing, nevertheless seemed to hint of something defective or abnormal in the constitution and blood [64].

It is not exactly an illness, but it is deleterious, nauseating, and poisonous. It is a nature depraved. Claggart cannot change his nature, as Satan, and, at this stage in his artistic career, Melville does not believe in reform; Melville is a conservative. The longstanding thesis that Melville is a rebel to the end must be qualified, if not negated. As Melville explores the nature of Claggart and even of both Budd and Vere, one begins to discern that Melville is not breaking with tradition or opposing authority; instead, Melville seems to surrender to the limits of possibility. Fixed in his ways, uneager to break from his ways, Claggart illustrates the depth of Melville's conservatism. Morally corrupt—a defect according to nature—Claggart prefers not to. Figures in Melville's art rarely change, and, particularly in *Billy Budd*, change is not an option. Melville's coming to terms with the nature of evil in large part determines the plot of the novella; this moral reckoning always has shaped Melville's art. Especially from *Typee, White-Jacket, Moby-Dick,* and now through *Billy Budd*, Melville cannot find resolution to the problem.

Vere

Melville's treatment of Billy all along has been highly symbolic such that the idea, content of Billy—his joy of life—suffers a defeat. However, with Vere's fatherly involvement after the verdict, Billy regains his heroic and joyous stature; in fact, because of Vere's tutorial, Billy becomes larger than life, and lives on in the hearts of men. Billy can only learn or grasp so much. How might Billy have gone to his death if Vere had not spoken to him privately, tenderly, and compassionately? Vere is not afraid of life, which James F. Farnham believes (364), but is drawn to it, drawn to Billy. There is no legal or naval justification for the Captain to be the one to inform Billy of the court's decision. He has taken an interest in Billy and has feelings for the sailor, which would be unusual for any high-ranking officer. An earlier example of this unusual precedent appears in *White-Jacket*. Jack Chase, a Handsome Sailor, speaks freely with his Captain. If Billy were a valet and worked for him, then it would be understandable. It is not Vere's role as commander to speak directly to Budd. Vere wants to tell Billy and is moved to spend time with him. Joseph Conrad in *Heart of Darkness* also has Marlow report, not dramatize, what Kurtz had taught him before he dies. Quite possibly, this episode in *Billy Budd* is yet another indication of Melville's anticipation of modernism. Melville gives the end result of Billy acting upon what he has learned from Vere, what Vere already persuaded his court officers and more in a way so that Billy could understand. The evidence that Billy has absorbed and lives out Vere's lessons is shown in Vere's behavior after the talk. Melville writes:

> The first to encounter Captain Vere in act of leaving the compartment was the senior lieutenant. The face he beheld, for the moment one expressive of the agony of the strong, was to that officer, though a man of fifty, a startling revelation. That the condemned one suffered less than he who mainly had effected the condemnation was apparently indicated by the former's exclamation in the scene soon perforce to be touched upon [115].

Vere's interview helps to stem mutiny. Billy does not slip or resist when he walks toward the noose. The moral necessity of punishment and the moral quality in Billy help both to keep mutiny at bay (the men repeat Budd's benediction, and obey orders thereafter) and to justify Vere. During the hanging, Vere is stiff and numb; in public, he does not become emotional, personal and does not break order.

It seems that Melville understands — and fights against — that to keep Billy's essential nature (without consciousness), the nature Melville loves, means that Billy cannot attain tragic stature. Melville insists on treating his material as tragic; in his own words, he envisages it as tragic. Billy enacts a tragic part in a tragedy, despite the apparent lack of quality of mind, the absence or weakness of his analytical or critical faculty. One key element of Melville's tragic vision is the need for great issues to inspire it. As Arthur Miller will promote in his essays on tragedy, even the common sailor can become a tragic figure: "Down among the groundlings, among the beggars and rakers of the garbage, profound passion is enacted" (35). Nonetheless, it is not enough. Melville recognizes the limitations of Billy's type (the Handsome Sailor) at the same time he wants to raise Billy to a higher standing.

Melville does want Billy to develop morally — which means to gain consciousness — but Melville is aware that thought itself is foreign, even deleterious to Billy. Hence, the important scene between Budd and Vere preceding the execution is important. A moral change seems to take place in Billy before us after that dialogue. Billy is not angry, resentful, or scheming; he is at peace. He is once again the "Peacemaker," the Handsome Sailor when he dies. He becomes a legend.

It must have been enormously challenging for Vere to discuss life and death matters with Billy. Vere had noted that his very own officers who led the drumhead court were limited in many ways. Once again, it must be said that Vere had to remind his officers of their basic functions as officers: loyalty to the crown and the necessities of war. Military ethics are different from civilian ethics, and more so when an artist dramatizes them in fiction. They are no longer men; they are transformed from ordinary men to subjects (objects) of the King. In the world of *Billy Budd*, one loses practically all choice and individuality when one dons the uniform. There are to be no exceptions; order must be preserved at all costs. Everything must appear in order, or else the men "would think that we flinch, that we are afraid of them — afraid of practicing a lawful rigor singularly demanded at this juncture" (113); Vere says, the crewmen "are familiar with our naval usage and tradition; and how would they take it" (112) if there were no punishment. The very nature of the system depends on it; chaos will rule. Melville notes, "Every sailor, too, is accustomed to obey orders without debating them" (87). An order is an order, and a precedent is a huge disrupter. Everything is set so that it is predictable and standardized. Vere believes in forms because they are "everything" (128). Personal feelings indicate weakness, and at a time when the Nore mutiny weakened the Navy, Vere cannot afford another; he certainly does not want to be another captain to fall victim and be humiliated by a rebellious crew.

Eventually the court officers grasped Vere's points — there was little time to begin with, given that French warships are nearby (112). Therefore, it required exceptional patience and understanding for Vere to explain difficult concepts in a simple manner quickly. Billy is not guileful or ironic; he is straightforward. Politics looms over everything, and larger forces shadow Vere and Budd; unfortunately but necessarily, they are the pawns on the King's chessboard. Why would Vere even bother to explain matters with Billy if he did not take interest in him? Why struggle to find the words, phrases so that Billy will understand? Billy depends upon Vere. Billy must die, but, with Vere's tutelage, he can die well.

It is then a test of moral strength for Vere and Billy: for Vere, a test of eloquence and concern, and for Budd, a test of self-esteem and courage. And each man succeeds and is able to face the inevitable. And each man's face tells how he has succeeded: "That the condemned one suffered less than he who mainly had effected the condemnation was apparently indicated" (115). The moral costs are high for Vere. I agree when Roger Shattuck raises an important point when defending Vere from the critical assaults on Melville's fictional character. Shattuck says, "It is essential to point out that the novel does *not* say: choose one interpretation or the other. Even Captain Vere, whom it is easy to see as an inflexible, unsympathetic martinet, knows that the situation is more complex than his official conduct can acknowledge.... Vere represents the attempt of an upright and intelligent man to come to terms with the intellectual currents of the nineteenth century: irreligion, science, evolution, democracy. The circumstances of Billy's court martial tax Vere to the limit" (432). He has ventured, risked his own well-being so that Billy can maintain his own; Vere sacrificed himself for Billy. It is not guilt or remorse that causes affliction for Vere; it is the pain of loss. I disagree with James F. Farnham's claim that "the death of Claggart is ultimately more disturbing to Vere's sense of himself and to his overall understanding of life than is the sacrificial death of Billy, even though Vere rejects Claggart emotionally. Vere seems to have more of himself at stake in Claggart's death than in Billy's, for he identifies more closely with the master-at-arms, whose role it is to enforce the law, than he does with the innocent victim of the law" (365). Unable as commander to save Billy's life, Vere as concerned individual rescues Billy from fear, confusion, and chaos. Vere's utter exhaustion testifies his own selflessness and commitment. His anguish is not crocodile tears; it is genuine grief. Vere's dying words — Billy's name — also speak his pain. Vere suffers the agonizing death that would have been Billy's: a restless, torturing death. Billy dies in peace. This sense of salvation is a Melvillean motif: Queequeg dies for Ishmael. Bartleby suffers and dies so the Lawyer can live.

A redeeming outcome of Vere's interview is the reemergence of Budd's joie de vivre. Facing impending death, Billy now glows as he always had; not conquered by guilt or fear, Billy is himself. He is carefree and vibrant. Melville notes, "Through the rose-tan of his complexion no pallor could have shown" (119). In his own way, Billy has come to understand why he must die — he has gained a level of consciousness. Melville earlier had described Billy's reaction to his impressments as happy-go-lucky. Billy's previous attitude toward fate was romantic and childish; he accepted whatever befell him. It would have been out of his nature to question. Nothing at that point could dampen his spirit. On the eve of his execution, he also yields to fate — he really has no choice — but has embraced it. He is at one with himself. Suffering and despair would have been Billy's fate, had been his fate, before Vere intervened. Whatever Vere had said clearly was unequivocal, gentle, and responsive. If Vere had not interposed, Billy surely would have died without courage. He would not have become a legend — an ideal, inspiring image, and American hero.

As a result Billy lives on in the imagination, in the future, as neither Ishmael nor Bartleby can. Melville offers a vision, a possibility which transcends the overwhelming bleakness of *Pierre* and *The Confidence-Man*; *Billy Budd* offers a hope not found in the earlier work. The immortality of art and a kind of religious vision subdue and redeem the growing tragic vision in the work; the joie de vivre can neutralize the inherent sadness of life. Life is not utterly bleak; there is something still to think about, assuaging the pain of life. Even though Billy deserves death, Billy is kept alive in art, and is passed on in memory. The reader comes to share in Billy's joie de vivre again; the reader remembers Billy's best qualities.

Vere's tangible success as teacher is Billy's peaceful sleep before execution. The glow of being the Handsome Sailor, of having the joie de vivre, has returned. Billy is Billy again but with a difference: birth of consciousness. Because Billy can sleep, it means that he is at peace, unafraid of his impending fate. It is not the exhausted sleep of despair; it is a safe, comforting, and deep sleep. Even in sleep, the joy of life is in evidence:

> Without movement, he lay in a trance, that adolescent expression previously noted as his taking on something akin to the look of a slumbering child in the cradle when the warm hearth-glow of the still chamber at night plays on the dimples that at whiles mysteriously forms in the cheek, silently coming and going there. For now and then in the gyved one's trance a serene happy light born of some wandering reminiscence or dream would diffuse itself over his face, and then wane away only anew to return [119–20].

Handsome is as Handsome does. Nothing can provoke or disturb that inner peace now; he is content and ready. Even the chaplain realizes that he can offer Billy nothing. The man of God realizes that catechism would be inappropriate for Billy. The clergyman is not pedantic or single-minded (narrowminded). I imagine the man of the cloth as living out Christ's lesson on following the Spirit of the Law rather than the Letter of the Law. It would be easy to overwhelm, shame, and terrify Billy. Instead, the priest shows restraint. In this manner, he and Vere are similar; they understand Billy's nature, and know they must speak and act accordingly. These men know that Budd committed a crime; however, they know too that he is innocent — according to his nature. They understand that his innocence is of a different sort, one not tainted by legal and military codes. As Melville writes, "since he felt that innocence was even a better thing than religion wherewith to go to Judgment, he reluctantly withdrew" (121). The joy of life will see Billy through. Religious matters — dealing with the metaphysical — are supercilious compared to the power of the inner life force.

The lasting (and ultimately the last) effect of Vere's words for Billy is Billy's own last words. Although in every other instance being a common sarcastic denunciation of the captain, Billy's final utterance signifies the high spirits that dwell in him. The threat of mutiny finally suppressed, a religious service follows after Budd's funeral. Both the execution and religious ceremony return order — form — to the crew. Vere's adage on forms emphasizes the necessity of routine, meaning, and rule. Without these standards, chaos rages. It is a time of war, which means disorder threatens all the time. What is to protect, defend against formlessness? If what seems to the drumhead court — average minds — as a harsh and unjust enforcement of the law is really what preserves the crew and officers from self-destruction. The law is the only means to save this limited, flawed system, and is the only available (viable) way to keep order; it is the best that Vere has at his disposal. It may not satisfy or please everyone. Even Vere himself does not like the brutality and objectivity of it, but far worse forces are on the horizon: French warships are on the prowl. For Vere the French Revolution is utter chaos. Enforced obedience holds the line and a quick order quells any "uncertain movement among the men" (127). The chaplain too with his "customary morning service" serves a vital component to maintain order. An unlikely duo, war and religion serve each other. God ultimately may not intervene or rule in this world, but the system of faith is obligatory to prevent full-out destruction. The military drum keeps the rhythm for the sacred music.

The warship *Athee* epitomizes the anarchy, formlessness of the French Revolution. Jean-Luc Nancy adds, "A ship called the *Athee* (the *Atheist*) leaves no room for doubt: the tragedy of Billy is that of Christ in a world without God — and perhaps, by that token, the tragedy of an art whose very art abandons it to the hatred of the world" (15). Its name suggests that rebellion is a denial of God. Mutiny disrupts order, as does the revolution as it ushers in chaos. Melville's implicit view of the Revolution implies an unfavorable one; he seems to consider it to be a hostile, treacherous, and nihilistic force. It eradicates the old order, but fails to replace it with a viable and methodic ruling system. Instead, it pulls society toward the destructive heart of hell. Without Law and God, the ultimate Lawgiver, man loses all restraint. The *Athee*, *Devastation*, and *Erebus* are the great destructive evils in the world warring against the principles of God, peace, and order. Anarchy and meaningless-ness are to be prevented at all costs. Vere in effect is killed by chaos, godlessness; however, without Vere, the *Bellipotent* does defeat the *Athee*. Order eventually overcomes formlessness. Vere's conviction about order becomes a profession of faith.

Vere's dying words, Billy's name, are prayer-like. They carry a religious emotional blessing in Billy's memory. His name will live on in legend, focusing on his goodness. It is the only lasting and sturdy offering to compensate for the false and libelous report implicating Billy as a vicious criminal. That the naval chronicle transforms Claggart into an innocent victim and Budd as a ruthless ringleader (Melville's original conception of Billy) demonstrates that the world distorts and perverts man. Truth becomes something worse than just relative; it can become meaningless. Not only is Melville motioning to the modern world but also a post-modern one. Billy's truer nature is memorialized in the closing ballad, and so Melville sees hope on the horizon; that Billy lives on in the imagination, art as a hero, the American Christ-like hero, stops the pull toward the abyss if the novel were to end immediately following his execution. Melville achieves muted victory, partial faith in the backdrop of a devastating skepticism. To believe, and not to believe: yes.

Conclusion

While few critics have noted in passing how many of Melville's characters seem bored, this project places boredom at the very center of Melville's philosophic musings and creative productions. Boredom is not simply a passing phase, but a growing and detrimental threat to most Melvillean protagonists. It encompasses deep psychological and ethical questions which, in his later art, fuse with the religious and theological. In his earlier art, Melville's own reliance on ill-defined and illusory expressions for boredom suggests his own hesitant and unsure understanding of boredom in his early artistic career. Only when he seizes upon boredom's damage to the soul does Melville articulate a mature vision. Once he discards conventional notions of evil in his art, Melville becomes more philosophic and artistic in his creative representations of boredom's devastating effects. The failures of work, friendship, and religion that increasingly plague Melville's characters point to the insidiousness of boredom. Overcoming his fear and irresolution concerning the darker implications of his material, Melville begins with *Moby-Dick* to accept that boredom is not simply to be ignored or downplayed. In Melville's mature work, it becomes increasingly clear that boredom kills not only time but souls. Boredom becomes then a determining force in Melville's art, an influence that past scholars have not acknowledged.

This project also disputes and amends the theoretical tradition of viewing boredom as somehow less dignified, hazardous, and significant. Given the rather complex nature of *boredom*, to splinter it into disparate notions and bewildering lexicon, and to insist on rigid constructs and abstruse diagnoses is to deny, constrict, and blunt its restless and existential complexion. Boredom is a force in its tidal-like action against the self: it ebbs and flows over the Melvillean protagonist's well-being, either pummeling the self's integrity or rising it toward consciousness and strength; boredom may vary in its strength and duration, but is an unified, although complicated, existential state.

Melville's literary vision of boredom reveals the awesome power of this beguiling and oftentimes confounding crisis. In its most basic sense, boredom is the decisive point in Melvillean consciousness when meaning is eroded;

the absence or destruction of meaning, whether it be short-lived or sustained, is the threat that sinks or swims Melville's major heroes. Boredom is a kind of psychological and moral crucible in which Melville tests his literary protagonists, measuring authenticity, maturity, and values. Experiencing a nautical calm for days, gazing into the dead brick wall, and wandering over the desert wastes of the Holy Land all give greater testimony to whatever profundity and stature that Reinhard Kuhn et al. theorize *ennui* or "modern boredom" to be; even the uneducated whaler and poor office worker suffer horribly, if not more so than the spoiled, dandified, and aristocratic European literary characters Kuhn focuses on. Given the austereness and forlornness of Melville's literary universe and his artistic understanding and dramatization of boredom, *boredom*, as concept, is consequential and terrifying. Reliance upon foreign words as *ennui* or even *acedia* to classify certain Melville heroes serves only to disown, muddle, and undermine unnecessarily both *boredom* and Melville's presentation of boredom.

And as Melville advances as artist, he realizes reluctantly but astutely the relationship between evil and boredom. Melville's unwillingness in the beginning of his artistic career to front evil stems mainly from his holding back through fear, uncertainty, and because of conflict with his own predilection for neat and affirming endings. This fear of evil both limited and restrained his initial artistic progress. Bridling his apprenticeship as artist significantly and at length, Melville's discomposure caused him to recoil, frustrating his efforts to explore fully emerging dark themes, taming his preliminary observations, thus making them less convincing, and jeopardizing his art's coherence, appeal, and success. To a certain degree, a kind of primness marks this early stage in Melville's artistic career. Even with the monumental breakthrough that is *Moby-Dick*, his later work still wrestles with this hesitancy; however, gaining in power, eloquence, and persuasiveness is his greater need in becoming a serious artist, which means confronting life's evil and tragedy. His youthful experiences as whaler and naval tar, which were branded in part by his witnessing of man's evil toward his fellow man, originating in large degree due to boredom, made it inevitable that he would contend with what he saw. In a short but key passage in *Typee*, Melville barely suppresses disgust and terror over his navy days:

> I formed a higher estimate of human nature than I had ever before entertained. But alas! since then I have been one of the crew of a man-of-war, and the pent-up wickedness of five hundred men has nearly overturned all my previous theories [203].

This actual experience haunted and in some ways slowed his progress until he finally dramatized it with mixed success in *White-Jacket*, which in essence is the precursor to his advancement into *Moby-Dick*. This phase in his development is characterized by his straining his material, not for effect, but lack of.

With *Moby-Dick*, Melville's capability became more pointed and his craft more elaborate and therefore more complicated. The battle was less with his audience — although this part of the conflict increasingly became a larger problem — than with his own self: pointing to moral crises is starkly different from delving into them. It is this challenge to his creative sensibility that provides a key tension in his art.

Aggravating Melville's initial imaginative unrest and imbalance is the latent hostility posed by boredom as theme. Particularly with his first set of South Pacific adventures, boredom is present and capable of becoming a devastating force although it is not readily apparent. Boredom's blackness has not shadowed Melville's creative disposition, and its negative energy only shows obscure signs of its emergence and development; boredom, it may be said, is lying dormant. Boredom's presence in Melville's juvenilia is best described as a haze shrouding it, a nearly invisible oppressive presence. What keeps boredom in check from awakening, and dilutes its energy of negation from crushing his characters are Melville's stronger romantic impulses: his heroes narrowly escape death, remaining unaware of deeper psychological meaning and resuming their picaresque and reckless exploits. There are in the early writing moments of burgeoning political and moral consciousness, but an overall lightness in style prunes any potential or significant growth; Melville is not in control of his material nor does he have a vision yet. The ambivalence Melville feels concerning the role of boredom should take snarls him.

White-Jacket is a partial achievement; its failings consist of artistic compromises: satisfying both his audience's and his own artistic need for optimism. Melville flinches from unnerving themes, and wavers in creative direction. In spite of these flaws, which, at times, sabotage any sense of accomplishment, the breakthrough is the conglomeration of Melville's key themes: growth of consciousness, metaphysics, religion, evil, and boredom. It is not a coherent, measured, or smooth integration; rather, it is coarse, unrefined, and rudimentary. *White-Jacket* is a forced attempt to collect all relevant themes: in a sense, this work is an embryo from which Melville's later work will develop.

As Melville unsuccessfully tries to suppress the manifestation of evil in his art, he too muffles the reach his theme of boredom is making in *White-Jacket*. Acts of antagonism, corruption, and wickedness largely emanate from man's irritation, frustration, and inability to cope with boredom. Melville certainly would have agreed with Kierkegaard that boredom is the root of evil.

Therefore, Melville's panic in the face of evil is also his timidity of the implications of boredom for his art. To come to terms with the knowledge of a Manichean universe was a huge dilemma for Melville to grapple with; not only does it challenge the very nature of Melville's system of literary values, but also his artistic vision of man. As a result, the theme of boredom functions as a stumbling block, an obstruction for Melville to gain his artistic footing in that conflict.

There is very little in Melville's art that truly anticipates *Moby-Dick*; not even the important "Hawthorne and His Mosses," given its brevity, sketchiness, and effusiveness, really prepares one for what is about to come. All that his early fiction achieves is simply to identify and chalk out what boredom may be, and his review of his fellow American's stories annunciates Melville's own "shock of recognition" of dark themes in his own work. Melville's shock is to recognize familiar but realized themes in a more mature, confident, and skilled artist, one who feels free in exploring disturbing and dark motifs. It is this sense of camaraderie that boasts his own fortitude but more importantly his craftsmanship. The influences of the Christian Bible, Dante, Shakespeare, Milton, Emerson, and Hawthorne, which in varying degrees were there from the near beginning, now bear their fruit. Melville's self-repression subsides, and the flood gates have opened. And the correspondence with Hawthorne certainly was a necessary catalyst for Melville's next phase. The leap from mere identification of boredom to the "deep diving" found in *Moby-Dick* and thereafter was mainly self-generated, and rooted in his own experiences and more so in his own reflections.

The Hurdle Overcome

Catapulting Melville into a new freedom as artist, his liberation from the confines of conventionalism, squeamishness, and self-doubt stimulates him finally to wield confidently his themes, especially of boredom. No matter how much *Mardi* may have revealed his potential, and may have indicated how imposing the threat boredom lodges toward the Melville hero, Melville's execution was cursory and inconsistent. His metaphysical tendencies in this novel, particularly in his treatment on boredom, manage to illustrate why boredom is so dangerous, and coordinate supporting motifs, showing in various ways how ethical, religious, and existential questions encompass boredom. Melville's inaugurating masterpiece, *Moby-Dick*, for the first time weaves those seemingly disparate elements into whole cloth; what Melville was struggling to articulate and dramatize was how boredom is the loss of meaning, how boredom attacks meaning and how man resists that loss or gives in. And through the incorporation of matters dealing with friendship, metaphysics, religion, and evil, Melville can now examine the force that negates man's life. Religious skepticism and Melville's need to find an affirming creed in life and God complicate the crisis his characters deal with the void left by boredom's destructive heart.

"Bartleby, the Scrivener" develops and emphasizes the failures to communicate, to connect, to extend oneself, and to forge bonds with others. Set on terra firma, there is no escape, no relief from the soul sickness of boredom. Nature or the outdoors no longer is a temporary respite for boredom. In past works, running away from home or fleeing from the captain was at best an enticing distraction; what seemed to be a triumph over restlessness really was delaying an inevitable reckoning. Bartleby's death extinguishes any hope in work and human relations and these two means to counter boredom are not beneficial, effective, or reliable. The spiritual emptiness reflected in both Bartleby and the Lawyer not only reveals the deep psychological and moral dynamics of boredom but the spiritual or religious factors, too. Melville's earlier response to boredom was to keep moving and working. As those strategies proved to be ineffective, he realized that there was little to combat boredom. When Bartleby was incapacitated with his soul-deep despair, Melville saw that there was no solution. Queequeg's love barely saved Ishmael from the jaws of death, and the Lawyer's love scarcely impressed Bartleby. Caught between the pull toward a watery or a land-locked demise, Melville's characters had few alternatives to choose from. Accepting that there was no solution, Melville matured as a tragic thinker.

Shifting his imaginative gaze from the water to terra firma, Melville's artistic treatment of boredom marks a new writing phase. Melville builds upon the metaphysical breakthroughs of *Moby-Dick* to dramatize the extent of boredom's withering effects on the soul; not only do the failures of enterprise, profession, and friendship constrict the Melville hero's ability to save himself from boredom, but the shortcomings of a faith in God or nature also deter him from integrity of the self. Melville has found a language, style, and confidence in which boredom's most troubling and repugnant features are no longer shielded by his fears of them; he is now a tragic artist. Because he has debunked the romantic appreciation (and thus illusion) of nature in *Moby-Dick*, he now can probe ever deeper, more than he had accomplished in his first masterpiece, the inner landscapes of his protagonists. The blandness, stillness, and lifelessness of nature all reflect the spiritual dryness that dwells within; the characters from his epic poem especially, Clarel and the Syrian Monk, are examples. The exterior world does not inspire hope or life and it cannot invigorate either of them. In the presence of nature, their sorrows are not redressed, doubts are not relieved, and troubles are not eased. For Melville, nature no longer can regenerate man's spirit, even in the Holy Land.

By returning to the sea, Melville also revisits the imprisoning qualities of being on a ship and being bored. This time, in *Billy Budd*, boredom reveals itself as a judgment of all of Melville's previous work; it dramatizes the intense battle between joy and despair, life and death, good and evil. *Billy Budd* is a work that settles a lifetime exploration of agnosticism; by exploring the theme of boredom, Melville indeed settles for uncertainty, that no answers are available, and that one cannot know God. This settlement for uncertainty is highly rare in others, and most people cannot grapple or accept that there is no answer or solution; it is taxing, and runs counter to the basic human impulse to know, to have an answer. Perhaps this is one reason why Melville's contemporary readers shrugged him off. By no means does this evaluation suggest an easy way out, of avoiding the issue. Melville is pointing toward modernism, literary assumptions that there are no confirmed absolutes, no hard-won assurance to feel secure.

Melville's settlement for uncertainty does not truly reach nihilism — complete and utter meaninglessness. Although, if the novel were to end with Billy's death, then the pull toward the abyss would be inevitable. Even Melville draws attention to this point in chapter 28 that Billy's life "has been faithfully given" but "the conclusion of such a narration is apt to be less finished" (128) if he did not pursue further and finish the story. A more satisfactory feeling arises with the last three chapters because it strengthens the sentiment that Billy's death was not in vain; it provides some meaning without straining the fact that he had to die. *Billy Budd* is not Melville's closure concerning his skepticism; rather, it is a confirmation or understanding that moral ambiguity presides in the world, yet another indication that Melville sees modernism in the horizon.

Just because Melville utilizes traditional Christian literary symbolism, summarizes specific Calvinistic doctrine, and uses biblical figures and stories, by no means do they suggest that Melville is a devout believer. These religious references are common literary devices, nearly commonplaces, and their use requires no faith on Melville's part. The last three chapters — the "sequel," as the narrator calls it (128) — encourages strongly the idea that Melville embraces acceptance of the Resurrection, given its secularization, and the sailors who collect Billy's belongings and turn them into relics, and one tar who composes a ballad, suggesting a kind of gospel, in Billy's memory suggest that Melville might have found some way to believe. Certainly old age and approaching death might encourage religious sentiment. The rich and evocative religious tropes and their dominance in the work do offer the possibility that, to some degree, Melville has some desire, need to believe. This feeling however is not that strong or convincing. In a journal entry describing his final meeting with Melville on 20 November 1856, Nathaniel Hawthorne writes, "He can neither believe, nor be comfortable in his unbelief; and he is too honest and courageous not to try to do one or the other. If he were a religious man, he would be one of the most truly religious and reverential" (651). Hawthorne's characterization is still a relevant and accurate assessment of the older Melville; this contradictory statement reflects the ambiguity and more importantly the agnosticism that mark Melville. Melville artistically dramatizes this ambiguity, and no easy or set answer can be derived.

If one sees in Vere's agony over condemning Budd to death as Melville's own, Melville's settlement for uncertainty was not easy. Parting with everything that Budd stood for, Melville realized how unlikely a Christ figure would succeed in his literary world. Fyodor Dostoevsky too understood that this type is doomed to fail. In *The Idiot* (1868), Dostoevsky is unable artistically to find a sustaining faith, and Prince Myshkin's symbolic function in the novel is to underscore that failing. Melville does not overwhelm his work with hope, little as it may be, and he curbs the failure that grips the work. Myshkin's tragic vision was too horrifying and realistic for Dostoevsky to find hope, and the inadequacy of God signals a harsher conclusion than Melville's final expression of agnosticism. If Dostoevsky endeavors to find faith, no matter how damaged or muted, Melville feels no such intense obligation to have one. Whatever hope implicit in Dostoevsky is played out and exhausted, and his work is far darker and more severe than Melville's. The feelings left with at the end of each work are starkly different. *The Idiot* is weighty and oppressive, while *Billy Budd* ends with Billy being cheerful before his execution, and maintains dignity throughout, indicating a hint of consciousness. The Russian novel is a deeper exploration of shared values, but the American work demonstrates the measure of strength in Melville pointing out optimism that Dostoevsky cannot. The Prince's traits are far darker and offer no true heritage. The power of Budd's personality is a lasting legacy, and inspires the sailors to commemorate him.

Boredom is a complicated literary, psychological, religious, and moral problem facing the individual in Melville's artistic universe. Boredom attacks the very foundations of the self, and functions as an index of consciousness, gauging recklessness, immaturity, and other failings as forerunners of existentially tragic outcomes. The meaninglessness that Melville's protagonists feel within, wrestle with, or flee from is the deep sense of nothingness and dread they experience when bored. Billy's legacy defies the worst that boredom can do to the soul. Melville manages to find some meaning in spite of the worst effects of boredom.

Bibliography

Adamson, Joseph. *Melville, Shame, and the Evil Eye: A Psychoanalytic Reading.* New York: State University of New York Press, 1997.

Adler, Joyce Sparer. *War in Melville's Imagination.* New York: New York University Press, 1981.

Altizer, Thomas. *The Gospel of Christian Atheism.* Philadelphia, Westminster Press, 1966.

Arnold, Matthew. "Dover Beach." In *The Norton Anthology of Poetry,* ed. Alexander W. Allison. 3rd ed. New York: W. W. Norton Company, Inc., 1983.

Arvin, Newton. *Herman Melville.* Westport, CT: Greenwood Press, 1950.

Auden, W. H. "Musee des Beaux Arts." *The Norton Anthology of Poetry.* Ed. Alexander W. Allison. 3rd ed. New York: W. W. Norton Company, Inc., 1983.

Barber, Patricia. "If Bartleby Were A Woman." Eds. Arlyn Diamond and Lee R. Edwards. *The Authority of Experience: Essays in Feminist Criticism.* Amherst: University Press of Massachusetts, 1977.

Berrios, German E. *The History of Mental Symptoms: Descriptive Psychopathology since the Nineteenth Century.* New York: Cambridge University Press, 1996.

Bewley, Marius. "Melville (1953)." *Ahab,* ed. Harold Bloom. New York: Chelsea House Publishers, 1991.

Bezanson, Walter. "Historical and Critical Note." *Clarel: A Poem and Pilgrimage in the Holy Land.* Eds. Harrison Hayford, Alma A. MacDougall, Hershel Parker, and G. Thomas Tanselle. Evanston: Northwestern University Press, 1987.

Bloom, Harold. "Introduction." *Ahab.* Ed. Harold Bloom. New York: Chelsea House Publishers, 1991.

"Boredom." *The Oxford English Dictionary.* 2nd ed. 1989.

Boudreau, Gordon V. "Herman Melville, Immortality, St. Paul, and Resurrection: From *Rose-Bud* to *Billy Budd.*" *Christianity and Literature* 52.3 (Spring 2003): 343–364.

Braswell, William. *Melville's Religious Thought: An Essay in Interpretation.* Durham, NC: Duke University Press, 1943.

Brodtkorb, Paul, Jr. *Ishmael's White World: A Phenomenological Reading of Moby-Dick.* New Haven: Yale University Press, 1965.

Brodsky, Joseph. "In Praise of Boredom." *On Grief and Reason: Essays.* New York: Farrar, Straus and Giroux, 1995.

Brown, Gillian. "The Empire of Agoraphobia." *Herman Melville: A Collection of Critical Essays,* ed. Myra Jehlen. Englewood Cliffs, NJ: Prentice Hall, 1994.

Bryant, John. *Melville and Repose: The Rhetoric of Humor in the American Renaissance.* New York: Oxford University Press, 1993.

Buell, Lawrence. "Ethics and Literary Study." *PMLA* 114.1 (Jan. 1999): 7–19.

_____. "What We Talk about When We Talk about Ethics." *The Turn to Ethics.* New York: Routledge, 2000.

Casarino, Cesare. *Modernity at Sea: Melville, Marx, Conrad in Crisis.* Minneapolis: University Press of Minnesota, 2002.

Chase, Richard. "The Maimed Man in the Glen." *Herman Melville: A Critical Study.* New York: Macmillian Publishing Co., Inc., 1949. Rpt. in *Critical Es-*

says on Herman Melville's Typee. Boston: G. K. Hall & Co., 1982.

Colatrella, Carol. *Literature and Moral Reform: Melville and the Discipline of Reading.* Gainesville, FL: University Press of Florida, 2002.

Cottingham, John. *On the Meaning of Life.* New York: Routledge, 2003.

Darwin, Charles. *The Autobiography of Charles Darwin, 1809–1882,* ed. Nora Barlow. Reissue ed. New York: W. W. Norton & Co., 1993.

Davis, Todd F. "The Narrator's Dilemma in 'Bartleby the Scrivener': The Excellently Illustrated Re-statement of a Problem." *Studies in Short Fiction* 34.2 (Spring 1997): 183–192.

Davis, Todd F., and Kenneth Womack. "Preface: Reading Literature and the Ethics of Criticism." Eds. Todd F. Davis and Kenneth Womack. *Mapping the Ethical Turn: A Reader in Ethics, Culture, and Literary Theory.* Charlottesville: University Press of Virginia, 2001.

Dening, Greg. "Performing on the Beaches of the Mind." *History and Theory* 41.1 (Feb. 2002): 1–24.

Derrida, Jacques. *Acts of Religion.* Ed. Gil Anidjar. London: Routledge, 2002.

Dillingham, William B. "Ahab's Heresy." *Melville's Later Novels.* Athens, GA: University Press of Georgia, 1986. Rpt. in *Ahab.* Ed. Harold Bloom. New York: Chelsea House Publishers, 1991.

Dilworth, Thomas. "Narrator of 'Bartleby': The Christian-Humanist Acquaintance of John Jacob Astor." *Papers on Language and Literature* 38.1 (Winter 2002): 49–75.

Dimock, Wai-Chee S. "'White-Jacket': Authors and Audiences." *Nineteenth-Century Fiction* 36.3 (Dec. 1981): 296–317.

_____. "Blaming the Victim." *Empire for Liberty: Melville and the Poets of Individualism.* Princeton: Princeton University Press, 1988. Rpt. in *Ahab.* Ed. Harold Bloom. New York: Chelsea House Publishers, 1991.

Doloff, Steven. "The Prudent Samaritan: Melville's 'Bartleby, the Scrivener' as Parody of Christ's Parable to the

Lawyer." *Studies in Short Fiction* 34.3 (Summer 1997): 357–361.

Douglass, Ann. "Moby-Dick and Pierre: The Struggle for Possession." *The Feminization of American Culture.* New York: Knopf, 1977. Rpt. in *Ahab.* Ed. Harold Bloom. New York: Chelsea House Publishers, 1991.

Dryden, Edgar A. *Melville's Thematics of Form: The Great Art of Telling the Truth.* Baltimore: The Johns Hopkins Press, 1968.

_____. *Monumental Melville: The Formation of a Literary Career.* Stanford, CA: Stanford University Press, 2004.

Duban, James. "From Bethlehem to Tahiti: Transcultural 'Hope' in *Clarel.*" *Philological Quarterly* 70.4 (Fall 1991): 475–483.

_____. *Melville's Major Fiction: Politics, Theology, and Imagination.* Dekalb, IL: Northern Illinois University Press, 1983.

Edwards, Jonathan. "A Faithful Narrative of the Surprising Work of God." *The Heath Anthology of American Literature, Volume 1,* 4th ed. Ed. Paul Lauter. New York: Houghton Mifflin & Co., 2001.

_____. "Personal Narrative." *The Heath Anthology of American Literature, Volume 1,* 4th ed. Ed. Paul Lauter. New York: Houghton Mifflin & Co., 2001.

Elliott, Emory. "'Wandering To-and-Fro': Melville and Religion." *A Historical Guide to Herman Melville.* Ed. Giles Gunn. New York: Oxford University Press, 2005.

Emerson, Ralph Waldo. "Friendship." *The Selected Writings of Ralph Waldo Emerson.* New York: The Modern Library, 1992.

_____. *The Journals and Miscellaneous Notebooks of Ralph Waldo Emerson, Volume VIII.* Eds. William H. Gilman and J. E. Parsons. Cambridge, MA: The Belknap Press of Harvard University Press, 1970.

Epicurus. "Evil." Comp. Bergen Evans. *Dictionary of Quotations.* New York: Wings Books, 1969.

Evans, K. L. *Whale!* Minneapolis: University Press of Minnesota, 2003.

Evelev, John. "'Every One to His Trade':

Mardi, Literary Form, and Professional Ideology." *American Literature* 75.2 (June 2003): 305–333.

Farnham, James F. "Captain Vere's Existential Failure." *Arizona Quarterly* (Winter 1981): 362–370.

Finkelstein, Dorothee Metlitsky. *Melville's Orienda*. New Haven: Yale University Press, 1961.

Fish, Stanley. "One University under God?" *The Chronicle of Higher Education* (7 Jan. 2005): CI.

Forst, Graham Nicol. "Up Wall Street Towards Broadway: The Narrator's Pilgrimage in Melville's 'Bartleby the Scrivener.'" *Studies in Short Fiction* 24 (Summer 1987): 263–270.

Franchot, Jenny. "Melville's Traveling God." *The Cambridge Companion to Herman Melville*. Ed. Robert S. Levine. New York: Cambridge University Press, 1998.

Gardner, John. *On Moral Fiction*. New York: Basic Books, Inc., Publishers, 1977.

Garland-Thomson, Rosemarie. "The Cultural Logic of Euthanasia: 'Sad Fancying' in Herman Melville's 'Bartleby.'" *American Literature* 76.4 (Dec. 2004): 777–806.

Gibson, Commodore William. "Life On Board a Man-of-War." *Harper's New Monthly Magazine* 46.274 (March 1873): 481–494. *Making of America*. 29 March 2005 <http://library8.library.cornell.edu/gifcache/moa/harp/harp0046/00495.TIF6.gif>.

Goldman, Stan. *Melville's Protest Theism: The Hidden and Silent God in Clarel*. DeKalb, IL: Northern Illinois University Press, 1993.

Goodstein, Elizabeth S. *Experience without Qualities: Boredom and Modernity*. Palo Alto, CA: Stanford University Press, 2005.

Grenberg, Bruce L. *Some Other World to Find: Quest and Negation in the Works of Herman Melville*. Urbana, IL: University Press of Illinois, 1989.

Guerard, Albert J. *Stories of the Double*. Philadelphia: Lippincott, 1967.

Hamilton, William. *Melville and the Gods*. Chico, CA: Scholars Press, 1985.

Hans, James S. "Emptiness and Plenitude in 'Bartleby the Scrivener' and *The Crying of Lot 49*." *Essays in Literature* 22 (Fall 1995): 285–299.

Harvey, Bruce A. "'Precepts Graven on Every Breast': Melville's *Typee* and the Forms of the Law." *American Quarterly* 45.3 (Sep. 1993): 394–424.

Hawthorne, Nathaniel. "Herman Melville: Journals and Letters." *The Portable Hawthorne*. Ed. Malcolm Cowley. New York: Penguin Books, 1976: 609–693.

_____. "Young Goodman Brown." *Mosses from an Old Manse*. New York: Modern Library, 2003.

Hayford, Harrison, and Hershel Parker. "Footnotes." *Moby-Dick: An Authoritative Text, Reviews, and Letters by Melville, Analogues and Sources, Criticism*. New York: W. W. Norton & Co., 1967.

Hayford, Harrison, and Merton M. Sealts. "Notes & Commentary." *Billy Budd, Sailor (An Inside Narrative): Reading Text and Genetic Text*. Eds. Harrison Hayford and Merton M. Selats. Chicago: University Press of Chicago, 1962.

Healy, Sean Desmond. *Boredom, Self, and Culture*. Rutherford, NJ: Fairleigh Dickinson University Press, 1984.

Helwig, Maggie. "Hunger." *This Magazine* (Feb. 1989). Rpt. in *The Norton Reader: An Anthology of Nonfiction*. Eds. Linda H. Peterson and John C. Brereton. New York: W. W. Norton & Co., 2004.

Herbert, T. Walter. *Moby-Dick and Calvinism: A World Dismantled*. New Brunswick, NJ: Rutgers University Press, 1977.

Holy Bible: King James Version (1611). Grand Rapids, MI: Zondervan, 2002.

Hove, Thomas. "Naturalist Psychology in *Billy Budd*." *Leviathan* 5.2 (Oct 2003): 51–65.

Howe, Irving. *The American Newness: Culture and Politics in the Age of Emerson*. Cambridge, MA: Harvard University Press, 1986.

_____. "The Idea of the Modern." *The Idea of the Modern in Literature and the Arts.* Ed. Irving Howe. New York: Horizon Press, 1967.

Hunt, Lester L. *"Billy Budd:* Melville's Dilemma." *Philosophy and Literature* 26.2 (Oct 2002): 273–295.

Jefferson, Thomas. "To Martha Jefferson." 21 May 1787. *The Family Letters of Thomas Jefferson.* Eds. Edwin Betts and James Adam Bear, Jr. Columbia: University Press of Missouri, 1966.

John, Richard R. "The Lost World of Bartleby, the Ex-officeholder: Variations on a Venerable Literary Form." *The New England Quarterly* 70 (Dec. 1997): 631–641.

Johnson, Bradley A. "Mind in the Maintop, Body in Bilge: Space and the Human Form in Melville's *White-Jacket.*" *ATQ* 14.4 (Dec. 2003): 243–257.

Kaul, A. N. "Herman Melville: The New-World Voyageur." *The American Vision: Actual and Ideal Society in Nineteenth Century Fiction.* New Haven: Yale University Press. Rpt. in *Critical Essays on Herman Melville's Typee.* Ed. Milton R. Stern. Boston: G. K. Hall & Co., 1982.

Kazin, Alfred. *God & The American Writer.* New York: Alfred A. Knopf, 1997.

Kenny, Vincent. *"Clarel."* A Companion to Melville Studies. Ed. John Bryant. New York: Greenwood Press, 1986.

_____. *Herman Melville's Clarel: A Spiritual Autobiography.* Hamden, CT: Archon Books, 1973.

Kier, Kathleen E. "An Annotated Edition of Melville's White-Jacket." Dissertation Columbia University. 1980.

Kierkegaard, Søren. *Either/Or, Part 1.* Eds. and trans. Howard V. Hong and Edna H. Hong. Princeton: Princeton University Press, 1988.

Klapp, Orrin E. *Overload and Boredom: Essays on the Quality of Life in the Information Society.* New York: Greenwood Press, 1986.

Kuebrich, David. "Melville's Doctrine of Assumptions: The Hidden Ideology of Capitalist Production in 'Bartleby.'"

The New England Quarterly 69 (Sept. 1996): 381–405.

Kuhn, Reinhard. *The Demon of Noontide: Ennui in Western Literature.* Princeton, NJ: Princeton University Press, 1976.

Lackey, Kris. "The Holy Guide-Book and the Sword of the Lord: How Melville Used the Bible in *Redburn* and *White-Jacket.*" *Studies in the Novel* 17.3 (Fall 1985): 241–254.

Lebowitz, Alan. *Progress into Silence: A Study of Melville's Heroes.* Bloomington, IN: Indiana University Press, 1970.

Levinas, Emmanuel. *Is It Righteous To Be? Interviews with Emmanuel Levinas.* Ed. Jill Robbins. Stanford: Stanford University Press, 2001.

_____. *Otherwise than Being; Or, Beyond Essence.* 1974. Trans. Alphonso Lingis. Pittsburgh: Duquesne University Press, 1998.

_____. *Totality and Infinity: An Essay on Exteriority.* 1961. Trans. Alphonso Lingis. Pittsburgh: Duquesne University Press, 1969.

Logan, Judy. "The Catnip and the Amaranth: Melville's Struggle with the 'Ever- encroaching Appetite for God.'" *Christianity & Literature* 51.3 (Spring 2002): 387–406.

Mahoney, M. Denis, Mother. *Clarel: An Investigation of Spiritual Crisis.* Washington: Catholic University of American Press, 1958.

Markels, Julian. *Melville and the Politics of Identity: From King Lear to Moby-Dick.* Urbana, IL: University Press of Illinois, 1993.

Martin, Robert K. *Hero, Captain, and Stranger: Male Friendship, Social Critique, and Literary Form in the Sea Novels of Herman Melville.* Chapel Hill, NC: University Press of North Carolina.

Mason, Ronald. *The Spirit Above the Dust: A Study of Herman Melville.* London: John Lehmann, 1951.

Matteson, John T. "The Little Lower Layer: Anxiety and the Courage To Be in Moby-Dick." *Harvard Theological Review* 81.1 (1988): 97–116.

McCall, Dan. *The Silence of Bartleby.* Ithaca: Cornell University Press, 1989.

McCarthy, Paul. *"The Twisted Mind": Madness in Herman Melville's Fiction.* Iowa City: University Press of Iowa, 1990.

Melville, Herman. "Bartleby, the Scrivener: A Story of Wall Street." *The Piazza Tales and Other Prose Pieces, 1839–1860.* Eds. Harrison Hayford, Alma A. MacDougall, and G. Thomas Tanselle. Evanston: Northwestern University Press, 1987.

_____. *Billy Budd, Sailor: An Inside Narrative.* Eds. Harrison Hayford and Merton M. Sealts. Chicago: University Press of Chicago, 1962.

_____. *Clarel: A Poem and Pilgrimage in the Holy Land.* Eds. Harrison Hayford, Alma A. MacDougall, Hershel Parker, and G. Thomas Tanselle. Evanston: Northwestern University Press, 1987.

_____. *Correspondence.* Eds. Harrison Hayford, Hershel Parker, and G. Thomas Tanselle. Evanston: Northwestern University Press, 1993.

_____. "Hawthorne and His Mosses." *The Piazza Tales and Other Prose Pieces, 1839–1860.* Eds. Harrison Hayford, Hershel Parker, and G. Thomas Tanselle. Evanston: Northwestern University Press, 1987.

_____. *Mardi and a Voyage Thither.* Eds. Harrison Hayford, Hershel Parker, and G. Thomas Tanselle. Evanston: Northwestern University Press, 1970.

_____. *Moby-Dick or The Whale.* Eds. Harrison Hayford, Hershel Parker, and G. Thomas Tanselle. Evanston: Northwestern University Press, 1988.

_____. *Omoo: A Narrative of Adventures in the South Seas.* Eds. Harrison Hayford, Hershel Parker, and G. Thomas Tanselle. Evanston: Northwestern University Press and Newberry Library, 1968.

_____. *Redburn; His First Voyage.* Eds. Harrison Hayford, Hershel Parker, and G. Thomas Tanselle. Evanston: Northwestern University Press and Newberry Library, 1969.

_____. "Timoleon." *Selected Poems of Herman Melville.* Ed. Hennig Cohen. New York: Fordham University Press, 1991.

_____. *Typee: A Peep at Polynesian Life.* Eds. Harrison Hayford, Hershel Parker, and G. Thomas Tanselle. Evanston: Northwestern University Press and Newberry Library, 1968.

_____. *White-Jacket or The World in a Man-of-War.* Eds. Harrison Hayford, Hershel Parker, and G. Thomas Tanselle. Evanston: Northwestern University Press and Newberry Library, 1970.

Merton, Thomas, and Czeslaw Milsoz. *Striving Towards Being: The Letters of Thomas Merton and Czeslaw Milosz.* Ed. Robert Faggen. New York: Farrar, Straus, & Giroux, 1996.

Milder, Robert. "Melville and the Avenging Dream." Ed. Robert S. Levine. *The Cambridge Companion to Herman Melville.* New York: Cambridge University Press, 1998.

Milosz, Czeslaw. *A Roadside Dog.* Trans. Robert Hass. New York: Farrar, Straus & Giroux, 1998.

_____. "Salagia." *To Begin Where I Am: Selected Essays.* Eds. Bogdana Carpenter and Madeline G. Levine. New York: Farrar, Straus & Giroux, 2001. Rpt. in *Beginning with My Streets: Essays and Recollections.* Trans. Madeline G. Levine. New York: Farrar, Straus & Giroux, 1991.

Nancy, Jean-Luc. "A-religion." *Journal of European Studies* (2004) 34.1/2: 14–18.

Nietzsche, Friedrich. *Beyond Good and Evil.* Trans. Helen Zimmern. *The Philosophy Nietzsche.* Ed. Willard Huntington Wright. New York: Modern Library, 1954.

_____. *Gay Science.* Trans. Josefine Nauckhoff and Adrian Del Caro. Ed. Bernard Williams. New York: Cambridge University Press, 2001.

Nownes, Nicholas L. "Narrative Representation and Self-Knowledge in Melville's *Typee.*" *ATQ* 11 (Dec. 1997): 323–338.

Nussbaum, Martha C. "'Finely Aware and Richly Responsible': Literature and the Moral Imagination." *Literature and the Question of Philosophy.* Ed. Anthony J.

Cascardi. Baltimore: Johns Hopkins University Press, 1987. 169–191. Rpt. in *Love's Knowledge: Essays in Philosophy and Literature*. New York: Oxford University Press, 1992.

Obenzinger, Hilton. *American Palestine: Melville, Twain, and the Holy Land Mania*. Princeton, NJ: Princeton University Press, 1999.

Olson, Charles. *Call Me Ishmael: A Study of Melville*. San Francisco: City Lights Books, 1947.

Otter, Samuel. *Melville's Anatomies*. Berkeley: University of California Press, 1999.

Parker, Hershel. *Herman Melville: A Biography, Volume 1, 1819–1851*. Baltimore: Johns Hopkins University Press, 1996.

Pascal, Blaise. *Pensees*. Trans. A. J. Krailsheimer. Revised Edition. London: Penguin, 1995.

Peretz, Eyal. *Literature, Disaster, and the Enigma of Power: A Reading of "Moby-Dick."* Stanford, CA: Stanford University Press, 2003.

Potter, William. *Melville's Clarel and the Intersympathy of Creeds*. Kent, OH: The Kent State University Press, 2004.

Raposa, Michael. *Boredom and the Religious Imagination*. Charlottesville: University Press of Virginia, 1999.

Reed, Naomi C. "The Specter of Wall Street: 'Bartleby, the Scrivener' and the Language of Commodities." *American Literature* 76.2 (June 2004): 247–273.

Reynolds, David S. "Melville's Whited Sepulchres: The Stylization of Reform." *Beneath the American Renaissance: The Subversive Imagination in the Age of Emerson and Melville*. New York: Knopf, 1988. Rpt. in *Ahab*. Ed. Harold Bloom. New York: Chelsea House Publishers, 1991.

Robertson-Lorant, Laurie. *Melville: A Biography*. New York: Clarkson Potter Publishers, 1996.

Rowlandson, Mary. *The Narrative of the Captivity and Restoration of Mrs. Rowlandson. The Heath Anthology of American Literature, Volume 1*. 4th ed. Ed. Paul Lauter. New York: Houghton Mifflin Co., 2001.

Russell, Bertrand. *The Conquest of Happiness*. New York: Liveright Publishing Corporation, 1996.

Ruttenburg, Nancy. "Melville's Handsome Sailor: The Anxiety of Innocence." *American Literature* 66.1 (Mar. 1994): 83–103.

Samson, John. *White Lies: Melville's Narratives of Facts*. Ithaca: Cornell University Press, 1989.

The Sayings of the Desert Fathers: The Alphabetical Collection. Trans. Benedicta Ward. Kalamazoo: Cistercian Publications, 1975.

Schechter, Harold. "Bartleby the Chronometer." *Studies in Short Fiction* 19.4 (Fall 1982): 359–366.

Schneidau, Herbert N., and Homer B. Pettey. "Melville's Ithyphallic God." *Studies in American Fiction* 26.2 (Autumn 1998): 193–211.

Scorza, Thomas J. "Tragedy in the State of Nature: Melville's *Typee*." *Interpretation* 8.1 (Jan. 1979): 103–120. Rpt. in *Critical Essays on Herman Melville's Typee*. Boston: G. K. Hall & Co., 1982.

Sedgwick, Eve Kosofsky. *Epistemology of the Closet*. Berkeley: University of California Press, 1991.

Seelye, John. *Melville: The Ironic Diagram*. Evanston, IL: Northwestern University Press, 1970.

Sewall, Richard B. *The Vision of Tragedy*. New Haven: Yale University Press, 1980.

Shakespeare, William. *Othello*. New York: W. W. Norton & Co., 2003.

Shattuck, Roger. "Guilt, Justice, and Empathy in Melville and Camus." *Partisan Review* 63.3: 430–449.

Shawcross, John T. "'Too Intellectual a Poet Ever To Be Popular': Herman Melville and the Miltonic Dimension of *Clarel*." Ed. Robin Grey. *Melville and Milton: An Edition and Analysis of Melville's Annotations on Milton*. Pittsburgh: Duquesne University Press, 2004.

Sherrill, Rowland A. "Melville and Religion." *A Companion to Melville Studies*. Ed. John Bryant. New York: Greenwood Press, 1986.

_____. *The Prophetic Melville: Experience, Transcendence, and Tragedy.* Athens, GA: University Press of Georgia, 1979.

Shurr, William H. *The Mystery of Iniquity: Melville as Poet, 1857–1891.* Lexington, KY: University Press of Kentucky, 1972.

Smith, Benjamin E. "Pronunciation of Alien Words." *The Century; A Popular Quarterly.* 32.6 (Oct. 1886): 967–968. *Making of America.* 29 Mar. 2005 <http://cdl. library.cornell.edu/cgibin/moa/moa-cgi?notsid=ABP2287–0032&byte=35274820>.

Spacks, Patricia Meyer. *Boredom: The Literary History of a State of Mind.* Chicago: University Press of Chicago, 1995.

Stanford, Raney. "The Romantic Hero and That Fatal Selfhood." *Centennial Review* 12.4 (Fall 1968): 440–443. Rpt. in *Ahab.* Ed. Harold Bloom. New York: Chelsea House Publishers, 1991.

Sten, Christopher. *The Weaver-God, He Weaves: Melville and the Poetics of the Novel.* Kent, OH: The Kent State University Press, 1996.

Svendsen, Lars. *A Philosophy of Boredom.* Trans. John Irons. London: Reaktion Books, 2005.

Taylor, Edward. "Christ's Reply." *The Heath Anthology of American Literature, Volume 1.* 4th ed. Ed. Paul Lauter. New York: Houghton Mifflin Co., 2001.

_____. "Meditation. Col. 2.17 Which are Shaddows of things to come and the body is Christs." *The Heath Anthology of American Literature, Volume 1.* 4th ed. Ed. Paul Lauter. New York: Houghton Mifflin Co., 2001.

Taylor, Mark C. *After Religion: Economies of Faith in Virtual Culture.* Chicago: University Press of Chicago, 1999.

_____. *Erring: A Postmodern A/Theology.* Chicago: University Press of Chicago, 1984.

_____. *Nots.* Chicago: University Press of Chicago, 1993.

Tennyson "The Lotos-Eaters." *The Norton Anthology of Poetry.* 3rd ed. Ed. Alexander W. Allison. New York: W. W. Norton & Company, Inc., 1983.

Thompson, Lawrance. *Melville's Quarrel with God.* Princeton: Princeton University Press, 1966.

Thomson, Shawn. *The Romantic Architecture of Herman Melville's Moby-Dick.* Madison, NJ: Fairleigh Dickinson University Press, 2001.

Thoreau, David Henry. *Walden and Resistance to Civil Government.* New York: W. W. Norton & Co., 1992.

Tocqueville, Alexis de. *Democracy in America.* Ed. Richard C. Heffner. New York: Signet Classics, 2001.

Toner, Jennifer DiLalla. "The Accustomed Signs of the Family: Rereading Genealogy in Melville's *Pierre.*" *American Literature* 70.2 (June 1998): 237–263.

Trotter, David. "Spitting Mad: Melville's Juices." *Critical Quarterly* 39.2 (Summer 1997): 23–38.

Twain, Mark. *Life On the Mississippi.* New York: Signet Classics, 2001.

Voltaire. *Candide.* 2nd ed. New York: W. W. Norton & Co., 1991.

Vincent, Howard P. *The Tailoring of Melville's White-Jacket.* Evanston: Northwestern University Press, 1970.

Warner, Charles Dudley. "Aspects of American Life." *The Atlantic Monthly* 43.255 (Jan. 1879): 1–9. *Making of America.* 29 March 2005 <http://cdl.library.cornell.edu/cgi-bin/moa/moa-cgi?notisid=ABK2934–0043&byte=269728520>.

Waugh, Evelyn. "Sloth." *The Seven Deadly Sins.* Ed. Angus Wilson, et.al. New York: William Morrow and Company, 1962.

Weil, Simone. *Gravity and Grace.* Posthumous 1952. Trans. Arthur Wills. New York: G. P. Putnam's Sons, 1952.

_____. "Factory Work." *The Simone Weil Reader.* Ed. George A. Panichas. New York: David McKay Company, Inc., 1977.

_____. "Human Personality." *Simone Weil: An Anthology.* Ed. Sian Miles. London: Virago Press Limited, 1986.

_____. "The Needs of the Soul." *Simone Weil: An Anthology.* Ed. Sian Miles. London: Virago Press Limited, 1986.

_____. *Waiting for God.* Posthumous 1951.

Trans. Emma Craufurd. New York: Perennial Classics, 2001.

Weinstein, Cindy. "The Calm before the Storm: Laboring Through *Mardi*." *American Literature* 65.2 (June 1993): 239–253.

Weinstock, Jeffrey Andrew. "Doing Justice to Bartleby." *ATQ* 17.1 (Mar. 2003): 23–42.

Weisberg, Richard. *Poethics and Other Strategies of Laws and Literature.* New York: Columbia University Press, 1992.

Wenke, John. *Melville's Muse: Literary Creation & the Forms of Philosophical Fiction.* Kent: Kent State University Press, 1995.

Wenzel, Siegfried. *The Sin of Sloth: Acedia in Medieval Thought and Literature.* Chapel Hill, University Press of North Carolina, 1960.

Whitman, Walt. "Democratic Vistas." In *Specimen Days & Collect.* New York: Dover Publications, 1995.

Widmer, Kingsley. *The Ways of Nihilism: A Study of Herman Melville's Short Novels.* Los Angeles: California State Colleges, 1970.

Woodward, C. Vann. *The Burden of Southern History.* Baton Rouge: Louisiana State University Press, 1993.

Wright, Nathalia. *Melville's Use of the Bible.* Durham, NC: Duke University Press, 1949.

Zlogar, Richard J. "Body politics in 'Bartleby': Leprosy, Healing, and Christ-ness in Melville's "Story of Wall-Street." *Nineteenth-Century Literature* 53.4 (Mar. 1999): 505–529.

Index